UNDERSTANDING EUROPEAN UNION LAW

Sixth Edition

Karen Davies

BPP   **REFERENCE USE ONLY**

Not to be removed from the Library

Sixth edition published 2016
by Routledge
2 Park Square, Milton Park, Abingdon, Oxon, OX14 4RN

and by Routledge
711 Third Avenue, New York, NY 10017

Routledge is an imprint of the Taylor & Francis Group, an informa business

© 2016 Karen Davies

First edition published by Cavendish Publishing 2001

Fifth edition published by Routledge 2013

British Library Cataloguing in Publication Data
A catalogue record for this book is available from the British Library

Library of Congress Cataloging-in-Publication Data
   Davies, Karen (Law teacher), author.
   Understanding European Union law / Karen Davies. – Sixth edition.
   pages cm
   Includes index.
   ISBN 978-1-138-77864-1 (pbk) – ISBN 978-1-138-77863-4 (hbk) –
   ISBN 978-1-315-77177-9 (ebk) 1. Law – European Union countries. I. Title.
   KJE949.D38 2015
   341.242′2 – dc23
   2015004501

ISBN: 978-1-138-77863-4 (hbk)
ISBN: 978-1-138-77864-1 (pbk)
ISBN: 978-1-315-77177-9 (ebk)

Typeset in Palatino by
Florence Production Ltd, Stoodleigh, Devon, UK

Contents

Table of Cases   *v*
Table of Legislation   *xvii*
Glossary   *xxiii*
Abbreviations   *xxxiii*

1   INTRODUCTION   **1**
   I.   The significance of EU law   1
   II.   The aims of this book   1
   III.   Your approach to studying EU law   2
   IV.   Finding resources on EU law   3
   V.   Beginning your studies   3
   VI.   Conclusions   6

2   THE CREATION OF A EUROPEAN UNION   **7**
   I.   The European Communities: why they were created
      and what do they comprise?   7
   II.   The development of the European Economic
      Community (EEC)   10
   III.   The EU today and in the future   22

3   WHO RUNS THE EU?   **25**
   I.   Power sharing in the EU   25
   II.   The institutional structure of the EU   29
   III.   Institutional balance, accountability and democracy
      in the EU   47
   IV.   Conclusions   50

4   SOURCES OF UNION LAW   **53**
   I.   Primary sources of EU law   54
   II.   Secondary sources of EU law   56

III. Case law of the Court of Justice of the European Union   64

IV. General principles of Union law   64

V. International agreements   69

VI. Conclusions   69

5 THE RELATIONSHIP BETWEEN UNION LAW AND NATIONAL LEGAL SYSTEMS   71

I. The doctrines of direct effect and supremacy   71

II. Conclusions   84

6 ENFORCING UNION LAW   87

I. Enforcing European law rights before national courts   88

II. Preliminary references and rulings   91

III. Enforcement actions against Member States (Arts 258–260 TFEU)   97

IV. Actions against EU Institutions: judicial review of the acts and omissions of Union bodies   102

V. Conclusions   113

7 FREE MOVEMENT OF GOODS   117

I. The elimination of pecuniary (monetary) barriers to trade   118

II. The elimination of non-pecuniary barriers to trade   124

III. Conclusions   139

8 FREE MOVEMENT OF PERSONS   141

I. Gaining the right to 'free movement'   142

II. Limitations on citizens' rights to free movement   149

III. Free movement: workers' rights (Arts 45–48 TFEU)   154

IV. Freedom of establishment and the provision of services   162

V. Enforcing rights to free movement   168

9 ASSESSMENT   171

I. Suggested approaches to coursework   171

II. Suggested approaches to revision   174

III. Examination technique   175

Index   *177*

Table of Cases

Adams v Commission (Case 145/83) [1985] ECR 3539; [1986]
  1 CMLR 506 .... 111, 113
Adeneler and Others v Ellinikos (Case C-212/04) [2006]
  IRLR 716 81
Adoui and Cornuaille v Belgian State (French Prostitutes case)
  (Cases 115 and 116/81) [1982] ECR 1665; [1982] 3 CMLR 631 150
Åklagaren v Hans Akerberg Fransson (Case C-617/10) [2013] 68, 69
Åklagaren v Percy Mickelsson and Joakim Roos (Case C-142/05)
  [20909] ECR I-4273 131
Alfons Lutticke v Commission (Case 48/65) [1966] ECR 19 108
Alpine Investments (Case C-384/93) [1995] ECR I-4101 168
Amministrazione delle Finanze dello Stato v San Giorgio
  (San Giorgio case) (Case 199/82) [1983] ECR 3595; [1985]
  2 CMLR 658 .... 89, 123
Amministrazione delle Finanze dello Stato v Simmenthal
  (Case 106/77) [1978] ECR 629 .... 73, 74
Arblade (Cases C-369 and C-376/96) [1978] ECR 629 168
Arsenal v Reed (No 2) [2003] 3 All ER 865 91

Barber v Guardian Royal Exchange (Case C-262/88) [1990]
  ECR I-1889; [1990] 2 CMLR 513 92
Bauhuis (Case 46/76) [1977] ECR 5 121
Bergaderm v Commission (C-352/98P) [2000] ECR 1-5291 .... 83, 111
Bettray v Staatssecretaris van Justitie (Case 344/87) [1989]
  ECR 1621; [1991] 1 CMLR 459 154
Bonsignore v Oberstadtdirektor of the City of Cologne
  (Case 67/74) [1975] ECR 297; [1975] 1 CMLR 472 150

Brasserie du Pêcheur SA v Germany; R v Secretary of
State for Transport ex p Factortame Ltd and Others
(Pêcheur and Factortame) (Cases C-46–48/93) [1996]
1 CMLR 889 . . . . 82, 90,
113, 163, 173
Bresciani (Case 87/75) [1976] ECR 129; [1976] 2 CMLR 62 121
Broekmeulen (Case 246/80) [1981] ECR 2311; [1982] 1 CMLR 91 . . . 92, 96
Bulmer v Bollinger [1974] 2 All ER 1226 93

Calpak (Cases 789 and 790/79) [1980] ECR 1949; [1981] 1 CMLR 26 . . . 105
Campus Oil Ltd v Minister for Industry and Energy
(Case 72/83) [1984] ECR 2727; [1984] 3 CMLR 544 . . . . 135, 138
Centrafarm v Sterling Drug (Case 15/74) [1974] ECR 1183;
[1974] 2 CMLR 480 137
Centrafarm v Winthrop (Case 16/74) [1974] ECR 1183; [1974]
2 CMLR 480 137
Centros Ltd v Erhvervs-Og Selskab-sstyrelser (Case C-212/97)
[1999] ECR I-1459 164
Centrosteel v Adipol (Case C-456/98) [2000] ECR I-6007 80–1
CIA Security International (Case C-194/94) [1996]
ECR I-2201 . . . . 81, 85
CILFIT Srl and Lanificio de Gavardo SpA v Ministry of Health
(Case 283/81) [1982] ECR 3415; [1983] 1 CMLR 472 . . . . 42, 94, 96
Cinéthèque v Federation des Cinemas Francais
(Cases 60 and 61/84) [1985] ECR 2605; [1986] 1 CMLR 365 127
Collins (Brian Francis) v Secretary of State for Work and Pensions
(Case C-138/02) [2004] ECR I-2703 152
Comet BV v Produktschap voor Siergewassen (Comet)
(Case 45/76) [1976] ECR 2043; [1977] 1 CMLR 533 . . . . 88, 90
Commission v Belgium (Case 149/79) (Re Public Employees)
[1980] ECR 3881; [1982] ECT 1845 160
Commission v Belgium (Cases 227–30/85) [1988] ECR 1; [1989]
2 CMLR 797 99
Commission v Council (Case 22/70) (ERTA case) [1971]
ECR 263 103
Commission v Council (Case 81/72) [1973] ECR 575 107
Commission v Denmark (Case 302/86) (Danish Bottles case)
[1989] ECR 4607; [1989]1 CMLR 619 128

Commission v France (Case 18/84) [1985] ECR 1339; [1986]
1 CMLR 605 133

Commission v France (Case 152/78) [1980] ECR 2299; [1981]
2 CMLR 743 137

Commission v France (Case 167/73) (French Seamen case)
[1974] ECR 359 169

Commission v France (Case 168/78) (French Spirits case)
[1980] ECR 347 . . . . 122, 123

Commission v France (Case C-265/95) [1997] ECR I-6959 125

Commission v Germany (Case 18/87) (Animal Inspection
Fees case) [1988] ECR 5427 121

Commission v Germany (Case 178/84) (German Beer case)
[1987] ECR 5427 . . . . 136, 138

Commission v Ireland (Case 113/80) (Irish Souvenirs case)
[1981] ECR 1625; [1982] 1 CMLR 706 134

Commission v Ireland (Case 249/81) (Buy Irish Campaign)
[1082] ECR 4005 . . . . 118, 125, 126

Commission v Italy (Case 7/68) (1st Art Treasures case)
[1968] ECR 423; [1969] CMLR 1 . . . . 118, 136, 138

Commission v Italy (Case 24/68) (2nd Art Treasures case)
(Statistical Levy case) [1969] ECR 193; [1971]
CMLR 661 . . . . 120, 121, 138

Commission v Italy (Case 101/84) [1985] ECR 2629; [1986]
2 CMLR 352 99

Commission v Italy (Case 228/91) [1993] ECR I-2701 . . . . 136, 138

Commission v Italy (Case C-110/05) [2009] ECR I-519 . . . . 131, 132

Commission v UK (Case 40/82) (Newcastle Disease case)
[1982] ECR 2793; [1982] 3 CMLR 493 138

Commission v UK (Case 124/81) (Re UHT Milk) [1983]
ECR 203; [1983] 2 CMLR 1 139

Commission v UK (Case 128/78) (Tachograph case) [1979]
ECR 419 96

Commission v UK (Case 170/78) [1980] 1 CMLR 716 122

Commission v UK (Case C-246/89R) [1989] ECR 3125; [1991]
3 CMLR 706 96

Conegate Ltd v HM Customs & Excise (Case 121/85) [1986]
ECR 1007; [1986] 1 CMLR 739 . . . . 134, 135, 138

Cordoniu v Council (Case C-309/89) [1994] ECR I-3605 105

Costa v ENEL (Case 6/64) [1964] ECT 585; [1964]
  CMLR 425 .... 43, 72, 73, 74, 93, 96, 173
Courage Ltd v Crehan (Case C-453/99) [2001] ECR I-6297 .... 84, 91
Cowan v Tresor Public (Case 186/87) [1989] ECR 195; [1990]
  2 CMLR 613 .... 167, 169
Cristini v SNCF (Case 32/75) [1975] ECR 1085 .... 159, 160

Da Costa en Schaake NV, Jacob Meijer NV and Hoechst-Holland
  NV v Nederlandse Belastingadministratie (Cases 28–30/62)
  [1963] ECR 31; [1963] CMLR 224 .... 64, 91, 94
Dano, Elisabeta and Florin Dano v Jobcenter Leipzig
  (Case 333/13) [2014] 147
De Agostini *see* Konsumentombudsmannen v De Agostini
Debauve (Case 52/79) [1980] ECR 833 167
Decker (Case C-120/95) [1998] ECR I-1831 127
Defrenne v Sabena (Case 43/75) [1976] ECT 455; [1976]
  2 CMLR 98 .... 76, 77, 85, 173
Dereci (Murat) and Others v Bundesministerium für Inneres
  (Case C-256/11) 145
Deutsche Grammophon v Metro (Case 78/80) [1971] ECR 487 137
Dillenkofer v Germany (Cases T-178, 179 and 188–90/94) [1996]
  ECR I-4845; [1996] 3 CMLR 638 83
Doughty v Rolls Royce [1992] 1 CMLR 1045, CA 79

EC v France (Case 90/79) [1981] ECR 283; [1981] CMLR 1 212 122
Echternach and Moritz v Netherlands Ministry for Education
  and Science (Case 389 and 390/87) [1989] ECR 723; [1990]
  2 CMLR 305 159
ENU v Commission (Case C-107/91) [1993] ECR I-599 108
Eridania v Commission (Cases 10 and 18/68) [1969] ECR 459 106
European Parliament v Council (Chernobyl case) (Case C-70/88)
  [1990] ECR I-2041; [1992] 1 CMLR 91 .... 33, 104
European Parliament v Council (Comitology case) (Case 302/87)
  [1988] ECR 5615 33

Familiapress (Case C-368/95) [1997] ECR 1-0000 129
Fink-Frucht v Hauptzollamt München-Landsbergerstrasse
  (Case 27/67) [1968] ECR 223 122

Foglia v Novello (Nos 1 and 2) (Cases 104/79 and 244/80)
  [1980] ECR 745; [1981] 1 CMLR 45; [1981] ECR 3045; [1982]
  1 CMLR 585 .... 94, 96
Forcheri v Belgium (Case 152/82) [1983] ECR 2323; [1984]
  1 CMLR 334 159
Ford Espana v Spain (Case 170/88) [1989] ECR 2305 121
Forster V IB Groep (Case C158/07) (2009) 1 CMLR 32 147
Foster v British Gas (Case C-188/89) [1990] ECR I-3313; [1990]
  2 CMLR 833 .... 79, 85, 173
Francovich and Bonifaci v Italy (Cases C-6 and 9/90) [1991]
  ECR I-5357; [1993] 2 CMLR 66 .... 82, 85, 90, 94,
                                                        97, 114, 173
Franz Grad v Finanzamt Traunstein (Case 9/70) [1970]
  ECR 825 .... 77, 78
Fratelli Constanzo (Case 103/88) [1989] ECR 1839 79
Fratelli Cucchi (Case 77/76) [1977] ECR 987 210 122

Gaal case C-7/94 [1996] ECR I-1031 159
Gebhard v Consiglio (Case C-55/94) [1995] ECR I-4165 . 156, 165, 166, 168
Geddo v Ente Nazionale Risi (Case 2/73) [1973] ECR 865 .... 125, 131
Germany v European Parliament & Council (Tobacco
  Advertising cases) (Cases C-233/94, C-376/98 and
  C-491/01) 28, 59
Gravier v City of Liège (Case 293/83) [1985]ECR 593; [1985]
  3 CMLR 1; [1985] 1 CMLR 432, Trib of Liège 66
Grimaldi v Fonds des Maladies Professionelles (Case C-322/88)
  [1989] ECR 4407 58
Groener v Minister of Education (Case 379/87) [1989] ECR 3967;
  [1990] 1 CMLR 401 155–6
Groenveld v Produktschap voor Vee en Vlees (Case 15/79) [1979]
  ECR 3409 132
Grzelczyk (Case C-184/99) [2001] ECR 1-6193 142

Handels-OG Kontorfunktionaernesforbund v Dansk
  Arbeejdsgiverforening (Danfoss case) (Case 109/88) [1989]
  ECR 3199 5, 6
Hauptzollamt Mainz v CA Kupferberg & Cie KG (Case 104/81)
  [1982] ECR 3641 77

Hoekstra (née Unger) v BBDA (Case 75/63) [1964] ECR 177;
  [1964] CMLR 546 .... 97, 154
Humblot v Directeur des Services Fiscaux (Case 112/84) [1985]
  ECR 1367; [1986] 2 CMLR 338 .... 123, 124

International Fruit Co v Commission (Cases 41–44/70) [1971]
  ECR 411; [1975] 2 CMLR 515 .... 105, 106
Internationale Handelsgesellschaft IHG v Einfuhr-und-
  Vorratsstelle für Getreide and Futtermittel (Case 11/70)
  ECR 1125; [1972] CMLR 255 .... 65, 66, 73, 74
Inuit Tapiriit Kanatami and Others v European Parliament
  and Council of the European Union (Case T-18/10) 106
Ioannidis Case (Case C 258/04) [2005] All ER (D)
  77 (Sep) 152

Jagerskiold v Gustafsson (Case C-97/98) [1999] ECR I-7319 754 118
Jégo Quéré v Commission (Case T-177/01) [2002] ECR II-2365 105
Johnston v Chief Constable of the RUC (Case 222/84) [1986]
  ECR 167 79
Jongeneel Kaas v Netherlands (Case 237/82) [1984] ECR 483 132

Keck and Mithouard (Cases C-267 and 268/91) [1993]
  ECR I-6097 .... 41, 64, 94, 128, 129,
                                                    130, 131, 132
Kempf v Staatssecretaris van Justitie (Case 139/85) [1986]
  ECR 1741; [1987] 1 CMLR 764 154
Knoors v Secretary of State for Economic Affairs (Case 115/78)
  [1979] ECR 399 165
Kobler v Austria (Case C-224/01) [2003] ECR I-10239 .... 83, 94
Kolpinghuis Nijmegen (Case 80/86) [1987] ECR 3639; [1989]
  2 CMLR 18 80
Konsumentombudsmannen v De Agostini (Svenska) Förlag AB
  and TV-Shop i Sverige AB (Joined Case C-34/95, C-35/95
  and C-36/95) [1997] ECR I-3843 130
Konsumentombudsmannen v Gourmet International Products
  (Gourmet Foods case) (Case C-405/98) [2001] ECR I-1795 ..... 130, 131

Levin v Staatssecretaris (Case 53/81) [1982] ECR 1085 .... 154, 161

Luisi and Carbone v Ministero del Tesoro (Joined Cases 286/82
and 26/83) [1984] ECR 377; [1985] 3 CMLR 52 167
Lütticke (Alfons) GmbH v Commission of the EEC (Case 48/65)
[1966] ECR 19 .... 97, 111, 113
Lyckeskog (Case 99/00) [2002] ECR I-4839 .... 93, 96

McCarthy (Shirley) v Secretary of State for the Home Department
(Case C-434/09) [2011] 3 CMLR 10 145
Mangold (Werner) v Rüdiger Helm (Case C-144/04) [2005]
ECR I-9981 81
Marleasing v La Comercial Internacional (Case C-106/89)
[1992] ECR I-4135; [1992] 1 CMLR 305 .... 80, 85
Marshall v Southampton and South West Hampshire AHA
(Marshall (No 1)) (Case 152/84) [1986] ECR 723; [1986]
1 CMLR 688 .... 78, 79, 81, 85
Marshall v Southampton and South West Hampshire AHA
(Marshall (No 2) (Case C-271/91) [1993] ECR I-4367; [1993]
3 CMLR 293 .... 89, 90, 97
Meilicke (Wienand) v ADV/ORGA FA Meyer AG
(Case C-83/91) [1992] ECR I-4871 .... 94, 96
Meroni case (Case 14/60 [1961] ECR 133 111
Metock (Blaise Baheten) and Others v Minister for Justice,
Equality and Law Reform (Case C-127/08) [2008]
ECR I-6241 144
Michel S v Fonds National de Reclassement Social des
Handicapes (Case 76/72) [1973] ECR 457 158–9
Mickelson v Roos, see Åklagaren v Percy Mickelsson and
Joakim Roos
Microban International Ltd and Microban (Europe) Ltd v
European Commission (Case T-262/10) 106
Morgan, Iris Butcher (Joined Cases C-11/06 and C-12/06)
[2007] ECR 1-9161 147

Ninni-Orasche (Franca) v Bundesminister für Wissenschaft,
Verkehr und Kunst (Case C-413/01) [2003] ECR I-13187 154
Nold v Commission (Case 4/73) [1974] ECR 491; [1974]
2 CMLR 338 .... 66, 68, 103
Nordsee (Case 102/81) [1982] ECR 1095 .... 92, 96

Officier van Justitie v Sandoz (Case 174/82) [1983] ECR 2445 .... 136, 138

O'Flynn v Adjudication Offi cer (Case C-237/94) [1996]
ECR I-2617 156

Pardini v Ministero del Commercio con L'Estero (Case 338/85)
[1988] ECR 2041 95

Parti Ecologiste 'Les Verts' v European Parliament (Case 294/83)
[1986] ECR 1339 103

Pfeiffer and Others v Deutsches Rotes Kreuz (Cases C-397–403/01)
[2004] ECR I-8835 81

Piraiki-Patraiki v Commission (Case 11/82) [1985] ECR 207 105

Plaumann v Commission (Case 25/62) [1963] ECR 95; [1964]
CMLR 29 .... 104, 105, 112

Procureur du Roi v Dassonville (Case 8/74) [1974] ECR 837;
[1974] 2 CMLR 436; [1975] FSR 191 .... 126–7, 128, 130,
131, 132

Pubblico Ministero v Ratti (Case 148/78) [1979] ECR 1629;
[1980] 1 CMLR 96 .... 78, 85, 173

R v Bouchereau (Case 30/77) [1977] ECR 1999; [1977] 2 CMLR 800 ... 150

R v Henn and Darby (Case 34/79) [1979] ECR 3795; [1980]
1 CMLR 246 .... 134, 135, 138

R v HM Treasury ex p British Telecom (Case C-392/93)
All ER (EC) 411; [1996] IRLR 300 83

R v HM Treasury ex p Daily Mail (Case 81/87) [1988] ECR
5483; [1989] 3 CMLR 713 183 164

R v Immigration Appeal Tribunal ex p Antonissen
(Case C-292/89) [1991] ECR I-745 152

R v London Borough of Ealing and Secretary of State for
Education and Skills, ex p Bidar (Case C-209/03) [2005]
ECR I-2119 .... 147, 159

R v MAFF ex p Hedley Lomas (Case C-5/94) [1996] ECR I-2553;
[1996] 2 CMLR 391 .... 83, 132

R v Secretary of State for Transport ex p Factortame Ltd
(Factortame (No 2)) (Case C-213/89) [1990] ECR 1-2433;
[1990] 3 CMLR 1 .... 74, 85, 90

R v Secretary of State for Transport, ex p Factortame Ltd and
others (Case C-221/89) [1991] ECR I-3905 .... 82, 163

R v Thompson and Others (Case 7/78) [1979] 1 CMLR 47 .... 135, 138

Razzouk and Beydouin v Commission (Cases 75a and 117/82)
[1984] ECR 1509 66

Reed case (Case 59/85) [1985] ECR 1283 148

Rewe-Zentral v Bundesmonopolverwaltung fur Branntwein
(Cassis de Dijon case) (Case 120/78) [1979] ECR 649; [1979]
3 CMLR 494 .... 127, 128, 129, 130, 131, 132,
133, 136, 138, 156

Rewe-Zentralfinanz v Landschwirtschaftskammer (San José Scale)
(Case 4/75) [1975] ECR 843; [1977] 1 CMLR 599 .... 136, 138

Rewe-Zentralfinanz v Landschwirtschaftskammer für das
Saarland (Case 33/76) [1976] ECR 1989; [1977] 1 CMLR 533 ..... 89, 90

Reyners (Jean) v Belgian State (Case 2/74) [1974] ECR 631;
[1974] 2 CMLR 305 .... 43, 76, 85, 166, 173

Rheinmuhlen-Dusseldorf (Cases 146 and 166/73) [1974]
1 CMLR 523 92

Richardt (Case C-367/89) [1991] ECR I-4601 135

Roberts v Tate & Lyle Industries (Tate & Lyle case)
(Case 151/84) [1986] ECR 703; [1986] 1 CMLR 714 78

Roman Angonese v Cassa di Risparmio di Bolzana Spa
(Case C-282/98) 169

Roquette Frères v Council (Case 138/79) [1980] ECR 3333 ..... 31, 61, 103

Rottman (Janko) v Freistaat Bayern (Case 135/08) [2010]
ECR I-1449 143

Royer (Case 48/75) [1976] ECR 497; [1976] 2 CMLR 619 .... 162, 164

Rutili v Ministre de l'Interieur (Case 36/75) [1975] ECR
1219; [1976] 1 CMLR 140 .... 66, 150

Sayag v Leduc (Case 9/69) [1969] ECR 329 110

Schloh (Bernhard) v Auto contrôle technique SPRL
(Case 50/85) [1986] ECR 1855 126

Schmidberger v Austria (Case C-112/00) [2003] ECR I-5659 128

Schneider Electric SA v Commission of the European
Communitie (Case T-351/03) [2007] ECR II-2237 112

Schoppenstedt v Commission (Case 5/71) [1971] ECR 975 .... 111, 112

Simmenthal SpA v Commission (Case 92/78) [1979] ECR 777;
[1980] 1 CMLR 25 .... 93, 110

Société Comateb v Directeur General des Douanes et Droites
  Indirects (Cases C-192–218/95) [1997] ECR I-165; [1997]
  2 CMLR 649 123
Société Roquette Frères v Commission (Case 26/74) [1976]
  ECR 677 113
Sotgui v Deutsche Bundespost (Case 152/73) [1974] ECR 153 160
Stanton v INASTI (Case 143/87) [1988] ECR 3877; [1989]
  3 CMLR 761 164
Stauder v City of Ulm and International Handelsgesellschaft
  (Case 29/69) [1969] ECR 419; [1970] CMLR 112 .... 66, 68
Steymann v Staatssecretaris van Justitie (Case 196/87) [1988]
  ECR 6159; [1989] 1 CMLR 449 154
Stork v High Authority (Case 1/58) [1965] ECR 405 .... 66, 68

Textilwerke Deggendorf (TWD) (Case C-188/92) [1994]
  ECR I-833 109
Thieffry v Conseil de L'Ordre des Avocats à la Cour de Paris
  (Case 71/76) [1977] ECR 765; [1977] 2 CMLR 373 164
Toepfer and Getreide-Import Gesellschaft v Commisson
  (Cases 106 & 107/63) [1965] ECR 405 105
Topfer v Commission (Case 112/77) [1978] ECR 1019 65
Torfaen Borough Council v B & Q plc (Case 145/88) [1989]
  ECR 3851 128
Trojani v Centre public d'aide sociale (Case C-456/02) [2004]
  ECR I-7573 163

UNECTEF v Heylens (Case 222/86) [1987] ECR 4097; [1989]
  1 CMLR 901 165
Unilever Italia v Central Foods (Case C-443/98) [2000]
  ECR I-7535 .... 81, 85
Union de Pequeños Agricultores v Council (UPA case)
  (Case C-50/00P) [2002] ECR I-6677 105
Union Royale Belge des Sociétés de Football Association
  ASBL v Bosman (the Bosman case) (Case C-415/93) [1995]
  ECR I-4921; [1996] 1 CMLR 645 .... 156, 169

Van Binsbergen v Bestuur van de Bedrijfsvereniging voor de
  Metaalnijverheid (Case 33/74) [1974] ECR 1299; [1975]
  1 CMLR 298 170

Van Duyn (Yvonne) v Home Offi ce (Case 41/74) [1974]
ECR 1337; [1975] 1 CMLR 1 . . . . 76, 78, 150

Van Gend en Loos v Nederlandse Administratie der
Belastingen (Case 26/62) [1963] ECR 1; [1963]
CMLR 105 . . . . 43, 64, 72, 73, 74, 75, 76, 77, 78,
80, 85, 91, 92, 96, 123, 173

Variola Variola SpA v Amministrazione delle Finanze
(Case 34/73) [1973] ECR 981 57

Vlassopoulou (Case 340/89) [1991] ECR 2357 165

Von Colson and Kamann v Land Nordrhein-Westfalen
(Case 14/83) [1984] ECR 1891; [1986] 2 CMLR 430 . . . 80, 85, 89, 97, 173

Wachauf (Hubert) v Bundesamt für Ernährung und
Forstwirtschaft (Case 5/88) [1989] ECR 2609 . . . . 67, 68

Walrave and Koch v Association Union Cycliste
Internationale (Case 36/74) ECR 12405; [1975]
1 CMLR 320 . . . . 166, 170

Wöhrmann (Milchwerke Heinz) & Sohn KG and Alfons
Lütticke GmbH v Commission of the European Economic
Community (Cases 31 and 33/62) [1962] ECR 501 110

Zambrano (Gerardo Ruiz) v Office national de l'emploi
(ONEm) (Case C-34/09) [2011] 2 CMLR 46 145

Zhu and Chen v Sec of State for Home Dept (Case C-200/02)
[2004] ECR 1-09925 144

Table of Legislation

CONVENTIONS AND TREATIES

Budgetary Treaty 1970 (First Budgetary Treaty) 23, 32, 54

Budgetary Treaty 1975 (Second Budgetary Treaty) 23, 32, 44, 54

Charter of Fundamental Rights of the European Union 2000 .... 18, 20, 67, 68, 69

EEC Treaty 1957 (Treaty of Rome) ... 10, 13, 54, 71, 72, 73
   Art 52 76
   Art 119 76

European Atomic Energy Community 1957 (EURATOM) Treaty 9, 10, 14, 54

European Coal and Steel Community Treaty 1951 (ECSC) (Treaty of Paris) 8, 9, 22, 26, 30, 54

European Convention on the Protection of Human Rights and Fundamental Freedoms 1950 (ECHR) 7–8, 15–16, 66, 67

Fiscal Compact Treaty 2011 (FCT) 20

Merger Treaty 1965 ..... 11, 22, 54

Single European Act (SEA) 1986 11–13, 23, 31

Treaty Establishing a Constitution for Europe (2004) 18, 23, 84

Treaty Establishing the European Community 2010 (TEC) (EC Treaty) 13, 16, 19, 102
   Art 10 .... 80, 89, 90
   Art 12 66
   Art 17 143
   Art 34 66
   Art 141 66
   Art 220 65
   Art 230 .... 17, 65, 105, 106, 109
   Art 288 65

Treaty of Accession 1951 (Treaty of Paris) (Belgium, France, Germany, Italy, Luxembourg, Netherlands) 8, 22

Treaty of Accession 1973
(Denmark, Ireland,
UK) 21, 23

Treaty of Accession 1981
(Greece) 21, 23

Treaty of Accession 1986
(Portugal, Spain) 21, 23

Treaty of Accession 1995
(Austria, Finland,
Sweden) 21, 23

Treaty of Accession 2004
(Cyprus, Estonia, Czech
Republic, Latvia, Lithuania,
Hungary, Malta, Poland,
Slovenia, Slovakia) 21, 23

Treaty of Accession 2007
(Bulgaria, Romania) 21, 23

Treaty of Accession 2013
(Croatia) 21, 23

Treaty of Amsterdam (ToA)
1997 .... 15–16, 23, 31, 54

Treaty of Lisbon (Reform
Treaty) 2009 ...... 4, 11, 18–20,
23, 31, 34, 47, 54,
60, 110

Treaty of Nice (ToN)
2000 .... 17, 23, 31, 54

Treaty on European Union
(TEU) 1992 (Maastricht
Treaty) ... 3, 4, 13–15, 23, 31, 54

Art 1 19

Art 2 .... 19, 48, 49

Art 3 .... 19, 29

Art 4 .... 25, 26, 29, 82, 90,
97, 101

Art 5 .... 25, 26, 29

Art 6 .... 19, 29, 67, 68

Art 7 61

Art 9 .... 19, 49, 142

Art 10 .... 19, 48, 49, 142

Art 11 .... 19, 49, 142

Art 12 .... 19, 49, 142

Art 13 .... 19, 29, 34

Art 14 46

Art 15 .... 34, 46

Art 16 .... 35, 36, 46

Art 17 .... 33, 46

Art 19 .... 35, 46, 64, 65

Art 47 .... 19, 69

Art 48 .... 19, 55, 56

Art 49 19

Art 50 19

Protocol No 2 (Application
of the Principles of
Subsidiarity and
Proportionality) 28

Protocol No 30 (On the
Application of the Charter
of Fundamental Rights) 68

Treaty on Stability, Coordination
and Governance in the
Economic and Monetary
Union (TSCG) 20

Treaty on the Functioning
of the European Union
2010 (TFEU) 3, 54

Art 2 .... 27, 29, 66

Art 3 .... 19, 25, 27, 29

Art 4 .... 19, 25, 27, 29, 80

Art 5 .... 25, 27, 29

Art 6 .... 19, 25, 27, 29

Arts 7–17 19

Art 17 39

Art 18 .... 66, 147, 153, 155,
159, 160, 163, 167

Art 19 66

Art 20 . . . 142, 143, 148, 153, 161

Art 21 . . . 141, 143, 145, 149, 153

Art 22 61

Art 24 . . . . 19, 142, 167–70

Arts 26–37 117

Art 26 . . . . 117, 141, 153

Arts 28–33 118

Art 28 118

Art 29 118

Art 30 . . . . 75, 119, 120, 121,
122, 123, 136

Art 31 61

Art 34 . . . . 72, 124, 125, 126,
127, 128, 129, 130,
131, 133, 134, 136,
138

Art 35 . . . . 124, 125, 126, 132,
133, 134, 138

Art 36 . . . . 124, 125, 126, 131,
132, 133, 134, 135,
137, 138, 139

Art 40 66

Arts 45–62 141

Arts 45–48 153

Art 45 . . . . 155, 157, 158, 160,
161, 166, 169

Art 46 . . . . 59, 60

Arts 49–62 169

Arts 49–55 . . . . 153, 162, 169

Art 49 . . . . 76, 163, 164, 165,
170

Arts 51–54 168

Art 51 . . . . 166, 168

Art 53 . . . . 165, 166

Art 54 . . . . 163, 164

Arts 56–62 . . . 153, 162, 166, 169

Art 56 . . . . 167, 170

Art 57 . . . . 167, 169

Art 62 168

Art 106 61

Art 110 . . . . 122, 123, 124

Art 113 59

Art 114 59

Art 157 . . . . 66, 76

Art 216 . . . . 69, 77

Arts 223–234 . . . . 30, 46

Art 225 31

Art 226 33

Art 227 33

Art 228 . . . . 33, 97

Art 230 32

Art 231 62

Art 234 33

Art 235 . . . . 34, 46

Art 236 . . . . 34, 46

Arts 237–243 . . . . 35, 46

Arts 244–250 . . . . 38, 46

Arts 251–281 . . . . 41, 46

Art 254 42

Art 256 43

Art 258 . . . . 40, 87, 97, 98,
99, 100, 101, 124,
170

Art 259 . . . . 87, 99, 100, 101,
124, 170

Art 260 . . . . 87, 99, 101, 124,
170

Art 263 . . . . 19, 28, 33, 37, 47,
65, 87, 102, 103, 104,
106, 108, 109, 110,
115, 171

Art 264 .... 87, 102, 107, 112

Art 265 .... 33, 87, 102, 108, 112

Art 266 .... 87, 107, 109

Art 267 .... 75, 78, 87, 91, 92, 93, 96, 109

Art 277 .... 110, 112

Art 279 102

Arts 282–284 .... 44, 46

Arts 285–287 .... 44, 46

Art 288 .... 56, 57, 58, 73, 77, 78, 103, 104, 105, 170, 173

Art 289 .... 19, 32, 47, 60, 61, 62, 63, 106

Art 290 .... 62, 63

Art 291 63

Art 294 .... 19, 36, 60, 61, 63

Arts 300–304 45

Art 300 45

Arts 305–307 45

Art 308 45

Art 309 45

Art 314 32

Art 340 .... 65, 83, 107, 110, 111, 112

Art 345 136

Art 352 59

Protocol No 2
(Application of the
Principles of
Subsidiarity and
Proportionality) 28

Protocol No 30 (On the
Application of the
Charter of Fundamental
Rights) 68

DIRECTIVES

Directive 70/50/EEC
(Restrictions on Imports) ... 124

Art 2(1) 124

Directive 76/207/EEC
(Equal Treatment) 78

Directive 93/7/EEC
(Return of Cultural Objects
Unlawfully Removed
from the Territory of
a Member State) 136

Directive 93/104/EC
(Working Time) 81

Directive 98/43/EC (Tobacco
Advertising) 59

Directive 2004/38
(Citizens' Rights of Free
Movement) 145, 161, 162, 167, 170

Art 2 .... 144, 148

Art 3 .... 144, 146, 148

Art 4 .... 146, 158

Art 5 .... 146, 158

Art 6 .... 146, 148, 152, 158

Art 7 .... 146, 152, 155, 158, 164

Art 8 155

Art 10 158

Art 12 .... 158, 159

Art 13 159

Art 14 152

Art 16 .... 146, 157, 158

Art 17 .... 157, 158

Art 18 158

Art 23 158

Art 24 .... 146, 147, 159, 160

Art 27 .... 151, 152, 160

Art 28 151

Art 29 150

Art 30 151

Art 31 151

Art 32 151

Directive 2005/36
(Recognition of Professional
Qualifications) 165

Directive 2006/123 (Services
in the Internal Market) 167

REGULATIONS

Regulation 1612/68/EEC
(Free Movement of
Workers) 155, 161

Regulation 3911/92/EEC
(Export of Cultural
Goods) 136

Regulation 492/11 (Freedom
of Movement for Workers
within the Union) 155, 158

**UNITED NATIONS
LEGISLATION**

Convention on the Rights
of the Child 151

Universal Declaration of
Human Rights 1948 66

Glossary

Acquis communautaire	The body of objectives, substantive rules, policies, laws, rights, remedies and case law fundamental to the development of the Union legal order.
Advocates-General	Assistants to the Court of Justice, having the same status as judges.
Assembly	Original name given to the European Parliament.
Budget	The Union's revenue and expenditure. The Commission is responsible for submitting a draft budget annually to the Council, which shares budgetary authority with the Parliament.
Charges having equivalent effect	Charges having an equivalent effect to customs duties and, as such, prohibited by Union law (Arts 34 & 35 TFEU).
Charter of Fundamental Rights	Charter setting out rights of EU citizens originally drafted in 2009 and given legal effect in December 2009 by the Treaty of Lisbon.
Citizenship	Citizenship of the Union is dependent on holding nationality of one of the Member States (Art 20 TFEU).
Co-decision procedure	The legislative procedure whereby the European Parliament was given the power to adopt acts jointly with the Council. Introduced by the TEU (Art 251 TEC). Now amended and renamed the 'Ordinary' legislative procedure by the Treaty of Lisbon (Arts 289 & 294 TFEU).
Comitology	The process by which the Commission is assisted by committees in the implementation of legislation (Arts 101 & 102 TFEU).
Committee of the Regions	A European Union body whose birth reflects Member States' desire not to respect regional and local identities and prerogatives and also to

	involve them in the development and implementation of EU policies.
Common Customs Tariff	The common customs duty encircling the EU, charged at the same level no matter where a product is cleared for customs (Art 28 TFEU).
Common policies	Includes policies on agriculture, commerce and transport, established to ensure common principles and aims throughout the Union.
Common market	The first stage towards the creation of the single market.
Competence	See 'Union competence'.
Competition rules	Union rules intended to ensure that competition in the Community is not distorted.
Conciliation Committee	Conciliation Committees may be set up by the Commission under the ordinary legislative procedure with the aim of reaching agreement between the Council and the Parliament in relation to a legislative proposal (Art 294 TFEU).
Consultation procedure	A legislative procedure under which the Council is bound to consult with the European Parliament and take its views into account.
Convergence criteria	Criteria that must be attained by those Member States wishing to join the European Single Currency.
Co-operation procedure	A legislative procedure, introduced by the SEA, giving the Parliament greater influence in the creation of Union legislation. No longer used.
COREPER	Name commonly given to the Committee of Permanent Representatives who carry out tasks on behalf of the Council. They also provide a forum in which legislation can be discussed and agreed.
Council	Often referred to as the Council of Ministers, it has no equivalent anywhere in the world. It is here that the Member States legislate for the Union, set its political objectives, co-ordinate their national policies and resolve differences between themselves and with other institutions.
Council of Europe	A non-EU organisation founded in 1949 and the author of the European Convention on Human

	Rights. Membership now comprises 47 European countries.
Court of Auditors	An EU Institution, it is effectively the taxpayers' representative, responsible for checking that the European Union spends its money according to its budgetary rules and regulations and for the purposes for which it is intended.
Court of First Instance	Established by the SEA, the Court took over some of the workload of the Court of Justice. Re-named the General Court by the Treaty of Lisbon.
Court of Justice of the EU	Provides the judicial safeguards necessary to ensure that the law is observed in the interpretation and application of the Treaties and, generally, in all of the activities of the Union. (Normally referred to as the 'Court' with a capital C.)
Customs Union	An area where barriers to trade have been eliminated, as exists between the Member States (Arts 28 TFEU).
Decisions	Union legislative acts which are binding upon those to whom they are addressed (Art 288 TFEU).
Decision making	The processes by which decisions are taken or legislative acts are created within the Union.
Deepening	The process of increased integration between the Member States.
Democratic deficit	Criticism levelled at the Union in relation to its perceived remoteness from the ordinary citizen, particularly in relation to the creation of legislation.
Direct applicability	A directly applicable provision of European law is one which takes effect within the Member States without the need for incorporation or implementation by national authorities.
Direct effect	A doctrine established by the Court of Justice providing that Union law may provide rights and obligations to individuals, enforceable in national courts (*Van Gend en Loos*).
Direct elections	Democratic elections held to elect the Members of the European Parliament (MEPs).

Directives	Legislative acts that oblige Member States to implement the aims contained within the directive by a stipulated date (Art 288 TFEU).
Distinctly applicable measure (DAM)	Term used to describe restrictive measures, enacted by Member States, which discriminate between nationally produced goods and those originating in other States.
Dualist State	A State, such as the UK, in which international law and national law are considered distinct and separate from one another.
Economic and Monetary Union	The process whereby the economic and monetary policies of the Member States are harmonised, culminating in the introduction of a single currency.
Economic and Social Committee	In accordance with the Treaties, the Committee advises the Commission, the Council and the European Parliament. The opinions which it delivers (either in response to a referral or on its own initiative) are drawn up by representatives of the various categories of economic and social activity in the European Union.
Effet utile	A principle of law developed by the Court of Justice to ensure effective enforcement of Union rules within the Member States.
Enlargement	See Widening.
EURATOM	European Atomic Energy Community created in 1957 in order to integrate the nuclear industries of the Member States, promoting safety, research, etc.
Euro	European unit of currency.
European Central Bank	An EU Institution and the decision-making body in relation to European Monetary Union, responsible for implementing the monetary policy of the Union.
European Coal and Steel Community	European Community created in 1951 in order to integrate the coal and steel industries of the Member States.
European Commission	A Community Institution which has three distinct functions: initiator of proposals for legislation, guardian of the Treaties, and the manager and

	executor of Union policies and of international trade relations.
European Community (EC)	Community originally created in 1957 by the Treaty of Rome. Once named the European Economic Community (renamed by the TEU) in order to integrate the economies of the Member States. Now part of the European Union (Treaty of Lisbon).
European Communities Act	Enacted in the UK in 1972 in order to incorporate the law of the European Union into the law of the UK.
European Convention on Human Rights	Signed under the aegis of the Council of Europe, which the Union is still in the process of acceding to, the Convention has been given legal effect by the Treaty of Lisbon.
European Council	The name given to the Heads of State of the Member States when they meet. Now formally recognised as an EU Institution.
European Central Bank	An EU Institution tasked with the role of administering the monetary policy of the Eurozone States.
European Investment Bank	The European Union's financing institution; it provides loans for capital investment, promoting the Union's balanced economic development and integration.
European Parliament	The directly elected democratic expression of the political will of the peoples of the European Union; the largest multinational Parliament in the world.
Functionalist approach	An early approach to integration taken by Europe i.e. industry by industry.
General Application	Under Art 288 TFEU, legislation which has 'general application' applies to everyone in every Member State.
General principles	A body of unwritten principles supplementing Union legislation and developed by the Court of Justice from the threads found in the Treaties, the laws of the Member States and international law.
Harmonisation	The process of approximation laws throughout the Member States in order to ensure the establishment and effective functioning of the internal market.

High Authority	The original name for what has become the European Commission.
Indirect effect	Doctrine developed by the Court of Justice requiring national courts to interpret national legislation in the light of European directives (*Von Colson*).
Indistinctly applicable measure (IDAM)	Restrictive measures enacted by Member States, which apply equally to domestically produced goods and those produced in other States.
Institutions	Seven Institutions that have been afforded powers by the Treaties in order to ensure aims set out in the EU Treaty are realised (Art 13 TEU).
Intergovernmental Conference	Conferences composed of the Heads of State the Member States.
Intergovernmental organisation	A body which reaches decisions through co-operation and consensus with its membership.
Intergovernmentalism	A theory of integration under which the Member States take decisions by co-operation and consensus.
Internal market	The creation of an internal market is the first of three stages in the creation of a EU, the others being monetary and political union. It involves uniting the markets of the Member States into a single economic area without internal frontiers.
Judicial review	Term used to describe the various actions available to the CJEU in order to review the legality of acts of the Institutions (Arts 263–266 TFEU).
Locus standi	The right to be heard in court proceedings.
Luxembourg Accords/ Compromise	Agreement reached, in 1966, following the French refusal to accept majority voting in the Council. It allowed Member States to request that decisions be reached by unanimity, rather than majority, when an issue was considered to be of major national interest.
Measures having equivalent effect	Measures having an effect equivalent to quantitative restrictions on trade and held to include State measures which have the potential to impact on trade between the Member States (Arts 34 & 35 TFEU and *Dassonville*).
Monist State	A State in which international law is incorporated into the national legal system as soon as it is ratified.

Multi-speed Europe	A term used to describe the system whereby a group of Member States is willing to make an advance in the assumption that other States will follow later. Also known as 'variable geometry'.
Official Journal	A publication of the European Union in which Regulations and Directives must be published, together with other legislative and non-binding acts.
Ombudsman	Every citizen of each Member State is both a national and a European citizen. One of the rights of all European citizens is to apply to the European Ombudsman if they are victims of an act of 'maladministration' by the institutions or bodies.
Preliminary reference	A term describing the procedure by which national courts may request a ruling from the Court of Justice on the interpretation of primary and secondary legislation and on the validity of secondary legislation (Art 267 TFEU).
Product requirement	National rules which relate to the intrinsic qualities of goods such as composition, size and weight.
Purposive method of interpretation	Method of legislative interpretation favoured by the Court of Justice in which the provision of Union law must be put into context and interpreted in the light of the law as a whole. Also alluded to as the teleological or contextual method.
Qualified majority voting	A procedure for reaching agreement in Council by which each Member State's votes are weighted to reflect the population of that State.
Quantitative restriction	Non-pecuniary restrictions placed on goods by virtue of their crossing a frontier, for example, quotas and total bans (Arts 34 & 35 TFEU).
Regulations	Legislative acts of the Institutions of the EU which take effect in all Member States without the need for enacting measures on the part of those States (Art 288 TFEU).
Schengen Agreement	An agreement between a number of Member States to abolish checks at common borders in order to achieve free movement of persons.

Selling arrangement	National trading measure which relates to the extrinsic qualitative of goods such as marketing and when or where goods can be sold (*Keck*).
Single European Act	Amending Treaty signed in 1986 by the Member States. Its main aim was to speed up integration in the (then) Community and it also laid down provisions relating to political co-operation.
Single market	An area in which most trade barriers have been removed, with common policies on product regulation, and freedom of movement of goods, persons, services and capital. Now commonly known within the EU as the 'internal market'.
Soft law	Rules which have no binding force, but which may nevertheless have practical effects.
Subsidiarity	A principle ensuring that decisions are taken as close as possible to the citizen in areas which are not in the exclusive competence of the Union.
Supranationalism	A theory of integration involving power moving from the Member States to the Institutions.
Supremacy	A doctrine developed by the Court of Justice, providing that, where Union law and national law conflict, Union law will take precedence.
Teleological	Derived from the Greek word *telos*, meaning 'end' or 'purpose'. A favoured method of interpretation of the CJEU.
Transparency	A term used by the institutions to denote openness in their workings. It includes a commitment to access to information.
Treaty of Amsterdam	An amending Treaty introduced in 1999. Its main aims are to place the interests of workers and citizens at the heart of the Union, to remove existing barriers to free movement while improving security, give the Union a greater voice on the world stage and ensure that the institutions are as effective and efficient as possible in preparation for enlargement.
Treaty on European Union	Signed in 1992, the Treaty not only amended TEC, but also created the European Union.
Treaty of Nice	Signed in 2000, came into effect in February 2003, an amending Treaty with the aim of facilitating the enlargement of the EU.

Twin pillars	The 'twin pillars' of direct effect and supremacy of EU law.
Two-speed Europe	See Multi-speed Europe.
Union competence	The Union is based on the principle of limited powers which are specifically attributed to it by the Treaties. Before the Union may take action, it must ensure that it has been provided with the authority to do so (Arts 2–6 TFEU).
Union law	The rules of the EU legal order including primary and secondary legislation, general principles of law and case law of the Court of Justice. Also known as the acquis.
Variable geometry	See Multi-speed Europe.
Widening	A term used to describe the enlargement of the EU.

Abbreviations

AG	Advocate-General
Art	Article
CCT	Common Customs Tariff
CFI	Court of First Instance (now General Court)
CHEE	charge having equivalent effect to a customs duty
CJEU	Court of Justice of the European Union (was ECJ)
CMLR	Common Market Law Review
CoA	Court of Auditors
CoR	Committee of Regions
COREPER	Committee of Permanent Representatives
DAM	distinctly applicable measure
DG	directorate-general
EC	European Community/European Council
ECB	European Central Bank
ECHR	European Convention for the Protection of Human Rights and Fundamental Freedoms/European Court of Human Rights
ECJ	European Court of Justice (now CJEU)
ECOSOC	Economic and Social Committee
ECR	European Court Reports
ECSC	European Coal and Steel Community
EEC	European Economic Community
EIB	European Investment Bank
EMU	European Monetary Union
EP	European Parliament
ESC	Economic and Social Committee
ESCB	European System of Central Banks

ET	Employment Tribunal
EU	European Union
EURATOM	European Atomic Energy Community
FCT	Fiscal Compact Treaty
GC	General Court (was CFI)
IDAM	indistinctly applicable measure
IGC	intergovernmental conference
IPR	intellectual property right
MEP	Member of the European Parliament
MHEE	measure having equivalent effect
MS	Member State
NATO	North Atlantic Treaty Organization
OEEC	Organisation for Economic Co- operation
OJ	Official Journal
QMV	qualified majority voting
QR	quantitative restrictions
RGM	relevant geographical market
SEA	Single European Act 1986
TEC	European Community Treaty
TEU	Treaty on European Union 1992 (Maastricht Treaty)
TFEU	Treaty on the Functioning of the European Union
ToA	Treaty of Amsterdam 1997
ToN	Treaty of Nice 2000
TSCG	Treaty on Stability, Coordination and Governance in Economic and Monetary Union

1 Introduction

I. THE SIGNIFICANCE OF EU LAW

The United Kingdom's (UK) membership of the European Union (EU) has resulted in EU law becoming an integral source of UK national law. Knowledge and understanding of the law of the EU is therefore indispensable to all lawyers in the UK in the same way in which knowledge of statute or common law is indispensable.

II. THE AIMS OF THIS BOOK

In recognition of the importance of EU law, it is vital that law students have a solid grounding in its principles. Many students, however, appear to find the study of EU law rather alarming, which is perhaps understandable given the differences of approach and terminology that often exist between the European Union's legal system and that of the UK.

Students of EU law should, however, take heart. The EU goes back little more than 50 years and has, in the main, developed with a set of specific aims in mind, which means that it is possible to approach it in a logical, incremental manner. That is not to say that the scope of EU law is narrow. Indeed, it is not and it would be impossible to cover all that it encompasses in any degree of depth in a single volume.

In recognition of the breadth of EU law, the content of most EU law courses is necessarily limited to the principal constitutional and institutional areas of the European Union's legal order, together with selected areas of substantive law.

Despite this approach, there are still huge areas of law to cover, and although there are a number of excellent textbooks providing detailed accounts of the law, such texts can be intimidating or overpowering and, consequently, rather daunting to the new student.

While this book aims to provide an account of the same constitutional and institutional principles together with important areas of substantive law, albeit in a less circuitous manner than many texts, a different approach has been taken. At the beginning of each topic, before the legal principles are examined, each area of law is put into context, thus allowing an understanding of relevant issues to be developed.

In addition, at the end of most sections, knowledge and understanding are consolidated by the provision of diagrams or flowcharts, highlighting the main points at issue, and/or 'thinking points' to encourage you to further develop your understanding. Finally, a chapter on assessment provides advice on approaching both coursework, revision and examinations.

This approach is intended to promote understanding of EU law as a whole, allowing students to develop a 'feel' for the subject and, hopefully, resulting in far less rote learning being necessary just before examinations!

III. YOUR APPROACH TO STUDYING EU LAW

Your approach to studying EU law can make all the difference to your enjoyment of the course and also to the end result. The subject of the UK's membership of the EU is one of keen debate in the media and it is almost impossible not to have formed some sort of opinion as to whether the UK should be 'in' or 'out'! Certain UK newspapers appear to thrive on discussion as to whether the EU should dictate the shape of the bananas we eat or whether hedgehog-flavoured crisps should be banned and it is often difficult to arrive at the study of EU law with an open mind. However this is an essential prerequisite to successful study.

During your course you will be expected to attend lectures and tutorials or seminars. Do not underestimate the importance of these as learning tools. We all learn in various ways, not only through what we read, but also by listening, seeing and doing. Reading a variety of texts, legal journals and so on is essential *but* attending lectures can focus the mind, provide an introduction to a topic, shed light on areas of confusion and afford an alternative point of view.

Similarly, seminar attendance has numerous advantages (and, of course, attendance is normally compulsory). Attendance allows various topics or points to be focused upon; provides opportunity for discussion; allows for clarification and is also likely to provide invaluable practice in answering exam-type questions. Be sure not to miss out on these valuable opportunities and don't delude yourself into thinking that you can 'get away with it' by not spending adequate time preparing for tutorials, as the loss will be yours alone.

IV. FINDING RESOURCES ON EU LAW

There is a wealth of sources of information on EU law. Those enrolled on a structured course will normally be provided with at least an outline list of appropriate reading.

Make sure you have an **up-to-date** copy of relevant EU legislation at the *start* of your course. (This can be found in an EU statute book or accessed online.) If used regularly, you will find it invaluable. The Treaty on the Functioning of the European Union (TFEU), Treaty on European Union (TEU) and secondary legislation are, in the main, very readable and you should *always* read the various Treaty articles and secondary legislation **as you study them. The value of reading primary source materials is often underestimated by students who are new to law but, as you wouldn't expect to complete a module on art appreciation without looking at a painting, why would you think that you can complete a law module without reading the law?**

In addition to more traditional sources of legal information, internet access has opened up a huge wealth of materials. The number of websites containing information on Union law appears to grow daily and it is a virtually impossible task to provide a comprehensive list. Do, however, take care only to consult those sites which are recognised legal databases such as LexisNexis or Westlaw. The EU also has its own website, which is a good place to begin, as it also provides a number of links to other relevant sites. The address of this site is **http://europa.eu.** Learning to negotiate the site may take a little time but the benefits can be enormous: TRY IT!

Furthermore, the EU Institutions produce a wealth of information on various aspects of the European Union, much of which is free to access. A list of such publications, together with details of how to order, can be found on the Europa website.

V. BEGINNING YOUR STUDIES

1. Coping with jargon

Law students often remark that, when they begin studying a particular branch of law, not only do they have to take on board new legal principles, statutes, case law and so on, but they also have to cope with legal jargon that is particular to that area of law. This is certainly true of EU law, and students new to the subject may find themselves confused by its terminology.

It is, however, important to recognise that lawyers (and other specialists) regularly use jargon as a form of shorthand when communicating with one another and so it is vital to get to grips with relevant terminology, as failing to do so can have serious consequences, for example, students who fail to break through the jargon may never fully understand the law beyond.

In order to overcome this problem this book provides a glossary of commonly used terms. Make life easier for yourself by consulting this at the beginning of your studies and also to refer to it throughout. The Europa website also has a Glossary, accessible at **http://europa.eu/legislation_summaries/glossary/index_en.htm**

2. EEC, EC or EU?

One important issue of terminology that needs to be addressed at the outset are the different names which have been afforded to 'Europe' over the years. Once quite commonly referred to as the 'common market', the formal names by which the EU has been known over the years are the European Economic Community (EEC), European Community (EC) and the European Union (EU).

The EEC was created by the Treaty of Rome in 1957. This community was subject to a change of name in 1993, following the enactment of the Treaty on European Union, 1992 (TEU, also commonly referred to as the Maastricht Treaty, after the city in which it was signed), when it became the EC. Confusingly, the TEU also created the EU. Further confusion arises because the EU was, at that time, a complex structure made up of a number of parts, *one* of which was the EC. The EC was part of the EU, but not the same as it! However, since the entry into force of the Treaty of Lisbon 2009, the EC no longer exists as an entity and has been superseded by the EU. Consequently, **all contemporary references should now be to the EU** and it is only when a historical perspective is being taken that the EEC or EC should be used. This should become clearer once Chapter 2 has been read and digested!

1957 The **European Economic Community** (EEC) is created by the Treaty of Rome

1993 The EEC becomes known as the **European Community** (EC) following the enactment of the Treaty on European Union (also known as the Maastricht Treaty)

2010 The EC becomes known as the **European Union** (EU) following the enactment of changes introduced by the Treaty of Lisbon

---

3. Dealing with case names

In addition to the often oblique terminology which has been adopted by the EU, students of EU law often find the names of the decisions of the Court of Justice of the European Union (CJEU) to be a nightmare!

When it is considered that the EU comprises 28 different States, and has almost as many official languages, it is understandable that case names should occasionally prove difficult to pronounce and spell. Few lawyers would pretend that Case 109/88, *Handels-OG Kontorfunktionaernesforbund v Dansk Arbeejdsgiverforening*, flows easily off either the tongue or the pen. Despair can be avoided however, once it is recognised that many EU law cases have 'nicknames' that are normally acceptable for use in examinations (but do check with your tutor). For example, the commonly used name for the above case is *Danfoss* which, I am sure you will agree, is quite manageable!

4. Make sure you know where you are going

Life can be made far easier if we know which direction we're going in. If we are unsure, then life can be very confusing. The same can be said of studying EU law. It is not sufficient to know that you are going to study EU law. In order to make studying as painless as possible, and even enjoyable (*yes!*), you need to have some knowledge of precisely what areas of EU law you are going to study, *why* you are studying them and also in what order various topics are going to be considered.

If you are provided with a module guide or handbook, such information is normally contained within it. Generally, undergraduate EU law courses follow a scheme, which is roughly that of this book (the figure on the next page illustrates this).

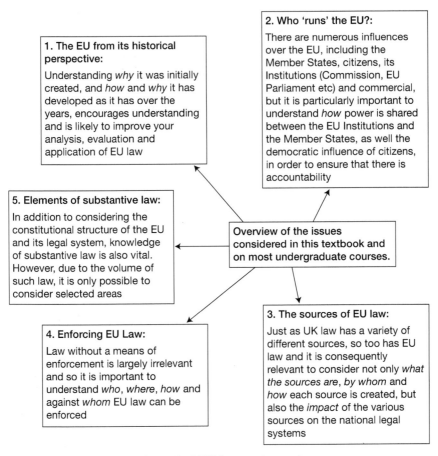

1. The EU from its historical perspective:

Understanding *why* it was initially created, and *how* and *why* it has developed as it has over the years, encourages understanding and is likely to improve your analysis, evaluation and application of EU law

2. Who 'runs' the EU?:

There are numerous influences over the EU, including the Member States, citizens, its Institutions (Commission, EU Parliament etc) and commercial, but it is particularly important to understand *how* power is shared between the EU Institutions and the Member States, as well the democratic influence of citizens, in order to ensure that there is accountability

5. Elements of substantive law:

In addition to considering the constitutional structure of the EU and its legal system, knowledge of substantive law is also vital. However, due to the volume of such law, it is only possible to consider selected areas

Overview of the issues considered in this textbook and on most undergraduate courses.

4. Enforcing EU Law:

Law without a means of enforcement is largely irrelevant and so it is important to understand *who*, *where*, *how* and against *whom* EU law can be enforced

3. The sources of EU law:

Just as UK law has a variety of different sources, so too has EU law and it is consequently relevant to consider not only *what the sources are*, *by whom* and *how* each source is created, but also the *impact* of the various sources on the national legal systems

Overview of a typical EU Law undergraduate course

VI. CONCLUSIONS

Hopefully, this book will not be seen as just another simplified or insubstantial text but rather as an introduction to the law of the European Union, ensuring that all who access it gain a firm foundation on which to build broader and deeper knowledge. No strong, high or enduring wall was ever built without a sound foundation being put in place first!

Remember that this book does not profess to contain all you will need to know about the law of the European Union but, hopefully, it will provide you with the desire and tools to develop your knowledge. Finally, **if there is something you do not understand, please ASK! Most tutors worth their salt will be only too pleased to help.**

2 The creation of a European Union

I. THE EUROPEAN COMMUNITIES: WHY THEY WERE CREATED AND WHAT DO THEY COMPRISE?

The best way to understand European Union (EU) law is to start at the beginning, which inevitably involves consideration of why the EU exists at all. The idea of a united Europe is certainly not a new one and a variety of leaders have, over the centuries, attempted to achieve European integration. In more modern times, it is possible to highlight the end of the Second World War, in 1945, as the catalyst which set in motion events that have led to the creation of the EU.

The economies of the various European states had been devastated by successive wars and the peoples of Europe were anxious to build a peaceful and more stable future for all. The United States of America saw a union between various European countries as a means of countering a perceived communist threat from the Eastern bloc and, consequently, provided financial aid to Europe under what is known as the Marshall Plan. In order to administer this programme of aid, the Organisation for Economic Co-operation was set up in 1948, inevitably involving co-operation between recipient countries. Other organisations such as the North Atlantic Treaty Organization (NATO), whose aims primarily related to defence, were also created and can be seen as early forms of modern co-operation among the countries of Western Europe.

1. The Council of Europe

Further co-operation between European governments led, in 1947, to the creation of the Council of Europe, an intergovernmental organisation (use the Glossary!) which adopted the European Convention on Human Rights

(ECHR) and established the European Court of Human Rights (ECtHR). *It needs to be strongly emphasised from the outset that this organisation was, and still is, SEPARATE from that which has become known as the European Union.* While undoubtedly performing a valuable role, particularly in the area of human rights, the Council of Europe fell short of what many felt was needed in order to stabilise inter-state relationships and ensure economic regeneration.

2. The First European Community: the European Coal and Steel Community (ECSC)

A plan based on economic co-operation in Europe was proposed by the French economist Jean Monnet and taken up by Robert Schuman, the then French Foreign Minister. This embryonic scheme took a functionalist approach (i.e. integration industry by industry) and involved the integration of the French and German coal and steel industries, as a means of stabilising the relationship between the two countries. The plan allowed the two industries to be closely monitored, ensuring that the capacity of states to secretly re-arm was reduced. However, as the idea also included ensuring security on a wider European basis, an invitation to participate was proffered to other European countries and the ECSC was finally created by the signing of the Treaty of Paris in 1951. This new Community had an initial membership of six, namely France, Germany, Italy, Belgium, Luxembourg and the Netherlands. (It is relevant to note that the then British Prime Minister, Sir Anthony Eden, had declared that the UK had no need to join, as it was *'well able to stand on its own two feet'* – a reference to the UK's assumed strong links with both the Commonwealth and the USA.)

The creation of the ECSC was significant, as it moved away from the more traditional intergovernmental (refer to the Glossary) system of co-operation between participating states. Four independent bodies – now known as the EU Institutions – were created to run the ECSC and the power to control the coal and steel industries was moved from the states to institutions comprising the High Authority, the Assembly, the Council and the Court of Justice. The new Community consequently had a supranational (Glossary), rather than intergovernmental, flavour. It is interesting to note that, although more than 50 years have gone by since this original transfer of sovereign powers from the Member States to the EU, as we shall see later, the extent of this transfer of authority still remains a matter of contention at times.

While the immediate focus of the ECSC was undoubtedly economic, that is, the creation of a common market in coal and steel, with common policies and the removal of all barriers to trade in those commodities, it should not be forgotten that the contracting States saw economic co-operation as a means to an end. Ensuring the longer-term aims of peace and European unity was the focus, if not the immediate emphasis, of the Community. This can be evidenced by reference to the Preamble to the Treaty of Paris, which provided that the establishment of an economic community was a 'basis for a broader and deeper community among peoples long divided by bloody conflicts; and to lay the foundations for Institutions which will give direction to a destiny henceforward shared'.

It should be noted that the Treaty of Paris expired in July 2002 and ECSC funds were transferred to the EU, to be used for research in sectors relating to the coal and steel industries.

3. Failed moves towards European Defence and Political Communities

Following the creation of the ECSC, further attempts at integration between the Member States were made, with plans being drawn up for a European Defence Community and European Political Community, involving the creation of a European army and a common European foreign policy. Agreement could not, however, be reached on these matters and it was not until 1956 that a way forward towards further integration was found. A report was published by an intergovernmental committee chaired by Paul-Henri Spaak, the then Belgian Foreign Minister, detailing plans for a further two communities, the European Atomic Energy Community (EURATOM) and the European Economic Community (EEC).

4. The European Atomic Energy Community (EURATOM)

The EURATOM Treaty was signed in Rome in 1957 by the same six countries that made up the ECSC. The object of this new community can be summarised as the furtherance of atomic energy for peaceful purposes, together with a commitment to uniform safety standards. Once more the control of each of the State's atomic industries was passed to four autonomous institutions, with the Assembly and the European Court of Justice being common to both the ECSC and EURATOM.

5. The European Economic Community (EEC)

Like EURATOM, the EEC was born as a result of the Spaak Report, and the treaty establishing the EEC – The EEC Treaty – was signed in Rome (hence often being referred to as the Treaty of Rome) by the same six contracting States, on the same day as the EURATOM Treaty. A further similarity lies in the fact that the new Community was to be administered by four bodies – or institutions – to which the Member States had delegated the right of independent action in certain specified areas. (Once more, the Court and the Assembly were shared between the three Communities.)

There was, however, a significant difference between the first two Communities and the EEC. Both the ECSC and EURATOM were limited in their scope, being functionalist in that they had as their aims the creation of a common market in coal and steel (ECSC) and in atomic energy (EURATOM), respectively. The EEC was significantly broader in its approach, in that it was created with the task of working towards integration of *all* aspects of the economies of its Member States, rather than integration of specific industries.

While the vehicle for integration was once more economic, the Preamble to the EEC Treaty continued to make it clear that the **longer-term goals were wider**, including a determination to 'lay the foundations of an ever closer union among the peoples of Europe'. It should be noted that this was very much in line with Monnet and Schuman's view that integration of the Member States' economies would spill over into other areas, namely political and social. It is, however, important to emphasise that the creation of the EEC meant that power to take decisions was **limited to specific, agreed areas only**, the most significant of which was in areas related to the creation of a common market.

II. THE DEVELOPMENT OF THE EUROPEAN ECONOMIC COMMUNITY (EEC)

The term 'European Communities' is used to denote all three Communities – that is the ECSC, EURATOM and the EEC. This should not be confused with 'European Community', which is the name which was later given to the EEC by the Treaty on European Union (TEU) in 1993. The Communities have not stood still since their inception and, in order to fully understand the present position, the major milestones in their development need to be considered, at least in outline.

1. The Merger Treaty 1965

The Merger Treaty, which came into effect in 1967, was the first amendment to the Treaties of Paris and Rome. Its main purpose was to merge the Institutions of all three Communities, creating a common Council of Ministers and a common Commission (formerly known as the High Authority). The remaining two Institutions, the European Parliament (EP, formerly the Assembly) and the Court of Justice (ECJ), already served all three Communities.

2. The Luxembourg Accords 1966

In 1965, France refused to attend Council meetings due to disagreement over the use of majority voting when taking decisions. This was resolved in 1966, when it was agreed that unanimous voting could be used where 'very important matters were at stake'. This agreement, known as the Luxembourg Accords, had no legal status but, in effect, gave States the right of veto in some matters.

3. The Single European Act 1986

The Single European Act (SEA), which came into effect in 1987, was the first substantial revision of the original EEC Treaty. While considerable early successes had been enjoyed, progress with regards to further integration had slowed to near-stagnation. This virtual standstill was blamed on a number of factors, both external and internal, including world recession, and the SEA can be viewed as a response to such problems.

The SEA contained a number of important provisions, both amending the original Treaties and also laying down new provisions for political co-operation between the Member States.

First, in an attempt to revitalise progress towards economic integration, the SEA set a date by which a 'single market' was to be achieved: 31 December 1992. Now referred to as the 'internal market', it was intended to take the EEC beyond being merely a Customs Union (i.e. an area where goods move freely without the need to pay customs duties) to an area with complete totality of economic activity. (You may find the terminology here a little confusing: the common, single and internal market are all terms which have been used to describe Europe's trading area. Under the changes introduced by the Treaty of Lisbon in 2009, all references should now be to 'internal market'.)

11

It was realised that the creation of a 'single market' would require substantial legislative activity by the relevant EU Institutions and, with this in mind, the SEA introduced a change to voting procedures within the Council. The use of qualified majority voting (QMV, whereby each Council member's vote was 'weighted', reflecting the population of the Member State that they represented) was significantly increased and, with the corresponding move away from the need for decisions to be agreed unanimously, the legislative process was effectively speeded up. In addition, the Commission was given a central role in the completion of the internal market, thereby increasing its influence on the development of the EEC.

The SEA amendments also attempted to ensure increased efficiency and democracy within the institutional framework. A Court of First Instance (CFI) was created to assist the overworked European Court of Justice (ECJ, formally known as the Court of Justice of the EU, or CJEU), while a new legislative procedure, known as 'co-operation', was introduced, providing the European Parliament (EP) with increased influence over the legislative process. The EP was also given the right of veto over the accession of new Member States. (Changes to the EP's functions were a response to calls for an enhanced role for the Institution following the introduction of direct elections to the European Parliament. The first elections took place in 1979 and were significant in that the EP became the first – and only – Union Institution to receive a **direct**, democratic mandate from the peoples of the EU.)

The SEA also formalised European political co-operation by recognising the European Council and providing for twice-yearly meetings. (A note of warning: take care not to confuse the European Council with the 'Council'. The European Council is a separate organisation created in 1974, with a membership composed largely of the Heads of State or Government of the Member States, while the Council is composed of representatives of each Member State at government-minister level. Neither should be confused with the Council of Europe (refer to the Glossary) which is **not** an EU Institution.)

In addition, the SEA also extended the areas of Community competence, formally recognising co-operation in economic and monetary union, social policy, economic and social cohesion (in an attempt to reduce disparities between regions within the Community), research and technological development and action on protection of the environment.

Finally, the Treaty referred to political co-operation, albeit outside formal Community structures, providing for the inclusion of the Commission and EP within the process and also for the development of co-operation in foreign policy and security fields (thus creating the forerunner of the 'three-pillared' EU, which is discussed below).

While the SEA was not without its critics, who decried it 'vague and ambiguous', it undoubtedly gave renewed momentum to plans for the economic integration of Europe and also laid important foundations for social and political integration. Institutional changes introduced by the Act supported the supranational nature of the Communities by increasing the influence of both the EP and the Commission while, at the same time, qualified majority voting (QMV) became the 'norm' in Council decision making, decreasing the influence of individual Member States.

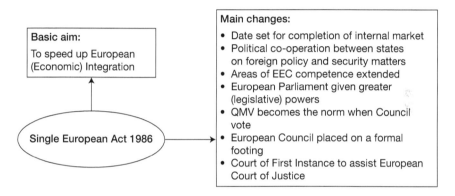

The Single European Act

4. The Treaty on European Union, 1992 (The Maastricht Treaty)

The Treaty on European Union (TEU), commonly known as the **Maastricht Treaty** after the Netherlands town where it was signed, was created with two broad aims in mind: first, to sustain the momentum created by the SEA and, second, the creation of a new organisation, albeit founded on the original Communities, to be known as the European Union (EU). The Treaty, which took effect in 1993, can be divided into two distinct areas: first, that which amended the original EEC Treaty and, second, that which created a new body – the European Union.

i. Changes to the original EEC Treaty

Significantly, the TEU renamed both the European Economic Community and the EEC Treaty, removing the word 'Economic' from both. (The EC Treaty became known as the **Treaty Establishing the European Community** or **TEC**.) It can be argued that the removal of this term was intended to indicate that, with the process of economic integration nearing completion, the European Community (EC) could now begin to concentrate on further integration in social and political fields.

The TEU also broadened the aims of the Community and provided for institutional and legislative changes, together with a timetable for the introduction of European Monetary Union (EMU). New areas of Community competence were introduced, while others were expanded. While the main changes are highlighted below, they will be further discussed, as appropriate, in later chapters.

The European Parliament's involvement in the legislative process was once more increased by extended use of the co-operation procedure and the introduction of a new procedure known as co-decision, which effectively allowed the EP to 'veto' legislative proposals. In addition, the Parliament was given a right of initiative with regard to legislation, once a monopoly enjoyed by the Commission. The EP was also given the power to appoint a European Ombudsman to investigate complaints relating to alleged maladministration on the part of the Institutions and their staff. Other changes involving the Institutions included formally recognising the Court of Auditors (CoA) as a Community Institution and the creation of a European Central Bank (ECB). (Further consideration of Union bodies is provided in Chapter 3.)

As part of an attempt to bring the Community 'closer to the peoples of Europe', the TEU introduced the concept of European citizenship, which is provided to all nationals of the Member States. (Discussed in further detail in Chapter 8.) With regard to issues relating to economic and monetary policy, the path towards EMU was further elaborated and a timetable set for its various stages, climaxing with the adoption of a single currency for the EU.

ii. Creation of the European Union

The TEU created a 'three-pillared' structure, *originally* comprising the following:

Pillar I, made up of the ECSC, EURATOM and the European Community (i.e. the European Communities);

Pillar II, which provided for the development of policies relating to foreign and security matters; and

Pillar III, relating to co-operation on justice and home affairs.

(Note that the specific content of these pillars was later subject to further change and has now been dismantled, as discussed in further detail below.)

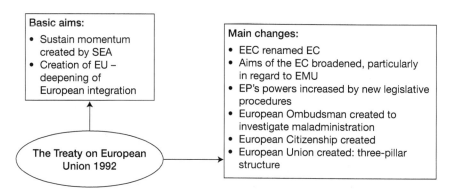

Basic aims:

- Sustain momentum created by SEA
- Creation of EU – deepening of European integration

The Treaty on European Union 1992

Main changes:

- EEC renamed EC
- Aims of the EC broadened, particularly in regard to EMU
- EP's powers increased by new legislative procedures
- European Ombudsman created to investigate maladministration
- European Citizenship created
- European Union created: three-pillar structure

The Treaty on European Union (The Maastricht Treaty)

In contrast to the EC, the original EU did not have separate legal personality and, in regard to Pillars II and III, there was no transfer of sovereign powers from the Member States to the Institutions. Instead, progress under Pillars II and III relied largely on co-operation and agreement between the States.

As with the SEA before it, the TEU was the subject of considerable academic analysis, not all of it complimentary. Commentators claimed, for example, that the structure of the Union had become too complex and fragmented and that 'opt-outs' afforded to some Member States reduced unity (e.g. the UK opt-out from the Social Chapter, negotiated by Prime Minister John Major, in 1991.) On the other hand, the Treaty was praised for measures such as increasing the role of the EP, widening the areas of European competence and increased flexibility.

5. The Treaty of Amsterdam 1997

The Treaty of Amsterdam (ToA), which came into effect in May 1999, has been described as a 'consolidating treaty', its main purposes being to improve processes, increase effectiveness and bring the EU closer to the ordinary person by making it more comprehensible.

Its provisions included a commitment to greater openness in the decision-making processes of the EU (transparency) and the recognition that the EU is based on respect for fundamental human rights, democracy and the rule of law. Indeed, membership of the EU was made contingent upon respect for such principles, and the Treaty also declared that the Union must respect human rights protected under the European Convention on Human Rights (ECHR). Any Member State found to be in 'serious and persistent' breach of such rights could now find its own rights, particularly those in regard to voting, suspended. (Protection of fundamental rights has now become an important area for the Union and is discussed in further detail in Chapter 3.)

The EC Treaty (TEC) was 'tidied up', with all obsolete provisions removed. This resulted in an almost complete renumbering of the Treaty. (*Take care*: it is important to note that texts and journals published prior to May 1999 are likely to refer to the 'old' numbering of the TEC. Also be aware that the Treaty of Lisbon, discussed below, has also resulted in further renumbering of provisions within both the TEU and TFEU.)

Specific changes to the TEC included a new non-discrimination provision that provided the EC with the authority to create secondary legislation aimed at combating discrimination based on sex, racial or ethnic origin, religion or belief, disability, age and/or sexual orientation. Member States were also encouraged to work together to combat unemployment, while areas such as public health and consumer protection were amended.

With regard to the Institutions, the EP was given yet further involvement in the legislative process as the use of the co-decision procedure (discussed in Chapter 4), included by virtue of the TEU, was expanded and simplified.

In an attempt to stem some of the criticisms levelled at the original Pillar structure, a number of changes were made to the content of the Pillars. Most significant among these changes was the transfer of policy on asylum, migration and judicial co-operation in civil matters from Pillar III to the Community pillar (Pillar I) and the renaming of the third pillar as 'Police and Judicial Co-operation in Criminal Matters'.

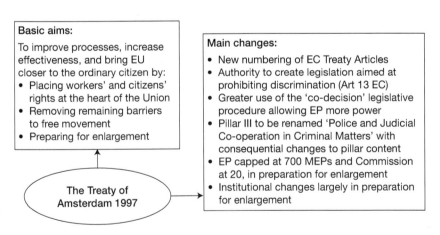

Basic aims:

To improve processes, increase effectiveness, and bring EU closer to the ordinary citizen by:
- Placing workers' and citizens' rights at the heart of the Union
- Removing remaining barriers to free movement
- Preparing for enlargement

Main changes:
- New numbering of EC Treaty Articles
- Authority to create legislation aimed at prohibiting discrimination (Art 13 EC)
- Greater use of the 'co-decision' legislative procedure allowing EP more power
- Pillar III to be renamed 'Police and Judicial Co-operation in Criminal Matters' with consequential changes to pillar content
- EP capped at 700 MEPs and Commission at 20, in preparation for enlargement
- Institutional changes largely in preparation for enlargement

The Treaty of Amsterdam 1997

The Treaty of Amsterdam

6. The Treaty of Nice 2000

The Treaty of Nice (ToN), which came into effect in February 2003, was enacted with the aim of facilitating, largely through institutional reform, the further enlargement of the EU.

The changes introduced by the ToN were described as 'modest' and even 'disappointing' and can be summarised as follows:

- *The decision-making process.* An extension of qualified majority voting in Council, together with a change of procedure, in that any decision needed to receive a specified number of votes (the 'threshold') *together with* the approval of a majority of Member States; a re-weighting of the votes in favour of the larger EU countries; increased use of the co-decision procedure, allowing the EP additional legislative authority.
- *The legal system.* In order to limit delays in obtaining judgments of the Court of Justice, a redistribution of responsibilities between it and the Court of First Instance (CFI, now known as the General Court).
- *Other institutional changes.* Limits were placed on the size of the Commission and EP. The EP was also placed on an equal footing with the Council and Commission in regard to judicial proceedings under Art 230 TEC (now Art 263 TFEU, discussed further in Chapter 6).

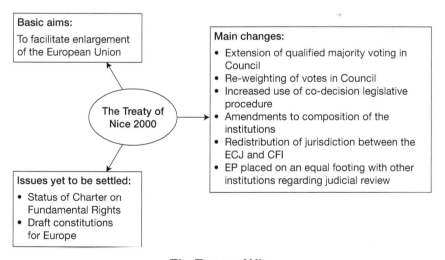

The Treaty of Nice

7. A Draft Constitution for Europe

Debate on creating a constitution for Europe was nothing new and the prospect had been considered at various times since the mid-1970s, with the most recent discussions culminating in the European Council agreeing the text of a 'Treaty Establishing a Constitution for Europe' in 2004.

In 2001, the Heads of State met at Laeken, Belgium for an IGC. (Remember to look up any unfamiliar abbreviations or terms in the list of abbreviations or glossary at the beginning of this book!) In what became known as the Laeken Declaration, the challenges facing the EU were set out. It was recognised, in particular, that the Institutions needed to bring themselves closer to the peoples of Europe by increasing democracy, transparency and efficiency, while the EU's role on the global stage was also in need of clarification.

The European Council, through the Laeken Declaration, set up a European Convention to consider such challenges, including the status of the EU's Charter of Fundamental Rights, and also to draft a 'Constitution for Europe'. The Convention was a move away from the norm – that is, discussion behind closed doors – to a far more public and transparent debate. Indeed, debate was opened to the public, while all official documents were also made public. In addition, the Convention set up numerous working groups and consulted with interested parties such as trade unions, employers' organisations and academics.

In 2003, after 16 months of intensive work, the European Convention produced a draft treaty establishing a 'Constitution for Europe'. This draft treaty was submitted to an IGC and, in October 2004, was unanimously agreed and signed by all Member States and candidate countries.

However, before the Treaty Establishing a Constitution for Europe could enter into force, it had to be ratified by all Member States. In 2005, the peoples of France and the Netherlands rejected the text of the Constitution. In the light of this, the European Council put ratification of the Constitutional Treaty on hold in order for a 'period of reflection' to take place. At a summit held in the summer of 2007, the proposed treaty was formally abandoned *but* it was also decided that moves towards reform would continue.

8. The Treaty of Lisbon 2009

As a result of Europe's continuing commitment to reform in order to meet the challenges of the twenty-first century, and despite the failure of the Draft Constitution for Europe, in December 2007, a **'Reform Treaty'** was agreed, by the Member States, in the city of Lisbon, Portugal. As a consequence of *where* it was agreed, the Treaty has since become known as the Treaty of Lisbon. The Treaty suffered an initial setback in June 2008, when it was rejected by the Republic of Ireland, but, following a second, successful Irish referendum in October 2009, the Lisbon Treaty finally took effect in December 2009.

The Council stated that the aim of the Treaty was completing 'the process started by the Treaty of Amsterdam and by the Treaty of Nice with a view to enhancing the efficiency and democratic legitimacy of the Union and to improving the coherence of its action'. Some of the most significant changes include giving the EU legal personality, which allows the Union to enter into agreements with third parties; increasing the use of qualified majority voting, as opposed to unanimous voting, when taking decisions (discussed further in Chapter 4) with the aim of increasing efficiency; introducing new 'jobs' (i.e. a permanent President for the European Council and a High Representative for Foreign and Security Policy to represent the EU in bodies such as the United Nations); changes to the Institutions, in terms of increasing their number from five to seven, size (size restrictions are placed

Administrative changes:	Policy and other changes:	Changes to law:
• *Change of name*: EC Treaty (TEC) changed to Treaty on the Functioning of the EU (TFEU) • Name of *European Court of Justice* changed to Court of Justice of the European Union • *Re-numbering* of Treaty Articles in both TFEU and TEC • *EU Institutions increased* from 5 to 7 (Art 13 TEU)	• Three-pillar *structure of EU changed* into a single framework (Art 1 TEU) • Union *values refined* (Art 2 and 3 TEU) • A number of TFEU *provisions recognised as having 'general application'* (Arts 7–17 TFEU) • Measures introduced intended to demonstrate EU commitment to democracy (Arts 9–12 TEU) • Shared *roles and powers of EU and Member States* clarified (Arts 3, 4 and 6 TFEU)	• EU given *legal personality* (Art 47 TEU) • Changes to *legislative procedures* (Art 48 TEU and 289, 294 TFEU, Art 24 TFEU (citizens initiative), State parliament given increased role (Art 12 TEU) • New provisions relating to *membership* of, and *withdrawal* from, EU (Arts 49–50 TEU) • Change to *Actions to Annul* (Art 263 TFEU) • Charter of *Fundamental Rights* given legal authority (Art 6 TEU)

Overview of main changes introduced by the Treaty of Lisbon

on the Commission and European Parliament), powers (e.g. the European Parliament's powers in regard to legislation will be put on an equal footing with those of the Council), and name (Court of Justice); merger of the Union's three-pillared structure into a single European Union; greater involvement for Member State Parliaments; greater clarity in power sharing between the Institutions and the Member States; greater emphasis on democracy (e.g. the introduction of a citizens' legislative initiative) and legal impact for the Charter of Fundamental Rights.

While each of these areas is dealt with in greater detail in the appropriate chapters of this text, the diagram also provides an overview of the main changes.

9. The Fiscal Compact Treaty (FCT)

In December 2011, in response to the debt crisis in the Eurozone, the European Council discussed the adoption of a 'Fiscal Compact' as part of an overall strategy to tackle the crisis. The UK vetoed its adoption and, consequently, the remaining Member States agreed to adopt it as an *international*, rather than an EU, treaty. In January 2012, 25 Member States (the UK and the Czech Republic were not parties to the agreement) formally agreed the Treaty (originally known as the **Treaty on Stability, Coordination and Governance in the Economic and Monetary Union (TSCG)**) and it was signed by 25 States in March 2012. The Treaty entered into force on 1 January 2013 with the aim of strengthening fiscal discipline in the euro area through the 'balanced budget rule' and the 'automatic correction mechanism'. It is legally binding as an international agreement and remains open to EU countries which did not sign it at the outset. The intention exists for it to be incorporated into the existing EU Treaties at some time in the future.

The FCT commits signatory States to introducing rules on budgetary deficits into their national constitutions, which has courted controversy, as it can be seen as a move away from the need for unity and unanimity among the EU Member States when taking decisions, reawakening arguments regarding the existence of a 'two-speed' Europe as it limits moves towards deeper economic integration to only 25 of the States. (For further, related, discussion on how the Member States, together with the Institutions, 'run' the EU, see Chapter 3.)

10. Enlargement

i. The UK's application for membership

By the early 1960s, the Member States of the Communities were beginning to enjoy the benefits of membership. A number of non-member countries, including the UK, were becoming aware of the benefits of membership and, in 1961, Britain made its first application to join. General De Gaulle, then President of France, made no secret of his hostility towards British membership, suggesting instead that the UK should continue its associations with the Commonwealth and the USA. The UK's application to join was consequently rejected.

A second UK bid to join in 1967 also failed and it was not until January 1973, following De Gaulle's resignation as French President, that the UK (together with Ireland and Denmark) was finally admitted.

ii. Further enlargement

In 1981, Greece joined the EEC, with Portugal and Spain raising the number of Member States to 12 by 1986. Austria, Sweden and Finland joined in January 1995, bringing the total to 15 Member States.

In May 2004, a further 10 States joined the Union, namely the former Eastern bloc countries of Estonia, the Czech Republic, Latvia, Lithuania, Hungary, Poland, Slovenia and Slovakia, together with Cyprus and Malta. This prompted Commissioner Gunter Verheugen to conclude that enlargement of the EU was a 'further step towards the fulfilment of an ideal that will bring peace, stability and democracy to the whole area ranging from the Baltic Sea to the Black Sea', demonstrating that the original goals for Europe are as relevant today as they were over half a century ago. In 2007 further enlargement occurred when Bulgaria and Romania joined, while in 2013 Croatia became the latest member of the EU.

At present, applications for membership have been received from a number of States, including Albania, Bosnia-Herzegovina, Iceland, Macedonia, Montenegro, Serbia and Turkey. They will, however, have to demonstrate that they meet the criteria for membership, known as the Copenhagen criteria, including a commitment to democracy, the rule of law, a market economy and adherence to the EU goals of political and economic union.

III. THE EU TODAY AND IN THE FUTURE

It should be evident by this stage that the EU is a complex structure. The Member States, while subscribing to the idea of an integrated Europe, do not always agree on the exact extent of such integration or on the means by which it should be achieved, and the issue of subsidiarity – or how power is divided between the Member States and the EU Institutions – continues to be a major issue. The *original* community, the ECSC, created in 1952, was designed as a first step in achieving lasting peace and increasing prosperity in a continent scarred by war. These aims have, by and large, been achieved: over half a century of peace together with the status of being one of the three most prosperous areas of the world are surely achievements to be proud of. However, the aims and objectives of the Union are constantly developing in response to both internal and external stimuli and the integration of Europe is far from complete.

Enlargement of the Union has itself presented significant challenges. The ambitious target of introducing a single currency throughout the Union continues to present a number of challenges, particularly in regard to European debt and global recession. In addition, a further deepening of European integration to include both wider political and social issues presents yet further challenges. Add to this the Union's attempts at establishing a global identity and your head is likely to be left reeling with the enormity of the tasks which lie ahead for Europe.

As Victor Hugo prophesied in 1894, 'A day will come when all the nations of this continent, without losing their distinct qualities or their glorious individuality, will fuse together in a higher unity and form the European brotherhood. A day will come when the only battlefield will be the marketplace for competing ideas. A day will come when bullets and bombs will be replaced by votes.'

Important dates and events in the creation of the EU

Apr 1951   Six States sign the Treaty of Paris establishing the ECSC

Mar 1957   The six sign the Treaties of Rome establishing the EURATOM and the EEC (in force Jan 1958)

Apr 1965   Merger Treaty is signed providing all three Communities with the same institutional structure

Jan 1966	Luxembourg Accords agreed
Apr 1970	First Budgetary Treaty signed, making major changes to the funding of the Communities
Jan 1973	Denmark, Ireland and the United Kingdom join the Communities
Dec 1974	Agreement on direct elections to the EP – a major step in ensuring a democratic Europe
Jul 1975	Second Budgetary Treaty signed
Jul 1978	European Council agrees on closer monetary co-operation
Jun 1979	First direct elections to the EP
Jan 1981	Greece joins the Communities
Jan 1986	Spain and Portugal join the Communities
Feb 1986	SEA signed with the aim of speeding up European integration (in force July 1987)
Feb 1992	TEU signed in Maastricht – creating the European Union (in force Nov 1993)
Jan 1995	Austria, Finland and Sweden join the Union
Oct 1997	ToA signed – consolidating Treaty aimed at enlargement and bringing EU closer to its citizens (in force May 1999)
Dec 2000	ToN signed. Main thrust was the reform of the Institutions in preparation for further enlargement (in force Feb 2003)
May 2004	Estonia, the Czech Republic, Latvia, Lithuania, Hungary, Poland, Slovenia, Slovakia, Cyprus and Malta join the EU
Jan 2007	Romania and Bulgaria join the EU
Oct 2004	Representatives of the 25 Member States sign the Treaty Establishing a Constitution for Europe
May 2005	France and the Netherlands reject the text of the Constitutional Treaty (finally abandoned during summer 2007)
Dec 2007	Representatives of the 27 Member States sign the Reform Treaty (now called the Treaty of Lisbon – ToL)
Dec 2009	ToL enters into force, amending the Maastricht Treaty (TEU) and amending and renaming the TEC – now Treaty on the Functioning of the European Union (TFEU)
Dec 2011	Agreement, among 25 Member States, in regard to the Fiscal Compact
Jul 2013	Croatia becomes the latest EU Member State

SOME ISSUES TO THINK ABOUT FURTHER

- Why was an integrated Europe seen as so important? What overarching aim(s) were all 3 Communities intended to achieve?
- What was the primary aim or emphasis of the original EEC Treaty? Did its short-term goals differ from its long-term aims?
- Why has it been necessary to 'develop' the European Communities/Union?
- What do you see as the main priorities for the EU in the future?
- Do you need to keep up to date with changes to the EU? How will you intend to do this?

3 Who runs the EU?

I. POWER SHARING IN THE EU

Since the first European community (the ECSC) was created, the Member States have delegated various powers to a number of bodies – largely the Institutions – who organised the day-to-day 'running' of the Communities on their behalf. Together, these Institutions fulfil many of the **functions of government**, taking decisions, creating laws and spending money on a joint (EU) basis – but *only* in areas in which they have been provided with the specific authority to do so by the Member States. (This is known as the principle of 'conferral' which is set out in Arts 4 and 5 TEU. The areas in which the EU has authority are set out in Arts 3 to 6 TFEU. You are *strongly* advised to read these Articles in order to gain a better understanding of how power is shared.) The Member States confer competence through the various treaties and retain the power to create and amend the constitutional and substantive rules of the EU in this way, as already discussed in Chapter 2 – and of course the Member States continue to be solely responsible in all areas that lie outside the competences of the EU.

Over the years, a number of theories have been put forward in an attempt to explain how power is, or should be, shared between the Member States and the Institutions. Consequently, the way in which power is divided – and among whom – is the main focus of this chapter.

1. Federalism, supranationalism and intergovernmentalism

There is no precise, agreed definition of federalism and a cursory examination of various federal systems throughout the world reveals that there are numerous different models. However, in its most basic form, **federalism** can be concluded as being the dispersal of power between different levels of government. Federalism has proved a tremendous influence on the governance of the EU and, as we will see, power within the EU is shared not only between Union (institutional) and Member State (national government) levels but also at regional and local levels, under the concept known as subsidiarity (discussed below). However, the question needs to be asked as to *how* power is shared between these various actors and consequently an understanding of the theories of supranationalism and intergovernmentalism becomes important.

Supranationalism occurs where the power to take decisions is concentrated at a level *above* that of participating Member States. As already touched upon, the Member States have created a number of institutions which have been given various powers that allow them to 'run' aspects of the Union. Decisions taken by the Union's Institutions can, as we shall see, take precedence over those taken by individual Member States and so the Institutions can be concluded as, in some circumstances, having supranational authority over individual Member States.

Intergovernmentalism on the other hand occurs where participating Member States retain the power to take decisions which allow the States to retain significant control over decision making. Within the EU, while the Member States have devolved power to the Institutions, they have also retained ultimate power for themselves, in that they have preserved the power to create and amend constitutional and substantive rules of the EU. The EU can therefore be said to also demonstrate intergovernmental tendencies.

Consequently, it can be concluded that governance of the EU displays a mix of both supranationalism and intergovernmentalism.

2. The division of competences (power) between the EU and its Member States

If it can be agreed that the power to govern the EU is shared, it becomes relevant to consider exactly *how* power is apportioned. Before there can be *any* EU involvement in a particular area, all Member States must have agreed to confer power on the Union: for example, before the Institutions could become involved in the running of Member States' coal and steel industries, the Member States first had to provide them with the authority to do so – which they did through enacting the ECSC Treaty. **It is important to be clear at the outset that any powers not conferred on the Union by the Treaties remain with the Member States (Art 4 TEU).**

Once power has been given, it then needs to be considered when and how that power can be executed. The TEU, in particular Arts 4 and 5, refers to this as the 'conferral of competence', while Art 2 TFEU goes into more detail, providing that there are three types of 'competence':

- **'Exclusive competence'**: relates to specific areas where *only* the EU Institutions may act (that is, take decisions which have legal impact).
- **'Shared competence'**: while this may appear to relate to specific areas where the Member States and the Union may both act, or come together to act, the situation is not as straightforward as it may appear, as the Member States may *only* act in these areas *if* the EU has:
  - not yet exercised its right to act; *or*
  - decided to *cease* exercising its right to act.

  Exactly when the EU **should** exercise, or cease to exercise, its right to act and when it should allow the Member States to act is governed by two important principles: *subsidiarity* and *proportionality*, which are discussed in more detail below.
- Finally, there are specific areas where the Member States have the right to act but where the Union may 'support, co-ordinate or supplement' the acts of its Member States.

Art 3 TFEU lists the *specific areas* in which the EU has exclusive competence, while Art 4 TFEU lists the areas in which the Union 'shares' competence with its Member States. Article 6 TFEU sets out the areas in which the EU has competence to 'support, co-ordinate or supplement' the acts of the Member States. However, the Treaty also sets out a number of areas which do not fall into any of these three areas of competence: for example, Art 5 TFEU sets out areas in which the Union may 'co-ordinate policies' or 'take initiatives'. As this may be difficult to digest at first, you are again **strongly** encouraged to carefully read all relevant Treaty Articles, which should assist in consolidating your understanding of power sharing within the EU. (While format and terminology may seem unfamiliar and off-putting at first, perseverance can only set you above those who have not persevered!)

3. The principles of subsidiarity and proportionality

Art 5 TEU provides that the application of the 'competences' discussed above is governed by two principles – those of **subsidiarity** and **proportionality**.

Specifically, the TEU states that in areas which do **not** come within the **exclusive** competence of the EU, the EU (through its Institutions) may **only** act if the objective(s) of any proposed action cannot be *effectively* achieved at national level (be that central, regional or local government), but where those objectives can be better achieved when action is taken at EU level.

This is the principle of **subsidiarity**. The principle can be seen as a means of avoiding over-centralisation and of ensuring that decisions are taken as closely as possible to the peoples of the EU thus, hopefully, bringing the EU and individuals 'closer together'. (Subsidiarity is not a new principle and was first articulated by the Court of Justice of the EU (CJEU) as a General Principle of EU law (further discussed in Chapter 4) and, in 1993, given formal recognition by the Maastricht Treaty (TEU)).

An alleged breach of the principle can result in a request for review being brought before the CJEU (under Art 263 TFEU), although the Court has appeared reluctant to consider the principle in any real depth, as consideration of Cases C-233/94 and C-491/01, *Germany v European Parliament & Council* (the *Tobacco Advertising* cases) demonstrates.

In terms of the EU legislative processes, the utility of the principle is reinforced by Protocol (No 2) on the Application of the Principles of Subsidiarity and Proportionality, which has been annexed to the TEU and TFEU by the Treaty of Lisbon. In particular, before proposing new legislation, the Commission is required to 'consult widely', taking into consideration the national implications of any such legislation. In addition, any draft act must be 'justified' by means of a statement demonstrating that both principles are being satisfied.

Significantly, the Protocol places national parliaments in the position of 'guardians' of the principle of subsidiarity, providing a procedure under which national parliaments may require a draft to be reviewed where its adherence to the principle is questioned. (Chapter 4 provides further detail on EU legislative procedures.) In addition, under jurisdiction afforded to it by Art 263 TFEU, the CJEU may also review the validity of legislative acts on grounds that there has been an infringement of the principle of subsidiarity. (Chapter 6 provides further detail in regard to this procedure.)

As already touched upon, Art 5 TEU also discusses the principle of **proportionality** in regard to the exercise of Union competences. In particular, it provides that Union action must not exceed what is *necessary* to achieve the objectives of the Treaties. Again, the principle was first developed by the Court of Justice as a General Principle of Union law.

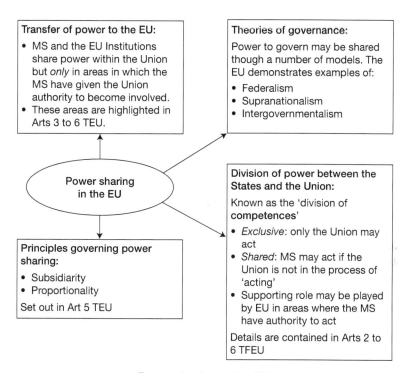

Power sharing in the EU

II. THE INSTITUTIONAL STRUCTURE OF THE EU

1. The Institutions and other Union bodies

Art 13 TEU provides that the tasks entrusted to the Union shall be carried out by seven Institutions, namely the European Parliament (EP), the European Council (EC), the Council, the European Commission (the Commission), the Court of Justice of the European Union (the ECJ or, more accurately, the CJEU), the European Central Bank (ECB) and the Court of Auditors (CoA). The Treaties have established several additional bodies such as the Economic and Social Committee (ESC) and Committee of Regions (CoR). As the Communities have grown and developed into the EU, so too have the Institutions grown and developed.

In order to understand the workings of the EU Institutions, each will be considered separately in terms of the role that it plays and also with regard to its relationship with the other Institutions.

2. The functions of government

It is worth taking a moment to consider the traditional division of the functions of government, that is: **legislative, executive** and **judicial**. In the UK, for example, each area is, in the main, fulfilled by separate bodies (under the doctrine of separation of powers: you are advised to research this UK constitutional principle) in order to check the potential for arbitrary government. No such division is attempted within the EU and the various roles of government are shared, rather than divided, among the Institutions. It is not possible, therefore, to declare any single Institution as, for example, the legislator of the EU.

3. The European Parliament (Art 14 TEU and Arts 223 to 234 TFEU)

i. Composition and functions

The European Parliament (EP – or Assembly, as it was originally known) was created by the ECSC Treaty in 1952. It consisted of 78 members who were *delegates nominated by the national parliaments*. While the role of a parliament traditionally involves a substantial legislative function, the EP's legislative role was initially extremely limited, providing little more than a forum for debate.

Today, the EP may be composed of a maximum of 750 members (known as MEPs), plus a President. Since 1979 the EP has, importantly, been directly elected through democratic elections held every five years in each Member State. It is the largest multinational parliament in the world, currently representing the interests of more than 500 million EU citizens. It has no permanent home and sits in Strasbourg for monthly plenary sessions, holds committee meetings and additional sessions in Brussels, while its General Secretariat is based in Luxembourg. All of the EU's major political parties are represented in the EP, with MEPs grouped together according to their *political affiliations, rather than by nationality.*

Remember that, due to its democratically elected status, **the European Parliament represents the interests of the citizens** of the EU and NOT those of the Member States.

ii. The legislative role of the EP

The process of enacting legally binding acts within the EU normally involves three of the EU's Institutions: the Commission, whose role is largely that of initiator and drafter of legislation (the EP may, however, request the Commission to submit proposals under Art 225 TFEU); the Council, which must normally provide its assent before legislation can take effect, and the Parliament, whose role has changed significantly over the years. Initially, the legislative role of the EP was extremely limited and largely confined to a process known as *'consultation'*. This procedure required that, before legislation could be adopted, the EP was to be consulted. While neither the Council nor the Commission was required to act on any opinions or proposals for change put forward by the EP, failure to consult could lead to legislation being declared void by the Court of Justice (Case 138/79, *Roquette Frères v Council*).

However, since the introduction of direct elections to the EP, the legislative power of the Institution has grown significantly. The Single European Act 1986 (SEA) introduced a process known as *co-operation*, which was seen as a first step in the extension of the powers of the democratically elected Parliament. Under this procedure, the EP was able to 'reject' draft legislation, which the Council was subsequently only able to adopt by unanimous agreement (the decision-making process known as 'unanimity'), rather than the more usual qualified majority voting (QMV is a system in which votes are weighted to reflect the population of each Member State). While not placing the EP on an equal footing with the Council in terms of the legislative power, the procedure increased the EP's influence, resulting in both the Council and the Commission becoming far more inclined to take into consideration the EP's point of view. It should be remembered, however, that following the SEA, the consultation procedure was still very much the norm and that the new co-operation procedure was initially limited in its application to relatively few areas.

The TEU further increased the EP's legislative powers by introducing a procedure known as *'co-decision'*. The main difference between the co-decision and co-operation procedures was that the former allowed the EP to veto, by absolute majority, a proposed legislative measure. The importance of the procedure from the Parliament's point of view was that it allowed the EP to prevent the Council from passing legislation without its agreement. It is important to note, however, that the use of the co-decision was again limited, the co-operation procedure becoming the norm under the Maastricht Treaty (TEU). The Treaty of Amsterdam (ToA) and the Treaty of Nice (ToN) both extended the use of co-decision, which again had the effect of increasing the influence of the EP in the European Union's legislative process.

Under the changes introduced by the Treaty of Lisbon the consultation procedure remains – but its use is extremely limited – while the use of the co-operation procedure has been discontinued. In addition, Art 289 TFEU provides that legislation can now be adopted by a procedure known as the *'ordinary'* legislative procedure, which is virtually identical to the co-decision procedure, which maintains the EP's status as 'co-legislator' with the Council. A further procedure, known as the *'special'* legislative procedure, has also been introduced by Art 289 TFEU. Both procedures are discussed in further detail in Chapter 4, as is the final legislative procedure, known as the *'consent'* (formally *'assent'*) procedure, which again is a rarely used procedure, under which the EP must provide its assent by majority.

iii. The budgetary role of the EP

Initially, the EP had, in line with its other legislative powers, a purely consultative role in relation to the (then) Community budget. In 1970, major changes were made with regard to the funding of the Communities and this coincided with the first major extension of the EP's powers through the 1970 and 1975 Budgetary Treaties.

Four Institutions have a part to play in the EU budgetary process. The Commission is responsible for drawing up a draft budget, which the Council and Parliament may adopt, while the Court of Auditors (CoA) provides an annual audit of spending. A draft budget will contain details of proposed compulsory and non-compulsory expenditure and also an estimate of revenue. Prior to the introduction of the Treaty of Lisbon, the Parliament only had the power to amend the sections of the budget relating to non-compulsory expenditure. However, under Art 314 TFEU, the EP's power was extended to include amendments to both areas of the budget. Where the draft budget cannot be agreed by the EP and the Council, a conciliation committee will be set up in order to promote consensus. If the EP and the Council decide to reject the draft budget, the Commission will be required to resubmit a second draft.

iv. The EP's supervisory role

As there is no strict separation of powers within the EU, the Treaties provide for a number of 'checks and balances' which are intended to ensure that no one Institution becomes too powerful. As part of this system, the Institutions all play a part in supervising each other, and one of the more important supervisory powers held by the EP is that which it has over the Commission. The EP is entitled to ask questions of the Commission and demand written answers (Art 230 TFEU) and since 1973 the Parliament has made time in its schedule for a regular 'question time' with regard to the work of both the

Commission and the Council. (While this power may be effective as a means of exposing wrongdoing, the Council, unlike the Commission, cannot be forced to reply to the EP's questioning.) The EP also debates, in open session, the Commission's Annual Report.

The EP also has the authority to require the Commission to resign *en bloc* (Arts 17 TEU and 234 TFEU). This power has, to date, never been used, probably because it has been seen as rather severe and, it is argued, in most circumstances the EP and the Commission consider themselves allies rather than adversaries. Also, until amendments were introduced by the Maastricht Treaty, the EP was unable to exert control over the appointment of new Commissioners and it would therefore have been rather pointless to sack the Commission when it had no control over who was to replace the outgoing Commissioners. New Commissioners must now, however, be approved by the EP before taking up office (Art 17 TEU).

The EP may exert supervisory powers over the acts of the other Institutions by instituting a legal challenge before the CJEU. This procedure, known as 'action to annul' (Art 263 TFEU, discussed in Chapter 6), provides that the EP may challenge any act having legal impact enacted by the other Institutions. It may similarly, under Art 265 TFEU, challenge the other Institutions should they fail to act when bound to do so under EU rules. While it was originally thought that the EP lacked *locus standi* to make a challenge (as can be evidenced by Case 302/87, *European Parliament v Council*, the *Commitology* case), in the later *Chernobyl* case (Case C-70/88, *European Parliament v Council*), the Court declared that the EP might bring such an action in circumstances where it was acting to protect its 'prerogatives'. The EEC Treaty was later amended by the SEA to formally acknowledge this right, and the ToN increased the EP's role, which is now comparable to that of the Commission and the Council.

The EP also enjoys supervisory powers in respect of allegations of maladministration: it may set up temporary Committees of Inquiry (Art 226 TFEU) to investigate such allegations – which may result from a complaint made by an individual under Art 227 TFEU – and also elect the European Ombudsman to receive complaints regarding possible maladministration against any EU body (Art 228 TFEU). At the conclusion of an investigation, the Ombudsman is required to report to the EP, which has no powers to correct the situation, but the process allows such maladministration to be brought to the attention of, for example, the media.

v. Conclusions

The EP, although initially weak, has been provided with substantially increased powers over time, largely as a result of its being directly and democratically elected. It can be argued that this is only right and proper, as it is the EP which enjoys the mandate of the peoples of Europe, and to continue to deny the Parliament a proper voice in Europe would have been to ignore the concept of democracy.

4. The European Council (Arts 15 to 16 TEU and Arts 235 to 236 TFEU)

First, it must again be emphasised that care should be taken not to confuse the European Council with either the Council (of the EU) or the **Council of Europe** (which **exists entirely separately from the EU**).

i. Composition and functions

Initially, the European Council (EC) was an informal body, composed of the Heads of state or government of the Member States, assisted by their Foreign Ministers, along with the President of the Commission. Their ad hoc meetings, known as summits, were formally recognised by the SEA, which required that the EC meet at least twice a year. Since the coming into force of the Treaty of Lisbon, summits must now take place twice every six months. The Treaty of Lisbon also made other significant changes, formally recognising the EC as an EU Institution (under Art 13 TEU). The EC has its own elected President (Art 15 TEU), which provides that the High Representative of the Union for Foreign Affairs and Security Policy also take part in its work. The EC has its base in Brussels.

The Maastricht Treaty gave the European Council a defined, if rather vague, role as providing the EU with 'the necessary impetus for its development' and providing that it 'shall define the general political guidelines thereof'. The body fulfils an important role in reaching agreement between the Member States should there be a failure to reach consensus at a lower level. It is also involved in the ratification of agreements (which must normally be reached by consensus: Art 15 TEU). It was agreement at EC level that led to the introduction of direct elections to the EP and also to the creation of a European unit of currency (the Euro), while the impetus for the creation of the European Union (following on from the European Communities) was a result of an ad hoc committee set up by the European Council (the Dooge Committee). In addition, major changes to the various Treaties have been preceded by summit meetings which, in turn, have led on to intergovernmental conferences (IGCs) from which amendments (agreed though unanimity) to primary legislation have emerged.

ii. Conclusions

The European Council can be seen as an important force within the EU, particularly in regard to developing policy and providing direction for the EU.

5. The Council (Art 16 TEU and Arts 237 to 243 TFEU)

i. Composition and functions

Formerly known as the Council of Ministers and, following the Maastricht Treaty, the Council of the European Union, the Council is comprised of one representative from each Member State, who is authorised to bind the government of that State. The composition of the Council has always been dependent on the subject matter under discussion: for example, if the Council is discussing matters relating to agriculture, each Member State's agriculture minister, or equivalent, will be present. Similarly, if transport matters are under discussion, transport ministers will be in attendance. Art 19 TEU provides for the Council to meet in 'different configurations', with a General Affairs Council ensuring the consistency of the work of each 'configuration'. (In addition, a Foreign Affairs Council 'shall elaborate the Union's external action', on the basis of guidelines set out by the European Council (EC). The Foreign Affairs Council is presided over by the High Representative of the Union for Foreign Affairs and Security Policy, who is an EC appointee. The Council's 'configurations', other than the Foreign Affairs Council, are led by a team of presidents, again appointed by the EC. It is the presidencies that decide what is discussed and when. It must again be emphasised that care should be taken not to confuse the European Council with either the Council (of the EU) or the **Council of Europe** (which **exists entirely separately from the EU**).

The Council is supported by a Committee of Permanent Representatives of the Governments of the Member States (known collectively as COREPER), which is responsible for 'preparing' the work of the Council (Art 16 TEU). COREPER consists of senior diplomats and it is instructive to note that it has been suggested that anything up to 90 per cent of all Council decisions are actually taken by COREPER before they reach ministerial level. In addition to COREPER, the Council also has a General Secretariat, which provides administrative support.

The Council represents *national* interests and, as a body, has characteristics of both a supranational and intergovernmental organisation. The ministers who form the Council are responsible to their national parliaments, yet they form part of the institutional body that makes decisions on behalf of the European Union. The TFEU provides that 'the Council shall, jointly with the European Parliament, exercise legislative and budgetary functions. It shall carry out policy-making and co-ordinating functions as laid down in the Treaties.'

The Council, along with the European Council, represents the interests of the governments of the Member States.

ii. The legislative role of the Council

The Council was once considered to be the principal legislator for the Communities. Following developments wrought by the amending Treaties, the Council now shares its legislative role with the European Parliament.

The main legislative procedure of the EU, through which the majority of legislative acts are now enacted, is known as the 'ordinary legislative procedure', as set out in Art 294 TFEU. Under this procedure, the Commission will submit a draft legislative proposal to both the Council and the EP and, in summary, if the two Institutions fail to reach agreement on the content of the proposal it will be abandoned, thus denying the Council the opportunity to push through legislation without the EP's approval, as it once could. While other legislative procedures exist, known as 'special' legislative procedures, these are limited to particular circumstances, as set out by the Treaties. (Further details on the EU's legislative procedures are provided in Chapter 4.)

iii. Decision making in the Council

In addition to its legislative powers, the Council sets political objectives, co-ordinates national policies and provides a forum where differences between the Member States may be resolved. When the Council is required to reach a decision – whether it relates to legislation or another matter – it does so by taking a vote. Over the years, three systems of voting have been used by the Council: **simple majority, qualified majority** or **unanimity**. Reaching a decision by simple majority requires that the majority of Council ministers support a proposal. This requires Member States to surrender a high degree of sovereignty, as they can easily be outvoted, and is consequently rarely used.

Initially, the favoured method of voting was unanimity, effectively allowing each Member State the power of veto. While this method is still used in very restricted areas, qualified majority voting (QMV) become the norm (Art 16 TEU). Under this method, each Member State's vote is 'weighted' to reflect the size of its population and this method of reaching decisions means that a Member State may find itself bound by a decision which it does not approve of. When, in 1966, the Council moved towards the regular use of QMV, France refused to attend Council meetings (known as the 'empty chair' policy), objecting to the resulting loss of sovereignty. This protest resulted in what has become known as the *Luxembourg Compromise* (or Accords, see Chapter 2), when it was agreed that, should a decision be required on an issue relating to 'very important interests' of a Member State, that State would be treated as having a right of veto. This had the effect of increasing the power of the Council, which represents Member State interests, and decreasing the influence of the Commission, which represents the interests of the EU as a whole. The effect of this 'veto' should not be over-emphasised however, as it is not recognised as having legal effect, although it has clearly encouraged the Member States to reach agreement through compromise whenever possible.

Previously, under QMV, a decision would normally have to receive at least 255 votes and be approved by the majority of the Member States. In addition, any member of the Council could request verification that the qualified majority represented at least 62 per cent of the total population of the EU. In November 2014 a change was introduced to the 'formula' for QMV, which is now referred to as 'double majority' voting. Normally, any decision now requires at least 55 per cent of the Council, representing at least 65 per cent of the EU population, to approve the measure. What the exact impact of this change will be is presently a matter of opinion but commentators have suggested that it will make decision making slightly faster, redistribute influence between the mid-sized States (less) and larger and smaller States (more), as well as having implications on the democratic legitimacy of the EU by increasing the transparency of the decision-making process.

iv. The other roles of the Council

In terms of the budget (which is a legislative act) the Council shares its role with the EP under a process which has already been set out above. The Council also co-ordinates the general economic policies of the Member States, while, in addition, the Council, in the same manner as the EP, exerts supervisory powers over the other Institutions by virtue of the judicial review procedures contained in the TFEU. This procedure, also known as 'action to annul' (Art 263 TFEU), is discussed further in Chapter 6.

v. Conclusions

Given its composition, it is clear that **the Council represents the interests of the governments of the Member States**, resolving issues of conflict and playing an important role in developing legislation.

6. The Commission (Art 17 TEU and Arts 244 to 250 TFEU)

Once known as the 'High Authority', the Commission's position within the institutional balance of the EU has varied considerably during its lifetime, fluctuating between being heralded as the 'embryonic European Government' and the less auspicious 'Community civil service'. The Commission's position in the institutional balance (discussed further below) has undoubtedly suffered as a result of the increased power enjoyed by the EP, and the 'Brussels bureaucrats' are often thought of as being held in low esteem by the general public – at least if the UK's popular press is to be believed – and publicity surrounding the Commission's *en bloc* resignation in 1999 (as a result of allegations of malpractice) did little to improve its reputation. On the whole, however, the Commission can be seen as a success, as the progress made with regard to European Union integration could not have been achieved without the Institution's input as motivator, monitor and negotiator.

The Commission represents the interests of the European Union as a whole.

i. The composition of the Commission

The Commission comprises 28 Commissioners, one from each Member State, who are appointed for a renewable period of five years. Commissioners, who must be EU citizens, are appointed under a procedure involving the Member States, the President of the Commission and the EP. The TFEU requires that each Commissioner be independent, not take instruction from any government or other body and act only in the interests of the EU. While a Commissioner who fails to fulfil the conditions of his/her appointment may be required to resign by the President of the Commission, the EP may also dismiss the Commission *en bloc*.

The membership of the Commission includes its President and the High Representative of the Union for Foreign Affairs and Security Policy. After first consulting the EP, the European Council proposes a President from among the Commissioners, who must then be formally elected by the EP. This is a particularly influential post, as the President will not only chair Commission meetings and attend the meetings of the European Council, but will also represent Europe at international summits. The High Representative is also proposed by the European Council and, in order to take up their role in the Commission as a Vice President, the High Representative has to appear before the EP for questioning and is then subject to the EP's vote of approval on the proposed Commission.

ii. The functions of the Commission

While the EP represents the interests of the citizens of Europe and the Council represents the interests of the Member States, the Commission represents the interests of the EU as a whole. This is reflected by Art 17 TFEU, which provides that the Commission must 'promote the general interests of the Union and take appropriate initiatives to that end'.

The Commission is divided into directorates-general (DGs), each headed by a director-general who in turn reports to a Commissioner with overall responsibility for the work of that DG. The DGs are divided by subject matter, for example, industry or matters relating to education, training and youth. Each Commissioner is supported by a cabinet and the Commission has a total staff of approximately 25,000.

The Commission is a multi-purpose organisation and its functions include the legislative, executive and quasi-judicial, as outlined below.

iii. The Commission's legislative role

The Commission plays a central role in the EU legislative process, its most important function being that of initiator of draft legislation. As has already been discussed above, in relation to the EP, the Commission will produce draft legislation which it then sends to the Council and the EP for their consideration and/or approval. The Commission further participates in the legislative process by amending legislative proposals in circumstances where either the Council or Parliament, or both, have failed to provide the necessary agreement, often reacting to amendments suggested by those Institutions.

Many of the Commission's proposals for legislation are a direct result of Council requests that various studies be undertaken and the EP may also request that the Commission submits legislative proposals on appropriate matters. The Commission publishes an annual programme outlining its legislative plans and listing legislative priorities for that year, thereby playing a part in planning the strategy for the EU as a whole. In addition, the Commission has been dubbed the 'motor for integration', due to its involvement in the development of policy. This can be evidenced, for example, by the Commission's White Paper entitled *Completion of the Internal Market* (COM (85) 310), which was significant in the shaping of the SEA.

The Commission also has the power, albeit in limited circumstances, to act alone in the making of EU legislation. In addition, the Council may delegate legislative powers to the Commission, once again in limited circumstances.

iv. The Commission's administrative and executive roles

Legislation, once enacted, must be implemented, and policy, once made, must be put into effect. The Commission's role is generally not one of direct action, as both policy and legislation are largely put into effect at national level, but to maintain a supervisory position, ensuring that the appropriate Member States' agencies comply. The Commission manages the EU's annual budget, including a number of funds such as the European Social Fund and, importantly, the European Agricultural and Guarantee Fund, which takes up a large proportion of the EU annual budget.

The Commission also has a central role in regard to the Union's external relations. The EU's effectiveness on a global level is enhanced by the Commission's role as negotiator of trade and co-operation agreements with countries or groups of countries outside the Union. The Commission, for example, represents the EU at the United Nations and its specialised agencies, such as the World Trade Organization.

v. The Commission's supervisory functions

The Commission has a number of supervisory (or quasi-judicial) functions. First, Art 258 TFEU provides the Commission with the power to investigate, and bring before the Court of Justice, any Member State that it considers to be in breach of its EU obligations. The Commission attempts to encourage the Member States to remedy a breach as informally as possible, through consultation and negotiation and an action before the Court is seen very much as a last resort. (This action is discussed in further detail in Chapter 6.)

Second, the Commission plays an important role in ensuring that EU competition rules are followed. For example, any undertaking (the favoured EU term for a firm or individual capable of economic activity) that attempts to distort trade within the Union may find itself in breach of EU law. Under Reg 17 (1956–62 OJ Spec Ed 87), the Commission was provided with the power to investigate possible breaches, provide formal decisions as to whether there has been an infringement and impose fines against any wrongdoers, a power which it now shares with appropriate bodies within the Member States. While the investigative and forensic powers of the Commission may be subject to judicial review, these functions provide the Commission with significant influence in relation to the development of EU policy.

In addition, the Commission, in the same manner as the other Institutions, exerts supervisory powers over the other Institutions by virtue of annulment procedures contained within the Treaty (discussed in Chapter 6).

vi. Conclusions

The Commission's functions elevate it far above that of an EU 'civil service'. It can be described as a *sui generis*, multi-functional organisation, with not inconsiderable influence over not only the day-to-day running of the Union, but also its development and direction. This said, its powers are not boundless and many are held under the discretion of the Council and the supervision of the EP.

7. The Court of Justice of the European Union (Art 19 TEU and Arts 251 to 281 TFEU)

The European Union is founded on the rule of law, and acceptance by the Member States, EU bodies and individuals of the binding nature of its 'rules' is fundamental to the Union's existence. Originally, the Court was known as the European Court of Justice (ECJ) and in November 1989 a Court of First Instance (CFI) was created to assist the ECJ in its tasks. The Court of Justice of the European Union (CJEU), as it has been known since the coming into force of the Treaty of Lisbon, is now made up of the Court of Justice, the General Court (GC, previously the CFI) and 'specialised courts'. The Courts sit in Luxembourg.

Although the rules of precedent do not apply to the CJEU, in reality the Court has, for the sake of consistency, tended to follow its past decisions. An infrequent example of the Court failing to follow its past judgments can be evidenced in the *Keck* judgment (Cases C-267 and 268/91, which is discussed in Chapter 7).

i. The composition of CJEU

The Court is made up of a number of personnel including judges and Advocates-General (AGs). Each court also has a President and a Registrar. While the judges act as decision-makers, AGs, who have no equivalent in the UK's legal system, assist the judges by delivering non-binding written opinions prior to the judges beginning their deliberations.

The number of judges composing the Court is dependent on the number of Member States: one judge per state, for a period of six years, renewable every three years. Both the TEU and TFEU emphasise that judges be 'persons whose independence is beyond doubt', and it is clear that judges must be independent of any government or interest group. As with all fixed-term appointments, it is possible that political pressure could be brought to bear on judges. The likelihood of this is reduced, however, as the Court's deliberations are secret, with a single ruling being delivered by the Court rather than individual judgments from each judge.

With regard to qualifications, the TFEU requires that judges must be individuals who 'possess the qualifications required for appointment to the highest judicial offices in their respective countries or who are jurisconsults of recognised competence'. While the UK has so far chosen to appoint domestic judges or legal practitioners, the Treaty allows academics to be appointed, and a number of other Member States have done so. In addition, the Court has eight AGs, with the rules of appointment and qualifications being the same as those for judges. All appointments are made by the Member States, following consultations with former Court judges.

The number of judges in the General Court must also include at least one judge from each Member State but this number may be increased (Art 254 TFEU). The General Court is also assisted by AGs.

ii. Functions and jurisdiction

Art 19 TEU set out the role of the CJEU rather succinctly, providing that it was to 'ensure that in the interpretation and application of this Treaty the law is observed'. The various actions that can be brought before the Court can be divided into direct actions and preliminary rulings. Direct actions include those brought by the Commission against Member States accused of failing to fulfil their EU obligations, and actions brought by the Institutions or individuals wishing to challenge the validity of legally binding acts of the EU (both are discussed in further detail in Chapter 6).

Preliminary rulings, on the other hand, are the result of requests by national courts requiring the Court to either interpret EU law or rule on its validity. National courts will make such requests where they have a case before them that revolves on a point of EU law (again, further considered in Chapter 6).

iii. Judicial activism and the Court's interpretive methods

It has been argued that the CJEU has used its rather broad jurisdiction to expand its role beyond that normally performed by a judicial body. The Court has adopted a purposive (also known as teleological or contextual), rather than literal, approach to interpreting EU law. As it explained in Case 283/81, CILFIT: 'Every provision of Community law must be placed in its context and interpreted in the light of the provisions of Community law as a whole, regard being given to the objectives thereof.' This has allowed the Court to take a major role in filling gaps in EU legislation which, in turn, has resulted in its being accused of usurping the role of both the EU legislators and policy-makers.

Such activism has been denied by both the Court and its supporters, who argue that the CJEU has gone no further than has been necessary to give effect to the Treaties, which are intended to provide no more than a legal framework for the European Union.

It cannot be denied that the Court has produced some particularly dynamic decisions and one has to look no further than Cases 26/62, *Van Gend en Loos* and 6/64, *Costa v ENEL* (in which the Court developed the central principles of Direct Effect and Supremacy, discussed in Chapter 5) to see the impact that the Court has had on the development of EU law. It has been argued, however, that the CJEU now plays a far less proactive role, perhaps because the EU's legal order has been adequately developed. (Although its activism in the development of protection of fundamental rights within the EU, discussed in Chapter 4 may belie this.)

iv. Procedure before the CJEU

Procedure before the Court can be divided into two stages – oral and written. Emphasis is placed on written submissions rather than oral, which are limited and short (which is probably advantageous as the case may be heard in any of the EU's official languages).

The written stage comes first, with relevant documents being communicated to all parties and published in the *Official Journal of the European Union* (OJEU, which is the official record of the EU). At the end of the written stage, cases may be argued orally in open court. Following this hearing the AG will deliver his or her opinion.

The judges, who may sit in plenary session (all judges) or in chambers, deliberate behind closed doors, delivering their judgment in open court. The judgment, which will be published in all official languages, will include the reasoning on which it is based. (It is worth noting that the AG's opinion is often very instructive and well worth reading. For example, if you struggle with the criteria necessary for direct effect (Chapter 5), consider reading the AG's Opinion in *Rayners v Belgian State*.)

v. The General Court

The General Court (GC), originally called the Court of First Instance (CFI), was established under the SEA as a means of relieving the excessive workload of the Court of Justice. The jurisdiction of the GC is set out under Art 256 TFEU.

vi. Conclusions

The importance of the CJEU in the development of the EU's legal system is well recognised. It is generally accepted that the Court has succeeded in constitutionalising the Treaties by articulating the relationship between the EU and its Member States and also between EU law and national legal systems. It has achieved this by putting 'flesh on the bones' of the Treaties and developing understanding of EU law and how it should be applied.

8. The European Central Bank (Arts 282 to 284 TFEU)

The European Central Bank (ECB) was created following the TEU (1992) and is now an Institution of the EU. It has been tasked with administrating the monetary policy of the Member States that have the euro as their currency (i.e. the 'Eurozone'). The ECB together with the national central banks make up the European System of Central Banks (ESCB).

The main role of the ECB is to maintain price stability within the Eurozone by ensuring that inflation is kept as low as possible. In addition it defines and implements monetary policy, controls foreign reserves and issues euro banknotes. It also works with national and international banking systems to maintain a stable financial system.

9. The Court of Auditors (Arts 285 to 287 TFEU)

The Court of Auditors (CoA) which, confusingly, is not a court at all as it has no judicial functions, was established by the Budgetary Treaty 1975, but it was not until the TEU came into effect that it was afforded the status of Union Institution. It comprises one member from each Member State. Both the Council and EP are involved in the appointment procedure and auditors must be appropriately qualified and their independence beyond doubt.

The CoA has been described as the **'taxpayer's representative'**, a 'watchdog' over the EU's money and as the Union's budget has increased, so has the prominence of the CoA, although it still remains 'low key' compared to the other main Institutions. Every Institution and body that has access to Union funds is subject to the scrutiny of the CoA and it provides a check that all legal requirements are observed and also that the Union is receiving value for money.

The CoA publishes an annual report, highlighting any areas where improvements are possible or desirable. It also provides the EP and the Council with a Statement of Assurance, which declares that EU money has been spent for the purposes intended.

10. Other Community bodies

The EU Treaties also make provision for a number of other bodies, the main ones of which will be considered very briefly.

i. The Economic and Social Committee (Arts 300 to 304 TFEU)

The Economic and Social Committee (ESC) is a **consultative** body which represents a variety of sectional interests. Its membership consists of up to 350 representatives drawn from a broad cross-section of European Union society, such as workers, employees, farmers, craftsmen, professionals, consumer groups and so on. Meetings are held on a monthly basis.

The TFEU requires that draft legislation, in specific policy areas, be referred to the Committee and that the majority of new EU laws of any significance are adopted only following input from the ESC.

ii. The Committee of Regions (Arts 300 and 305 to 307 TFEU)

The Committee of Regions (CoR) was established by the TEU (1992) to represent regional and local interests. Like the ESC, it has a membership of up to 350, drawn from around the Member States. It must be consulted by the Council and Commission where the Treaties so specify.

As national barriers break down and borders between the Member States become more open as a consequence of the internal market, the creation of a CoR can be seen as a response to people's fears of over-centralisation. The CoR has direct experience of how EU policies affect the everyday life of citizens and its expertise allows it to bring a powerful influence to bear.

iii. European Investment Bank (Arts 308 to 309 TFEU)

The European Investment Bank (EIB) is the EU's financing Institution, providing long-term loans for capital investments which promote the Union's economic development and integration. It supports regional development and its loans are often accompanied by grants from the EU's Structural and Cohesion Funds.

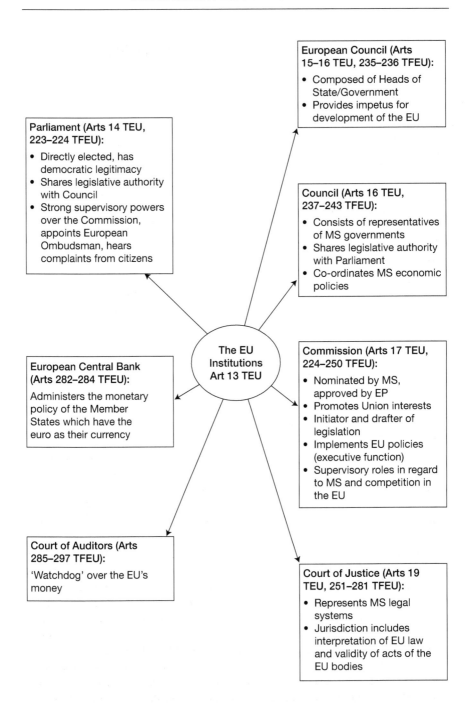

European Council (Arts 15–16 TEU, 235–236 TFEU):

- Composed of Heads of State/Government
- Provides impetus for development of the EU

Parliament (Arts 14 TEU, 223–224 TFEU):

- Directly elected, has democratic legitimacy
- Shares legislative authority with Council
- Strong supervisory powers over the Commission, appoints European Ombudsman, hears complaints from citizens

Council (Arts 16 TEU, 237–243 TFEU):

- Consists of representatives of MS governments
- Shares legislative authority with Parliament
- Co-ordinates MS economic policies

The EU Institutions Art 13 TEU

European Central Bank (Arts 282–284 TFEU):

Administers the monetary policy of the Member States which have the euro as their currency

Commission (Arts 17 TEU, 224–250 TFEU):

- Nominated by MS, approved by EP
- Promotes Union interests
- Initiator and drafter of legislation
- Implements EU policies (executive function)
- Supervisory roles in regard to MS and competition in the EU

Court of Auditors (Arts 285–297 TFEU):

'Watchdog' over the EU's money

Court of Justice (Arts 19 TEU, 251–281 TFEU):

- Represents MS legal systems
- Jurisdiction includes interpretation of EU law and validity of acts of the EU bodies

The institutional structure of the EU

III. INSTITUTIONAL BALANCE, ACCOUNTABILITY AND DEMOCRACY IN THE EU

1. Institutional balance or how the Institutions share power

As already discussed, power within the EU is shared between the Member States and the bodies which have been set up to perform Union functions (basically the Institutions). In addition to considering power sharing between the Member States and the Institutions, it is also important to consider how the Institutions share the power afforded to them.

As has been previously highlighted, the Institutions of the EU represent different interests: the European Parliament represents the interests of European citizens, the Council represents the Member States' interests, in particular the governments of those States, while the Commission represents the interests of Europe as a whole. Consequently, it is vital that the powers and influence of these Institutions are carefully balanced in order that no one Institution – or the interests which they represent – becomes too powerful, overshadowing the interests of the others.

Originally, the powers of the Council and the Commission dwarfed those of the EP. In terms of legislative power, for example, the EP's role was mainly that of debating legislative proposals, with little opportunity to exert significant control over what did, or did not, become law. The original, effectively subordinate, role of the EP can also be further evidenced by consideration of the supervisory procedure known as 'action to annul' (Art 263 TFEU, discussed in Chapter 6) under which the EP, unlike the Commission and Council, was unable to challenge the validity of the acts of the other Institutions.

However, the growth in the EP's powers has been considerable over the years. Following the introduction of direct elections to the European Parliament in 1979, the authority of the Institution has increased with every subsequent amending Treaty. The changes resulting from the Treaty of Lisbon further expanded EP's role as co-legislator with the Council, as the 'ordinary legislative procedure' (Art 289 TFEU) has become the default procedure for the majority of EU legislation. Similarly, in respect of its ability to challenge the legal acts of the other Institutions (Art 263 TFEU, discussed in Chapter 6), Parliament is now on a par with the Commission and Council. The EU's budgetary procedures have further increased the EP's power over the years and it now enjoys parity with the Council in this area also.

Similarly, the EP's influence has increased through its supervisory role over the Commission.

However, as power is finite, it should be remembered that as the EP's role has increased, the power of the other main Institutions has been somewhat reduced. The Council is no longer the 'main' legislator of the EU, nor does it have sole power to give assent to all areas of the EU budget. Similarly, due to the Commission's being subject to the supervisory powers of the EP, its influence has also been kept in check, thus ensuring that no one Institution has the potential to exert inappropriate influence within the EU.

2. Legitimacy, accountability and democracy in the EU

The issues of legitimacy of the EU, the accountability of its Institutions and democratic standards within the EU are inextricably linked. As already explained above, the Institutions fulfil the main functions of government within the Union. These functions are shared among the Institutions and, in order to remove the potential for arbitrary government, not only do the powers enjoyed by the Institutions have to be divided – or balanced – appropriately but accountability of the Institutions is also fundamental to the legitimacy of the EU. Similarly, the accountability of those who take decisions is fundamental to the issue of democracy within the Union.

Democracy, in its simplest form, can be loosely defined as government by the people, *usually* through elected representatives (which is known as **'representative democracy'** and on which the EU is founded (Art 10 TEU. Also consider Art 2 TEU)). In terms of the EU this was seen as problematic as, originally, none of the EU Institutions was *directly* elected by its citizens – the EP and Commission were nominated by the Member States and the Council, although composed of ministers, was still considered rather distant from the electorate. Added to this was, for the majority of citizens, a lack of physical proximity and also the complaint that the Institutions lacked transparency, taking decisions out of the public eye and thus reducing their accountability. Consequently, a common complaint was that Europe suffered from a 'democratic deficit'.

The EU has, however, worked hard to reduce this 'deficit'. In terms of the Institutions, direct election of MEPs was seen as enormously significant, with the powers of the EP being appreciably extended to reflect their mandate, as has already been highlighted above. Decision making in the Council has also become more democratic, with the introduction and increased use of QMV (qualified majority voting), under which each Member State's voting capacity is determined largely by the size of its population. In addition, the accountability of the EU Institutions has been extended through increased transparency in terms of decision making: for example, EU documents are now far more accessible, while the development of the principle of subsidiarity, also already considered above, has reduced the possibility of illegitimate expansion of the Institutions' powers.

The Treaty on European Union now emphasises the importance of democracy by explaining that it is one of the foundational values of the Union (Art 2 TEU) and setting out the democratic principles on which the EU is based (Arts 9 to 12 TEU), highlighting not only that the EU is founded on representative democracy but that every citizen has the right to participate in the democratic life of the Union (**participative** democracy). In particular, in terms of leadership of the EU, the EP and Council gain more influence over the Commission through the process of appointing the Commission President. In terms of legislation, the influence of the EP is once more increased, as the use of the 'ordinary' legislative procedure (once known as the co-decision procedure) is extended to new areas, while the use of QMV (now 'double majority' voting) has been similarly extended. Transparency is improved in the Council, as meetings involving debate on

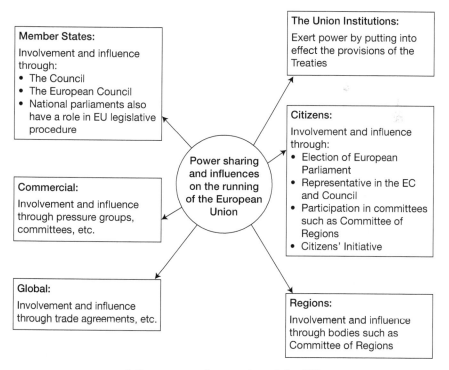

Influences on the running of the EU

legislation are held in public, allowing national governments to more effectively supervise their representatives.

Commentators have argued that the Union should not be expected to achieve democracy as experienced within Member States. This, it is contended, is due to the nature of the decisions taken within the EU, the lack of interest shown by its citizens in electing their European Parliament representatives and also because accountability can be achieved through other means (for example, through the checks and balances built into the EU system of governance, such as actions to annul, adherence to the principles of subsidiarity, proportionality and respect for fundamental rights and so on, all of which are discussed in further detail elsewhere). However, as the EU continues to expand and move into new areas of competence it would appear that improving democracy, accountability and therefore legitimacy is still somewhat of a priority.

IV. CONCLUSIONS

Once the Member States took the decision to organise the Communities (now European Union) in a manner which involved the creation of Institutions to 'run' Europe on their behalf and carry out the day-to-day functions of government, it became important to clarify how power should be shared between the Member States and the Institutions, who would 'staff' these bodies, how roles would be allocated to and between them, and also how far their powers should extend. These issues are important because they strongly impact on democracy and accountability in the EU and, consequently, its legitimacy.

When attempting to understand – and memorise for examinations – the roles of the Institutions, it is helpful to think of them in terms of the traditional roles of government; that is, legislative, executive and judicial (or quasi-judicial). Similarly, it is also important not to forget that each of the main Institutions represent different interests – those of citizens (EP), the Member States (Council) and European interests as a whole (Commission) – which should be helpful when trying to understand why it is so important that no single body becomes too powerful.

It is also essential to understand that the Member States, while allocating power to the Institutions, are the ultimate authorities in terms of the EU. Consequently, the allocation of competences between the Member States and their Institutions is a priority. While the Institutions may be tempted to allow their powers to 'creep' into areas which have been reserved for the Member States, it is important to understand how the Treaties ensure that this is not going to happen!

SOME ISSUES TO THINK ABOUT FURTHER

- There are a number of theories of governance: what are they and how do they apply to the EU?
- How, and on what basis, are powers within the EU distributed between the Member States and its Institutions?
- How, and on what basis, are powers distributed between the Institutions?
- What does the term 'democracy' mean to you? Is the EU 'democratic'? Does it need to be, given that the EU is involved in limited areas only?
- What does the term 'subsidiarity' mean in terms of European Union governance? What do the Treaties have to say about the principle of subsidiarity?

4 Sources of Union law

In order to develop an understanding of European Union law, its sources need to be examined. **EU law can be divided into two basic categories: primary and secondary**. The primary source of EU law is the various Treaties, both those that were enacted in order to create the original European Communities (i.e. the Coal and Steel Community, EURATOM and the European Economic Community) and also those that have been enacted in order to *amend* the original Treaties. (An overview of these Treaties is provided in Chapter 2.) The Treaties provide a framework of policies and rules (think of them as a skeleton), which are then fleshed out by the other sources of law.

Secondary sources *include* secondary legislation (take care not to confuse these two sources), as enacted by the EU Institutions, case law, which comes from the judgments of the Court of Justice of the EU (CJEU), general principles of EU law and international agreements entered into by the EU.

Each of these sources will be considered in turn.

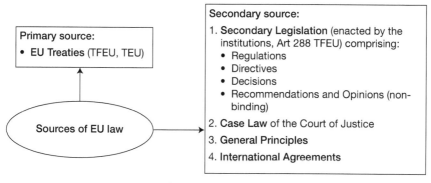

Sources of EU law

I. PRIMARY SOURCES OF EU LAW

The primary source of EU law is the Treaties. Three separate Treaties originally created three separate European Communities, namely:

1 Treaty Establishing the European Coal and Steel Community, 1951 (ECSC, commonly called the Treaty of Paris);

2 Treaty Establishing the European Atomic Energy Community, 1957 (EURATOM, also called the *First* Treaty of Rome); and

3 Treaty Establishing the European Economic Community, 1957 (EEC, also called the Treaty of Rome and *renamed* the Treaty Establishing the European Community (TEC) by the Treaty on European Union (TEU) and more recently the Treaty on the Functioning of the European Union (TFEU) by the Treaty of Lisbon).

In addition, the Treaty on European Union, 1992 (TEU, also known as the Maastricht Treaty) created the European Union in 1993. (Note: the dates given for the various Treaties are the years in which they were signed, rather than the years in which they came into effect, which may differ.)

The most important Treaties from the perspective of the European Union *today* are, of course, the TFEU and the consolidated version of the TEU, as they are the Treaties which set out the framework on which the EU is now based. DO TAKE CARE NOT TO CONFUSE THESE TREATIES!

There have also been a number of Treaties enacted which have **not provided 'stand-alone' law** but which have been enacted in order to **amend** the EEC/TEC and TEU. These include the Merger Treaty 1965; the Budgetary Treaties 1970 and 1975; the Single European Act (SEA) 1986; the Treaty on European Union[1] (TEU) 1992 (also known as the Maastricht Treaty); the Treaty of Amsterdam (ToA) 1997; the Treaty of Nice (ToN) 2000; and the Treaty of Lisbon 2007.

The Treaties, along with secondary legislation, are divided into 'articles', which basically perform the same function as 'sections' in UK legislation. They can be written thus: Art 249 TFEU, with the last few letters demonstrating which Treaty the article is contained in. (Don't leave out the treaty name: you wouldn't leave out the name of an act when referencing UK law, as the citation would be incomplete, and it's the same in the EU.) It is important to remember that in the 'hierarchy' of EU law the Treaties

---

1 It should be noted that the TEU could be included in either list as not only did it amend the then EC Treaty, but it also created the EU.

sit at the top and should always be the first source consulted when researching EU law.

i. Protocols and declarations

Protocols and declarations are often found annexed to the Treaties. Protocols are integral and enjoy Treaty status. Declarations, however, are not binding but instead are normally intended to inform or assist in interpretation of the various Treaties.

1. Revising primary legislation

The Member States hold the ultimate authority to develop and amend treaties. Under procedures refined by the Treaty of Lisbon, an amendment to the Treaties (i.e. the TEU or TFEU) may be introduced by one of two legislative procedures: the Ordinary Revision Procedure or the Simplified Revision Procedure, both of which are set out in **Art 48 TEU**.

In *outline*, under the **Ordinary Revision Procedure**, a Member State, the European Parliament (EP) or the Commission may initiate the procedure by submitting a proposal for amendment to the Council, who will then notify all Member States of the proposal while also submitting it to the European Council (EC). The EC may then convene a Convention, composed of representatives of national parliaments, Heads of State, the EP and the Commission, to consider the proposal. Alternatively, should the EC, together with the EP, feel that a Convention is not necessary, the proposal can be put before an intergovernmental conference (IGC: refer to Glossary) comprising representatives of the Member States. Before any amendment can come into effect, it must be ratified by the Member States in a manner that accords with their individual constitutions. Once ratified, the amendments will come into effect on an agreed date. If not all Member States have ratified but, after two years, a minimum of four-fifths of the States have ratified the amendment, the matter must once more be referred to the EC.

However, should an amendment proposal relate to Part Three of the TFEU (which relates to Union Policies and Internal Actions, seen as a 'less sensitive' area), the **Simplified Revision Procedure** may be used. In outline, under this procedure the EC may adopt an amendment, normally by unanimity, after consulting with the EP and Commission (and ECB, if in regard to a monetary issue). The EC must notify the Member States of the proposed amendment and, if no opposition to the amendment is voiced within six months, the EC may adopt the amendment provided the agreement of the EP is also given.

1. The Ordinary Revision Procedure

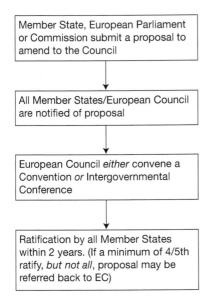

Member State, European Parliament or Commission submit a proposal to amend to the Council

↓

All Member States/European Council are notified of proposal

↓

European Council *either* convene a Convention *or* Intergovernmental Conference

↓

Ratification by all Member States within 2 years. (If a minimum of 4/5th ratify, *but not all*, proposal may be referred back to EC)

2. The Simplified Legislative Procedure

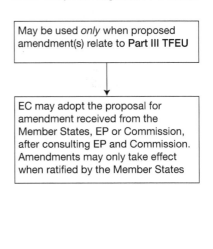

May be used *only* when proposed amendment(s) relate to **Part III TFEU**

↓

EC may adopt the proposal for amendment received from the Member States, EP or Commission, after consulting EP and Commission. Amendments may only take effect when ratified by the Member States

Amending primary legislation (Art 48 TEU)

II. SECONDARY SOURCES OF EU LAW

1. Secondary legislation

Art 288 TFEU provides that: 'To exercise the Union's competences, the Institutions shall adopt regulations, directives, decisions, recommendations and opinions.'

i. Regulations

Art 288 TFEU further provides that: 'A regulation shall have general application. It shall be binding in its entirety and directly applicable in all Member States.'

The fact that regulations have '**general application**' and are '**binding in their entirety**' means that they will be effective *throughout* the EU, in every Member State and in full. Regulations must be published in the Official Journal (Glossary) and come into force on the date specified by the regulation or, if no such date is specified, on the 20th day following its publication.

'**Direct applicability'** means that regulations automatically take effect in each Member State **without the need for national implementing measures.** The CJEU has gone as far as to provide that Member States must not pass any incorporating measures (Case 34/73, *Variola*), as this could result in a Member State placing its own interpretation on the regulation.

Regulations are used to achieve **uniformity** of law throughout the EU.

ii. Directives

Art 288 TFEU provides that: 'A directive shall be binding, as to the result to be achieved, upon each Member State to which it is addressed, but shall leave to the national authorities the choice of form and methods.'

Directives differ from regulations in a number of important ways. First, they do *not* have general application and need not be addressed to all Member States. Additionally, they are *not* directly applicable and, *normally*, the rights and obligations created by them **only become effective once they have been incorporated into national law** by the appropriate national authorities. They do, however, place an obligation on addressee Member States to ensure that a particular aim is achieved by a particular date, leaving national authorities to decide on the exact implementation details. Such autonomy allows a far greater degree of flexibility, providing Member States with the opportunity to introduce a measure in the manner best suited to each State.

Directives are the chosen method of legislating where **harmonisation,** rather than uniformity, of law is the aim.

iii. Decisions

Art 288 TFEU provides: 'A decision shall be binding in its entirety. A decision which specifies those to whom it is addressed shall be binding only on them.'

A decision is similar to a regulation in that it has direct applicability, requiring no national implementation in order to take effect. However, decisions do not have general application and consequently on have impact on addresses. All decisions must be published in the Official Journal, taking effect on a prescribed date or on the 20th day following publication.

iv. Recommendations, opinions and 'soft' law

Unlike regulations, directives and decisions, recommendations and opinions are **not legally binding**.

Art 288 TFEU provides that they have no binding force, although they are **persuasive** and should be taken into account by national courts (Case C-322/88, *Grimaldi*). Such sources of law are sometimes known as 'soft law'. Other sources of soft law may include guidelines or codes of conduct issued by the Union's Institutions.

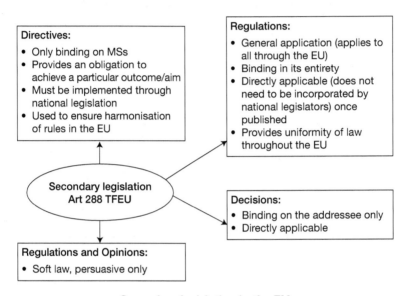

Secondary legislation in the EU

2. Enacting secondary legislation

All binding secondary legislation is subject to review by the CJEU, which may adjudicate on its validity. It is particularly important that **correct procedures** are followed when creating such legislation, as failure to do so may render the legislation invalid. (Judicial review, through 'actions to annul', of legally enforceable acts of the Institutions is further discussed in Chapter 6.)

i. The main actors in the enactment of secondary legislation

The enactment of secondary legislation normally involves four bodies: the Commission, who take responsibility for initiating and drafting new legislative proposals, the European Parliament and the Council, whose assent is normally required before legislation can come into effect, and, finally, national parliaments, who consider legislative proposals in order to ensure that they comply with the principle of subsidiarity.

In addition, a number of other groups may be involved in the process, for example, in certain circumstances the European Central Bank may adopt legislative acts, while the EU's advisory bodies such as the Economic and Social Committee (ESC) may be involved in a consultative capacity.

The roles of the main bodies are discussed further, below.

ii. The legal base for the creation of secondary legislation

EU legislators must demonstrate that they have the necessary **authority** to enact secondary legislation. Such authority will derive from a treaty article empowering the Institutions to legislate. This is known as the '**legal base**'.

The choice of legal base will depend on the subject matter of the proposed legislation. If, for example, the EU wishes to legislate on the free movement of workers, the legal 'authority' for doing so is provided by Art 46 TFEU. However, should the EU wish to enact secondary legislation in relation to taxation, Art 113 TFEU provides authority to do so. Where no such specific law-making powers are provided, Art 352 TFEU *may* provide a general power to legislate. (*TIP*: take out your copy of the TFEU and read these articles NOW! This will most certainly assist your understanding.)

All secondary legislation should contain a statement as to the legal basis on which it is based and it is vitally important that the correct legal base is used, as the validity of the legislation will be open to challenge under the judicial review procedure (specifically, action to annul, Chapter 6) if the wrong base is used. An example of this can be found in Case C-376/98, *Germany v Parliament & Council* (*Tobacco Advertising* case), where the legal base used to enact Directive 98/43/EC (which imposed a general ban on tobacco advertising) was given as Art 114 TFEU (then Art 95 TEC). The CJEU held that the incorrect legal base had been used and the Directive was consequently declared void.

iii. Legislative procedures

Before looking at the specific procedures under which secondary legislation may be enacted, it is important to briefly consider the need for collaboration between all interested parties, both in the planning of legislative strategies and in regard to the content of new acts. Consultation and co-operation between various parties allows the interests of Member States, citizens, the EU as a whole and a variety of pressure groups to be taken into consideration and is essential to ensure the democratic nature of the decision-making processes within the European Union. It should therefore be understood that the whole issue of law making may be far more complex than it first appears. Not only do the competing interests of the Institutions have to be balanced, but also the competing interests of the various groups within the Institutions, such as the various Member States, political parties and so on.

The EU legislative process has tended to be complicated, providing a number of different procedures by which secondary legislation may be enacted. This has been due, in the main, to additional procedures being developed over the years in order to increase the legislative power of the European Parliament (a point already touched upon in Chapter 3).

The question of *which* legislative procedure should be followed in any one set of circumstances is answered by the legal base. For example, if the EU wishes to enact legislation relating to the free movement of workers the legal base (Art 46 TFEU) will be the decisive feature, rather than the form that the legislation is to take – the procedure will not differ if a directive were to be proposed rather than a regulation.

The main, or 'default', legislative procedure is the '**Ordinary**' legislative procedure, while '**Special**' legislative procedures include a 'Consultation' procedure, 'Consent' procedure, the 'Council and Commission acting alone' and the 'Commission acting alone'. Each is discussed, in outline, below.

The 'ordinary' legislative procedure (Arts 289 and 294 TFEU)

This procedure, previously known as the 'Co-decision' procedure prior to the enactment of the Treaty of Lisbon, was introduced by the TEU to enhance the legislative power of the EP. The complex procedure, which is now the main legislative procedure by which EU acts are adopted, involves the Commission sending a legislative proposal to both the Council and the EP. If both the Council and the EP approve the proposal, it will be adopted.

Should consensus not be reached, this signals the beginning of a stage whereby the proposal may be subject to a 'to-ing and fro-ing' between the Council and EP. If agreement still cannot be reached, a conciliation committee will be convened by the Commission in an attempt to draw up a legislative act which is acceptable to both the EP and Council. If this cannot be achieved within six weeks of the Committee being convened, the proposal will fail. If a joint text is agreed, it will again be put before both Institutions for their approval.

'Special' legislative procedures (Arts 289 and 294 TFEU)

'Special' legislative procedures relate to specific circumstances highlighted by the Treaties, where the 'Ordinary' procedure need not be followed.

The Commission acting alone

This method is rarely used and it is sufficient to say that it involves the Commission acting without intervention from the other EU Institutions. (An example of the use of this procedure may be found under Art 106 TFEU, relating to competition rules.)

The Commission also enjoys delegated legislative power. Although not strictly a legislative procedure, the Council may, through parent legislation, authorise the Commission to enact regulations in specific areas such as agriculture and competition; this allows legislation to be enacted quickly in areas that are highly regulated.

The Council and Commission acting alone

Here the Council may adopt a proposal from the Commission without having to refer to any other authority. An example of this procedure may be found under Art 31 TFEU, which allows the Council to fix Common Customs Tariffs, following a proposal from the Commission.

The 'Consultation' procedure

Under this procedure, which was found in the original EEC Treaty, the Commission may put forward a proposal to the Council who, in turn, must consult the EP. No obligation is placed on either the Council or the Commission to follow the EP's opinion. Note, however, that the resulting legislation may be annulled should the EP not be consulted (Case 138/79, *Roquette Frères v Council*).

An example of the Consultation Procedure can be found under Art 22 TFEU, in regard to the rights of EU citizens.

The 'Consent' procedure

In a small number of areas, the positive approval of the EP is required before the Council can adopt a proposal. This procedure, originally introduced by the SEA, affords the EP an absolute power of rejection. An example of its use can be found under Art 7 TEU.

While it is important to get to grips with the procedures by which the Union's Institutions may enact secondary legislation, there is far more to the legislative process than mere practice.

3. Voting procedures

When Institutions have to take legislative decisions, the voting procedures used are of significance as different options available can impact on the influence exerted by participants. The various voting methods available to the Institutions are as follows:

- *Simple majority*. Under this procedure each participant (but not those who are absent) is given a **single vote** and a decision is reached on the basis of the largest number of votes received. An argument against this voting method is that the rights of the minority may be sidelined. This is a method through which the **Commission** reaches its decisions.

- *Absolute majority*. This method requires that **over half** of all those with a vote (including any absentees) must agree before a proposal can be carried. Majority voting is the method adopted by the **European Parliament** (Art 231 TFEU), although whether it be by simple or absolute majority will depend on the specific requirements of the Treaty.

- *Qualified majority (QMV)*. QMV has been a feature of EU decision making since the birth of the EEC in 1957. Under this process, votes are weighted according to the population of each Member State. This form of voting has been considered the most democratic and is the method under which the **Council** takes decisions, *unless* otherwise provided by the Treaties. In November 2014 this procedure has been amended to include a greater 'population element' under which a **double majority** is needed to adopt proposals i.e decisions in the Council need the support of 55 per cent of Member States (15 out of 28 EU States) representing a minimum of 65 per cent of the EU's population.

- *Unanimity*. Before agreement can be reached under this procedure, **all participants must agree**. While this system demonstrates solidarity and unity, it can also significantly increase the time taken to achieve agreement and so is limited in its use to issues of high importance. This method of voting also allows participants to 'veto' a decision.

i. Delegated acts

Art 289(3) TFEU defines legislative acts as 'legal acts adopted by legislative procedure' that is by means of the legislative procedures outlined above. However the Treaty, by means of Art 290 TFEU, also allows the EP and the Council to delegate the power to adopt 'non-legislative' acts to the Commission, thereby creating a new category of legal act: **delegated acts**.

Art 290 defines such non-legislative acts as 'acts of general application' which 'supplement or amend non-essential elements of the legislative act'. Such delegated power is strictly limited; only the Commission can be delegated such authority and the Institution must act under the conditions set by the legislator(s) (i.e. EP and/or Council), who may revoke the delegated act or limit its duration. Delegated acts are typically used to specify technical details or to provide the opportunity for later amendment to legislation.

ii. Implementing acts

While the implementation of EU law within the Member States is normally the responsibility of the States, it will sometimes be necessary to ensure that legislation is implemented uniformly across the Member States. In such circumstances, Art 291 TFEU confers such implementing powers on the Commission.

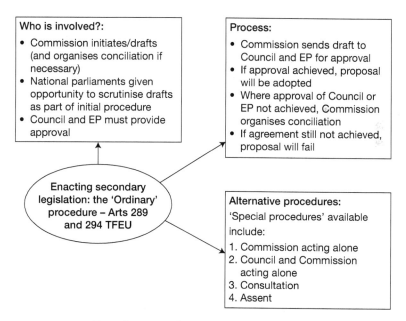

Enacting secondary legislation in the EU

III. CASE LAW OF THE COURT OF JUSTICE OF THE EUROPEAN UNION

The CJEU's function, as provided by Art 19 TEU, is to 'ensure that in the interpretation and application of the Treaties, the law is observed'. As the treaties and secondary legislation can be imprecise or insufficiently comprehensive, this has provided the CJEU with the opportunity to significantly contribute to the corpus of European Union law.

The importance of the Court's case law should not be underestimated. By virtue of its favoured purposive, or teleological, method of interpretation (use your Glossary!) – and its jurisdiction to provide preliminary rulings (discussed in Chapter 6) – the Court has, virtually single-handedly, **developed the EU's legal system, constitutionalised the Treaties and filled in gaps in legislation**. While there is no formal system of precedent, with the Court being free to depart from its own past decisions should it see fit, in the interest of consistency this has seldom occurred. (For an example of the Court departing from its past decisions consider cases C-267 and 268/91, *Keck*, discussed in Chapter 7.) With regard to the relationship between the Court's decisions and national courts, the Court's decisions *do* have a precedential value, as can be evidenced by the Court's dicta in Cases 28–30/62, *Da Costa* (discussed in Chapter 6).

The case of *Van Gend en Loos* (Case 26/62) epitomises the importance of the case law of the CJEU, demonstrating the Court's approach to its role and also the extent of its impact. It is consequently strongly recommended that students read this judgment and consider its consequences (discussed further in Chapter 5).

IV. GENERAL PRINCIPLES OF UNION LAW

General principles of law, which can be found in all advanced legal systems not just that of the EU, have the function of assisting where written sources of law are not sufficiently comprehensive. The General principles of EU Law have been developed by the CJEU and have been used to 'flesh out' law found in the treaties and secondary legislation.

General principles have been held to include equality (and/or non-discrimination), fundamental rights, proportionality, subsidiarity and legal certainty, many of which have gone on to be formally recognised by later inclusion in the treaties.

1. The function and status of general principles

General principles have been used by the CJEU to assist in the interpretation of EU legislation and also as a factor when considering the validity of secondary legislation (an example of which is Case 112/77, *Topfer v Commission*, which you may wish to research further). In addition, they can provide a restraint on the activities of the Member States (for example, Case 11/70, *Internationale Handelsgesellschaft (IHG)*).

The Court has been creative in developing these principles, using the purposive method of interpretation and discovering them as 'threads' running through:

- EU Treaties;
- the national laws of the Member States; and
- international law.

The CJEU justified its actions by referring to three Treaty articles which, it argues, gave it the necessary authority, namely:

- Art 220 TEC (now Art 19 TEU), which provided that the Court 'ensure that in the interpretation of the Treaties the law is observed', the term 'law' in this context being understood to mean more than the written sources of law contained in the Treaties;
- Art 230 TEC (now Art 263 TFEU), which provided 'infringement of the Treaties or any rule of law relating to their application'. 'Any rule of law' in this context has been interpreted to be a reference to law other than that contained in the Treaties; and
- Art 288 TEC (now Art 340 TFEU), which referred to 'general principles common to the laws of the Member States'.

In order to provide a flavour of how these principles have been developed and applied, a number of important examples will be considered in turn below.

2. Equality – 'discovered' in the Treaties

The Treaties refer to the principle of equality on a number of occasions and this is an example of the Court developing a general principle by bringing together 'threads' found in the Treaties.

While Art 12 TEC (now Art 18 TFEU) prohibited discrimination on the grounds of nationality, Art 34(2) TEC (now Art 40 TFEU) prohibited discrimination between producers or consumers within the EU. In addition, Art 141 TEC (now Art 157 TFEU) provided for equal pay between men and women, and the Court, on the basis of these 'threads', developed the more general principle of non-discrimination.

The Court went on to use the principle to prohibit discrimination based on grounds such as nationality (Case 293/83, *Gravier v City of Liège*) and gender (Cases 75a and 117/82, *Razzouk and Beydouin v Commission*).

The principle of equality or non-discrimination is now formally supported by the TFEU (Arts 2 and 19), which provide the EU with the authority to legislate in order to prohibit discrimination based on 'sex, racial or ethnic origin, religion or belief, disability, age or sexual orientation'.

3. Fundamental rights – 'discovered' in national and international law

When the EEC Treaty was originally enacted it contained no mention of protection for human rights. This is quite understandable, given its largely economic emphasis, together with the fact that human rights issues were already being addressed by both the United Nations, through its 1948 Universal Declaration of Human Rights, and also by the Council of Europe, who created the European Convention for the Protection of Human Rights and Fundamental Freedoms (ECHR) in 1950.

The Court of Justice initially resisted any involvement in this area, holding that they had no jurisdiction and that protection of such rights was a matter for individual Member States (Case 1/58, *Stork*). However, once the Court began to develop the principle of supremacy of EU law over national law (discussed in Chapter 5) it recognised the potential for national rules protecting human rights to be undermined if unsupported by the EU and, in Case 29/69, *Stauder*, explained that protection for fundamental human rights was a general principle of EU law.

This approach was confirmed in Case 11/70, *Internationale Handelsgesellschaft (IHG)*, in which the CJEU provided that rights guaranteed under (German) **national law** were also protected by what was then the EEC, and in further cases, such as Case 4/73, *Nold*, the CJEU confirmed that the Court drew inspiration from the constitutional principles 'common to the Member States'.

In Case 36/75, *Rutili*, the Court developed the matter further by providing that rights found in the **ECHR** would be protected by the EU, while in

Case 5/55, *Wachauf*, the Court held that, when implementing Community (now EU) issues, all Member States must respect fundamental rights.

Support for the Court's approach was provided by the other EU Institutions in the Joint Declaration of the European Institutions, 1977, while the judicial activism of the CJEU was apparently vindicated by the reference to fundamental rights in the Maastricht Treaty (TEU 1992). The position of the ECHR within EU law, however, presented some difficulties and, despite the Court of Justice making it clear that the ECHR was of significance in its development of the EU's position on the protection of fundamental rights within the EU, the Court, in its Opinion 2/94 on Accession, provided that the ECHR did not bind the EU and that the Treaties did not provide authority to accede to its Human Rights Charter.

In 2000, the European Parliament drafted a '**Charter of Fundamental Rights**', a persuasive rather than legally binding statement of the EU's position on human rights. While the Charter did not introduce any rights not already broadly recognised in the Treaties, secondary legislation or judgments of the Court of Justice, it made them more easily identifiable. (The Charter contains rights and freedoms under six titles: Dignity, Freedoms, Equality, Solidarity, Citizens' Rights, and Justice.)

Since that time the Charter has been given legal effect (by the Treaty of Lisbon) and now enjoys the same legal status as the Treaties (Art 6 TEU.) In addition, Art 6 TEU also gave the EU the **authority to accede to the ECHR** while at the same time stating that accession will 'not affect the Union's competences'.

Representatives of the membership of both the Council of Europe and the EU have now produced a draft agreement on the accession of the EU to the ECHR. However, in order for accession to take place, the opinion of the CJEU on the compatibility of the draft agreement with the EU Treaties will need to be sought. In addition, the Council of the EU will have to unanimously adopt a decision authorising the signing of the agreement, while all EU Member States will have to ratify it, as will the EU. The Council of Europe will also need to adopt the agreement. In the meantime, where the Charter contains rights that stem from the Convention, their meaning and scope will need to be treated as the same.

i. Scope and enforcement of the Charter

As already touched upon above, Art 6(1) TEU provides that the Charter has 'the same legal value as the Treaties'.

Further, Art 51(1) of the Chapter provides that the 'provisions of this Charter are addressed to the institutions, bodies, offices and agencies of the Union with due regard for the principle of subsidiarity and to the Member

Initially: **Community Treaties fail to mention FR**: unsurprising as the Communities are largely economic in nature and protection already available under the European Convention on Human Rights (ECHR) created by the Council of Europe
– **Court of Justice** upholds this approach (Case 1/58, *Stork v High Authority*)

Change of Attitude: Court of Justice explains that protection of FR is enshrined in the General Principles of EU law (based on the law of the MS and international treaties such as ECHR) (Case 26/29, *Stauder v Ulm*, Case 11/70, *Internationle Handelsgesellschaft (IHG)* and Case 4/73, *Nold*). Member States must also respect FR when implementing EU law (Case 5/88, *Wachauf*)

Support for the Court of Justice's position on FR: Joint Declaration by the Institutions in 1977. FR referred to in amending Treaties (TEU 1992)

Impact of the ECHR in EU: While Court of Justice recognises ECHR as a source of the EU General Principle of FR, the Court provides that the ECHR does not bind the EU (then EC) and that the EC does not have the power to accede to the ECHR (Opinion 2/94 on Accession). TEU refers to ECHR

– **Draft Charter of Fundamental Rights produced in 2000**: Charter is persuasive rather than binding
– **Charter given legal effect** by the Treaty of Lisbon and now has same weight as Treaties (Art 6 TEU)

Application: The Protocol on the Application of the Charter of Fundamental Rights provides that nothing in the Charter creates rights applicable to the UK or Poland. Charter places an obligation on the Institutions and Member States not to 'act in a manner which conflicts with the Charter' (Art 6 (1) TEU). Following *Case C-617/10, Akerberg*, the Charter applies to situations falling within the 'scope of EU law', as opposed to strictly limiting it to situations concerning national law intended to 'implement EU law'

The future: EU has been given the authority to accede to the ECHR (Art 6 TEU). What this will mean is somewhat uncertain as TEU also provides that accession will '*not affect the Union's competences*'. The Protocol on the Application of the Charter of Fundamental Rights also provides that nothing in the Charter creates rights applicable to the UK or Poland

Overview of the development of the protection of fundamental rights in the European Union

States only when they are implementing Union law.' From this it can be seen that the Charter places an obligation on both the EU and its Member States not to act in a manner which conflicts with the Charter.

The duty with regard to the EU means that its Institutions and other bodies must ensure that they do not violate the rights contained in the Charter when they take action – for example, when creating EU policy and law. With regard to the Member States, the extent of the duty is illustrated in Case C-617/10, *Akerberg*, where the Court of Justice took a broad interpretation of Art 51(1), explaining that the Charter applies to situations falling within the 'scope of EU law', as opposed to strictly limiting it to situations concerning national law intended to 'implement EU law'.

As the Charter has the same legal impact as the Treaties, the rights contained within it can be enforceable in the same way as other sources of EU law (discussed in Chapter 6).

V. INTERNATIONAL AGREEMENTS

The EU enjoys legal personality (Art 47 TEU) and Art 216 TFEU confirms that the Union may enter into agreements with third countries or international organisations which may be binding on the Institutions and on the Member States.

VI. CONCLUSIONS

European Union law is an evolving legal system, containing rules that provide rights, obligations and remedies. It has evolved over time and continues to develop in response to the needs and objectives of the EU. Contained in numerous sources, it is made up of rules which effectively provide the EU's constitution, direction on how the Union is to be administered and also the substantive law of the EU. Once this has been understood, the time is right to consider the relationship that exists between EU law and the law of its Member States.

SOME ISSUES TO THINK ABOUT FURTHER

- Which of the EU Treaties were 'amending' treaties? Which contain the principles and rules by which the EU is presently governed?
- How do the various sources of secondary legislation differ from one another?
- From what source do legislators obtain the necessary authority to enact secondary legislation? How is secondary legislation enacted? Is there a different procedure for each type of legislative act?
- What role(s) do the general principles of EU law play?

5 The relationship between Union law and national legal systems

I. THE DOCTRINES OF DIRECT EFFECT AND SUPREMACY

The status of EU law within the legal systems of the various Member States is of fundamental importance, and there are a number of questions that must be answered before an understanding of Union law and its impact can be fully gained.

First, it is necessary to consider which source of law will take precedence should there be a conflict between EU law and national law. Second, it is necessary to consider the effect of EU law in the Member States, who receives rights and obligations under it and whether, where and how such rights may be enforced.

1. The original position

Perhaps rather surprisingly, the founding Treaties did not directly address these questions and the Member States originally assumed that EEC law would have the same domestic effects as other sources of *international* law. This resulted in the status of the EEC Treaty being determined by each Member State's own constitutional rules.

In dualist States (such as the United Kingdom), *international* law is only binding on individuals if it has been adopted by the national authorities and made part of domestic law. In such States, it was therefore considered that the EEC Treaty would bind the state but not provide enforceable rights to individuals unless specifically incorporated.

On the other hand, in monist States (such as the Netherlands), once ratified, international law automatically forms part of the national legal system. In Member States with such constitutional rules, it was consequently assumed that EEC law automatically became part of that State's domestic legal system. As a result, the status – and impact – of EEC law varied from State to State.

The CJEU, however, took a different approach to the question of the impact of Union law and developed two principles, which later become known as the 'Twin Pillars upon which the Community rests', namely, direct effect and supremacy. Each will be considered in turn.

2. The doctrine of supremacy of Union law

Member States have two legal systems with which to contend – that of national law and that of EU law. It therefore needs to be considered which source of law should be applied in cases of conflict between these two sources. As the Treaty is largely silent on this issue (although implicit in a number of provisions) it has been left to the CJEU to provide guidance.

i. The creation of the doctrine of supremacy

While the Court did not address the issue of supremacy of EU law directly in Case 26/62, *Van Gend en Loos* (*Van Gend*), it explained that Union (then Community) law constitutes a 'new legal order . . . for the benefit of which the States have limited their sovereign rights, albeit within limited fields'. (The Court's judgment resulted in Union law (what is now Art 34 TFEU) being applied, rather than the conflicting national (Dutch) law, which was set aside by the domestic court.)

It is clear from the Court's dicta that it was recognised that to allow Member States to apply conflicting national law rather than Union law would severely undermine the ability of the EU to achieve its aims. Thus, the doctrine of the supremacy (or primacy) of Union law was established.

ii. The development of the doctrine

The implications of the doctrine of supremacy were not fully addressed until Case 6/64, *Costa v ENEL*. In this judgment the Court confirmed that where national law and EU law conflict, EU law must take precedence, even where the national law has been enacted subsequent to EU law, thus ruling out the possibility of national law taking precedence under the concept of 'implied repeal' (i.e. a constitutional principle recognised in the UK under which legislation is presumed to have been repealed by later, conflicting, legislation).

The Court provided a number of arguments in support of its dicta. First, it confirmed that EU law is an integral part of domestic legal systems, also providing that Member States had created this new legal system by limiting their sovereign rights and transferring power to the EU.

Drawing heavily on the spirit and aims of the (then EEC) Treaty, the Court pointed out that the uniformity and effectiveness of Union law would be jeopardised should national law be allowed to take precedence. In addition, the Court argued that the obligations undertaken by the Member States would be 'merely contingent' rather than 'unconditional' if they could 'be called into question by subsequent [national] legal acts'.

The Court also referred directly to the text of the EEC Treaty to support its judgment. Although the original Treaties did not – and the TEU and TFEU still do not – provide directly for the supremacy of European law, the Court of Justice has argued that Art 288 TFEU, which provides for the direct applicability of regulations, would be meaningless if Member States could negate their effect by enacting subsequent, conflicting legislation.

While *Van Gend* and *Costa* dealt with the theoretical principle of supremacy, the Court had little to say on the practical application of the concept. A serious threat to the supremacy of EU law was revealed in Case 11/70, *Internationale Handelsgesellschaft (IHG)*, when the German Administrative Court voiced its concern over the legal foundations on which the principle of supremacy was based. The German Court's disquiet revolved around its concern that fundamental rights contained within the German constitution could be overruled by European law. The CJEU made it clear that EU law is supreme over *all* forms and sources of national law, while wisely softening the blow by declaring that the Union recognised such fundamental rights as an 'integral part of the general principles of law' whose protection would be ensured 'within the structure and objectives of the Community' (now Union).

In Case 106/77, *Amministrazione delle Finanze dello Stato v Simmenthal*, as a result of a preliminary reference, the CJEU was required to consider whether a national court should dis-apply conflicting national legislation, even in situations where that court had no domestic jurisdiction to do so (in Italy, this function was only to be carried out by the Constitutional Court). The Court provided that where conflict arises between national and European law, the national court is required to give immediate effect to EU law and not wait for a ruling from the Constitutional Court.

This judgment is important, in that it confers on all domestic courts' jurisdiction that they may not have under domestic law. Once more, the European Court emphasised the need for such action in order to ensure the effectiveness of Union law.

A further example of the jurisdiction of national courts being extended by Union law can be found in Case C-213/89, *R v Secretary of State for Transport ex p Factortame Ltd* (*Factortame* (*No 2*)). In this case, the CJEU explained that a national rule must be set aside by a national court if that rule interferes with an EU law right. This can be seen as an additional example of the practical consequences of the doctrine of supremacy.

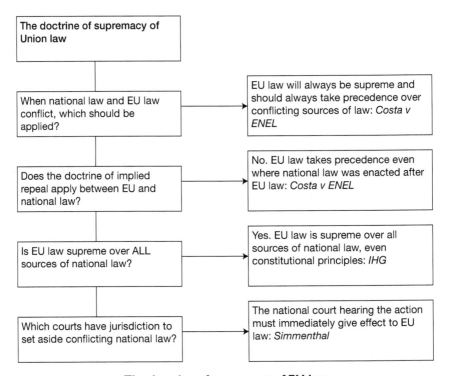

The doctrine of supremacy of EU law

3. The doctrine of direct effect of EU Law

i. The creation of the doctrine

The CJEU provided a ground-breaking judgment in Case 26/62, *Van Gend en Loos* (*Van Gend*). Van Gend imported goods from Germany into the

Netherlands and was required, by Dutch law, to pay customs duty on the goods to the Dutch authorities. The importers challenged the legality of the duty, claiming that it was an infringement of what is now Art 30 TFEU. The Dutch tribunal referred the question to the CJEU under the preliminary reference procedure (Art 267 TFEU, discussed in Chapter 6).

In order to arrive at its decision, the Court of Justice drew heavily on its purposive method of interpretation (Glossary), relying not only on the wording of the Treaty, but also on the spirit and aims of the Union (then, Community). In its judgment, the Court declared that the Union constituted a new legal order of international law, which conferred both rights and obligations on individuals, as well as on the participating Member States, without the need for implementing legislation. The Court further concluded that national courts must protect such rights. In other words, the Court of Justice provided that EEC law (now EU law) had direct effect, which can be seen as a two-pronged concept under which:

- EU law provides individuals, as well as Member States, with rights and obligations; and
- such rights and obligations are enforceable by national courts.

From this judgment, which was opposed by a number of Member States, **it can be concluded that the Court was motivated by the need to ensure the integration, effectiveness and uniformity of EU law.**

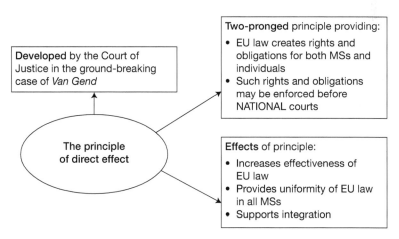

The doctrine of direct effect of EU law

ii. The conditions for direct effect

The Court explained in *Van Gend* that not all Treaty articles would be capable of direct effect and it is now clear that any provision must first fulfil a set of criteria if it is to be directly effective (these criteria will hereafter be called the *Van Gend* criteria, for ease of explanation). It should be noted that some sources may refer to the '*Reyners* criteria' after the case in which they were first listed together (in the AG's Opinion in the case). The *Van Gend* criteria require that in order to have direct effect, the legal provision must be:

- *clear and precise* – it is logical that if law is to be enforceable, both parties must be clear as to what their respective rights/obligations are. The CJEU has therefore declared that a provision must be 'sufficiently clear and precise' before being capable of direct effect. This does not necessarily mean that the whole provision must comply: for example in Case 43/75, *Defrenne v Sabena*, it was held that only part of Art 119 EEC (now Art 157 TFEU) fulfilled this criterion but that part was still held to have direct effect;
- *unconditional* – a provision will not be unconditional if the right it provides is in some way dependent on the judgment or discretion of an independent body unless that discretion is subject to judicial control (an example of this may be found in Case 41/74, *Van Duyn*);
- *not subject to any further implementing measures on the part of either the Union or national authority* – this criterion would appear to have been subject to a liberal application by the Court, as can be demonstrated in Case 2/74, *Reyners*. In this case, based on the wording of the Treaty, it had been anticipated that secondary legislation would have to be enacted before the objectives contained in Art 52 EEC (now Art 49 TFEU) would provide rights to individuals. However, the Court declared the provision to be directly effective, explaining that to do otherwise could result in individuals being denied their EU law rights.

iii. Direct effect of different sources of Union law

The doctrine of direct effect has been further developed and expanded upon over the years and the important developments are set out below.

Direct effect and Treaty articles

As we have already seen above, the question of whether the principle of direct effect applies to Treaty articles was considered in the judgment of *Van Gend en Loos* and it is now well accepted that all Treaty articles are capable of direct effect, **providing** that they comply with the *Van Gend* criteria. In addition, the Court has provided that rights and obligations contained in Treaty articles may be enforced both against the State **and** public bodies (known as *vertical* **direct effect**: *Van Gend*) and against private bodies and individuals (known as *horizontal* **direct effect**: Case 43/75, *Defrenne v Sabena*).

Direct effect and regulations

Article 288 TFEU (TIP: read this Treaty Article very carefully) would appear to give regulations direct effect. The Article states that a regulation 'shall be binding in its entirety and directly applicable in all Member States'. (Direct applicability, which should not be confused with direct effect, has been interpreted as meaning that a provision requires no implementation or further action by the States in order for it to take effect in national law.) While all regulations are directly applicable (as are Treaty articles), the Court confirmed in Case 9/70, *Franz Grad*, that regulations would only be directly effective when they fulfil the *Van Gend* criteria. As with Treaty articles, **regulations may be enforced both vertically and horizontally.**

Direct effect and decisions

Decisions, as regulations, are directly applicable, but Art 288 TFEU provides that they can be binding on those to whom they are addressed (whether that be Member States, corporations or individuals). The Court of Justice has held that decisions will be directly effective, providing they fulfil the *Van Gend* criteria, against an addressee (Case 9/70, *Franz Grad*).

Direct effect of international agreements

This is a controversial and complex area, outside the scope of this book. It is sufficient to conclude that, in an attempt to ensure that Member States respect any commitments arising from such agreements, the Court has ruled that international agreements may have direct effect if the circumstances are appropriate (Case 104/81, *Kupferberg*. It is also instructive to read Art 216 TFEU).

Direct effect and directives

This has proved to be a particularly controversial area. Article 288 TFEU provides that: 'A directive shall be binding, as to the result to be achieved, upon each Member State to which it is addressed, but shall leave to the national authorities the choice of form and methods.'

Directives are therefore *not* directly applicable, as they require implementation into national law by each State's legislative body. Consequently, directives do not appear to provide rights to individuals **until** they have been incorporated – and then through national incorporating legislation, rather than through the directive itself – although they *do* place obligations on Member States.

Despite the wording of Art 288 TFEU, which would appear to preclude directives from being directly effective, the CJEU has held that where a directive has not been properly implemented into national law, it may still give rise to direct effects (*Franz Grad* and *Van Duyn*).

The Court has confirmed that in order for directives to be directly effective, they must satisfy the *Van Gend* criteria. While the first two criteria present few problems, it would appear that the final criterion is impossible to satisfy. However, once the date on which the directive *should* have been implemented has passed, the CJEU has shown itself willing to conclude that this criterion has also been satisfied (Case 148/78, *Pubblico Ministero v Ratti*).

The Court has argued that this approach results in directives being both more effective and also stops Member States from relying on their own 'wrongdoing' should they fail to incorporate a directive into domestic law. This development has not been without its critics however, who argue that to allow directives direct effect removes the intended distinction between regulations and directives.

In response to such criticism, the CJEU has explained that directives are distinct as they may **only be enforced vertically** (that is, against the State) and **not** horizontally (that is, against individuals) (Case 152/84, *Marshall v Southampton and South West Hampshire AHA* (*Marshall* (No 1)).

In the *Marshall* case, Miss Marshall wished to enforce rights emanating from the Equal Treatment Directive (Council Directive (76/207/EEC)), against her employer. She attempted to do this in the appropriate national court, i.e. an employment tribunal (ET). The ET made a preliminary reference to the CJEU (under Art 267 TFEU), asking whether Ms Marshall could rely on the Directive. The Court replied that she could, as her employers were a public body and therefore part of the State – in other words, she could rely on the *vertical* direct effect of the Directive.)

This requirement has the unfortunate effect of discriminating between individuals who wish to enforce their rights against a State or public body, as compared to those wishing to pursue the same rights against a private body. The problem can be illustrated by consideration of Case 151/84, *Roberts v Tate & Lyle Industries* (the *Tate & Lyle* case), which mirrored the circumstances of *Marshall* (No 1). Ms Roberts also wished to enforce rights emanating from the Equal Treatment Directive but, as she was employed by a private corporation as opposed to an emanation of the State, her rights were unenforceable.

4. Developing the effectiveness of directives

i. Vertical direct effect: a wide interpretation of 'State'

In an attempt to circumnavigate the problem highlighted above, the CJEU has shown itself willing to adopt the widest possible definition of 'State'.

As already discussed, the Court has been willing to recognise a Health Authority as part of the State (in *Marshall No 1*), while in Case 103/88, *Fratelli Constanzo*, regional and local government were also considered to be within the definition. In Case 222/84, *Johnston v Chief Constable of the RUC*, the Chief Constable was also recognised as being part of the state – or an 'emanation of the State' as it has become known.

In Case C-188/89, *Foster v British Gas*, the Court of Justice provided some **guidance** (note: these are not criteria) on what could be considered an 'emanation' by explaining that a directive may be relied upon against organisations or bodies which:

- have been made responsible for providing a public service; and/or
- are subject to the authority or control of the State; and/or
- have special powers beyond those which result from the normal rules applicable to relations between individuals.

These guidelines (note: they are *not* criteria), while failing to provide an inclusive definition of 'State', have nevertheless proved helpful by making it clear that something *more* than mere control is necessary.

This conclusion is supported by the Court of Appeal's dicta in *Doughty v Rolls Royce* (1992). Although Rolls Royce was, at the time of the action, wholly owned by the British State, it was not considered an 'emanation of the State' as the company neither provided a public service nor had any of the 'special powers' referred to in *Foster*. Note that it is for the national courts to decide whether a defendant is an emanation of the state or not.

ii. Indirect effect or the 'interpretive obligation'

The CJEU's refusal to allow the horizontal direct effect of directives has without doubt lessened their effectiveness as legislative instruments. In an attempt at remedying this, the Court has developed a principle which has become known as 'indirect effect' or 'the interpretative obligation'.

The basic principle

In Case 14/83, *Von Colson*, the Court reminded Member States of their duty, provided under Art 10 TEC (now Art 4 TFEU), to 'take all appropriate measures . . . to ensure the fulfilment of the obligations arising out of this Treaty' and also to 'facilitate the achievement of the Community's tasks'. The Court went on to explain that such obligations also bind all the authorities of the States including, for matters within their jurisdiction, the national courts. Consequently, an obligation is placed on national courts to interpret and apply national law in a manner which is consistent with the wording and purpose of directives.

This judgment has been the subject of much academic criticism as, it is argued, it requires national courts to supplement the role of the domestic legislator. The principle has also been criticised for allowing the direct effect of directives via the 'back door', without the need to ensure that the restrictive *Van Gend* criteria are fulfilled.

The principle has, however, undoubtedly succeeded in enhancing the effectiveness of unimplemented and/or incorrectly implemented directives, while at the same time placing another obstacle in the path of Member States who fail to comply with their obligations.

The development of the doctrine of indirect effect

The *Von Colson* judgment left a number of questions unanswered with regard to the exact extent of the principle of 'indirect effect'.

In Case 80/86, *Kolpinghuis Nijmegen*, the Court made it clear that it would not be possible to interpret national legislation in the light of a directive should this result in conflict with any of the general principles of Union law, such as non-retroactivity or legitimate expectation (Chapter 4 provides consideration of General Principles). Thus, it is clear that there are limits on the application of indirect effect, and national courts need only interpret national law to conform with directives 'in so far as it is possible'.

In Case C-106/89, *Marleasing*, the CJEU confirmed that national legislation, which has been interpreted by a national court in the light of a non-implemented or incorrectly implemented directive, can be relied on, not only by an individual against a State, but also against another individual and even where such national law pre-dates a directive and was not intended to implement it. This would appear to be allowing unincorporated directives to be enforced against individuals, thus achieving 'horizontal direct effect' in all but name. However, the decision in *Marleasing* has been tempered in Case C-456/98, *Centrosteel*, where the CJEU provided that a directive cannot of itself impose criminal liability on individuals in the absence of proper implementing legislation. Further, the Court has confirmed that the interpretive duty only arises once the date for implementation has passed (Case C-212/04, *Adeneler and Others*).

Academics have highlighted that indirect effect is the *most used* means of ensuring proper effect of incorrectly or unimplemented directives **and its importance should not, consequently, be underestimated.** The Court has regularly reaffirmed its importance and, in joined Cases C-397–403/01, *Pfeiffer and Others* (a case relating to the 'Working Time Directive'), provided that 'the requirement for national law to be interpreted in conformity with Community law is inherent in the system of the Treaty . . . to ensure the full effectiveness of Community law . . .'.

iii. 'Incidental' or 'triangular' effect

Despite the Court of Justice's decision in *Marshall* (*No 1*) prohibiting the horizontal direct effect of directives, in Case C-194/94, *CIA Security International* the Court appeared to allow the equivalent of horizontal effect to directives, albeit in limited manner. It would seem that where an individual attempts to demonstrate that national law conflicts with a directive, and such illegality is proven, the Court has signalled that EU law (i.e. the directive) must be applied – even where this has an impact on a third party, *providing* that no legal obligations are imposed directly on the individual(s) as a result. Once more, the CJEU cited the enhanced effectiveness of directives as its aim in allowing this.

Other cases in which this principle has been utilised include Case C-443/98, *Unilever Italia* and Case C-201/02, *Wells*. However, due to its limitations, it should be noted that the 'incidental effect' of directives is likely to arise only in very limited circumstances.

iv. Additional thoughts on the source of an EU right or obligation

While the matter of the relevant source of a right or obligation (that is, whether the right in question emanates from a treaty article or regulation, for example) is rarely problematic, Case C-144/04, *Mangold* is worth taking a moment to consider. In this case it appeared that the source of the claimant's right was a Directive, the expiry date of which had not yet passed. Consequently, the Directive could not have direct effect but, as the right in question related to a matter of discrimination, the Court of Justice provided that the right could emanate from the General Principle of Non-discrimination, as opposed to the Directive in question.

It is consequently worth bearing in mind that the source of a right/ obligation may not always be as straightforward as it may first appear to be!

5. State liability for damages (the *Francovich* principle)

In view of the limitations placed on the direct effect of directives, and despite the possibility of enforcing rights under the principle of indirect effect, a number of barriers may still exist with regard to the enforcement of rights emanating from a directive (for example, there may be no national law to interpret or interpretation may simply not be possible due to the wording of the national legislation being very precise).

In Cases C-6 and 9/90, *Francovich and Bonifaci v Italy (Francovich)*, the Court of Justice held that, should a Member State fail to incorporate a directive into national law, an individual who suffers damage as a consequence may claim compensation from that State, thereby ensuring greater effectiveness of directives.

This right to compensation was, however, subject to a number of criteria, namely:

- the directive must be intended to confer a right on citizens;
- the content of the right must be identifiable by reference to the directive;
- there must be a causal link between the State's breach and the damage suffered.

The Court's judgment in *Francovich* reinforces Member States' obligations under Art 4 TEU and also provides a further incentive to Member States to ensure that EU law rights are not denied to individuals.

i. The development of State damages

The *Francovich* ruling has been of immense importance to Union law and the principle has been clarified and extended in a number of later cases. While in *Francovich*, the CJEU's decision related to a Member State's failure to fulfil its obligations in relation to directives, in joined Cases C-46 and C-48/93, *Brasserie du Pêcheur SA v Germany; R v Secretary of State for Transport ex p Factortame Ltd and Others (Pêcheur and Factortame)*, the Court confirmed that damages could also be available in situations where a Member State had failed to fulfil obligations derived from *other* sources of Union law. Once more, however, the Court explained that certain criteria must be fulfilled:

- the rule of law infringed must be intended to confer rights on individuals;
- the breach must be sufficiently serious;
- there must be a direct causal link between the States breach and the damage caused.

The Court also provided that the principle applied to whichever organ of a State was responsible for the breach or omission, whether it be legislative, executive or, controversially, judicial (as in Case C-224/01, *Kobler v Austria*).

ii. The Court of Justice's interpretation of 'sufficiently serious'

With regard to what will constitute a 'sufficiently serious' breach, the Court has put forward various factors that may be taken into account, including the following:

- the degree of clarity and precision of the EU rule that has been breached (if the rule is imprecisely worded, the breach will not be sufficiently serious: Case C-392/93, *R v HM Treasury ex p British Telecom*);
- the 'intentionality' or 'voluntariness' of the infringement and the damage caused (intentional fault is not essential: Cases T-178, 179 and 188–90/94, *Dillenkofer v Germany*);
- the degree of discretion provided to the Member State by the provision (where there is no, or limited, discretion, the infringement of law in itself may be sufficient to establish the existence of a sufficiently serious breach: Case C-5/94, *R v MAFF ex p Hedley Lomas*).

By allowing individuals to bring such actions before their national courts, it should be evident that the CJEU has once more enhanced the effectiveness of EU law. The development of actions for damages against the Member States can be compared with the availability of actions for damages against Union Institutions, which have been provided for by the Treaty (Art 340 TFEU, discussed in Chapter 6) and it is quite clear that the Court has been influenced by Art 340 TFEU in regard to the way in which State damages have been developed. (For those wishing to consider the development of the parallel principles developed between State and Union liability, Case C-352/98P, *Bergaderm v Commission* is recommended reading.)

iii. Expansion of the principle to actions against private parties

In addition to the *Francovich* principle being expanded beyond non- or ineffective implementation of directives to any sufficiently serious breach of Union law by a Member State, it would now appear that such actions for damages may also be available against *private* bodies. This can be evidenced by Case C-453-/99, *Courage Ltd v Crehan*. In this case an individual sought to bring an action against another individual for damage suffered as a result of a breach of EU competition law. *As no national remedy was available for the breach*, the Court of Justice confirmed that an action may be brought under the *Francovich* principle, not just against Member States but against private individuals/bodies that cause loss to another through breach of Union law.

II. CONCLUSIONS

Membership of the EU has resulted in States having an additional source of law to contend with – that of the EU. Perhaps rather surprisingly, the Treaties give little guidance as to the interaction between national and Union law and it has been left to the CJEU to interpret which source of law is supreme in situations of conflict and also what effects EU law may have within national legal systems. (It is interesting to note, however, that if the Constitutional Treaty had been given effect, it *would* have contained a statement on the effect of EU law, under what was known as the 'primacy clause'.)

Relatively early in the life of the EEC, the Court of Justice was prepared to explain that Union law is not like other sources of international law. Not only is EU law supreme but it also provides rights and obligations to both States and individuals alike, which can, in turn, be enforced before national courts. The development of principles such as direct effect and supremacy have resulted in the Court of Justice being criticised for its 'judicial activism' and for usurping a role that should have been left to the Union's legislators.

While the principles discussed above may appear simplistic and obvious, it should, however, be recognised that their effect on the EU has been profound, elevating its relevance and ensuring its uniform effectiveness throughout the Union.

NOTE: Chapter 9 provides tips on how to approach problem questions relating to supremacy, direct effect, and the alternatives to direct effect, which will hopefully support your approach to answering seminar questions, coursework and examinations.

DIRECT EFFECT of Union Law (Note: EU law also enjoys SUPREMACY)
What is the source of the EU right?

- **Treaty Article or Regulation:** Enforceable before national court IF source satisfies the 3 *Van Gend/Reyners* criteria (if not, right may not be enforceable through direct effect). Capable of vertical and horizontal d/effect (*Defrenne*)

- **Decision:** Enforceable against addressee only IF 3 *Van Gend/Reyners* criteria satisfied (if not, right may not be enforceable)

- **Directive:** More problematic. Enforceable only IF 3 *Van Gend/Reyners* criteria are satisfied. Implementation date also must have passed (*Ratti*). Only enforceable vertically against a State (*Marshall*). Note the broad interpretation of 'State' (guidance on what may be an emanation of the State provided in *Foster v British Gas*)

ALTERNATIVES TO DIRECT EFFECT: Where direct effect is not available, consider:

1. **Indirect effect (interpretive obligation):** National law may be interpreted in light of an unincorporated directive once date for implementation has passed (*Von Volson*) in so far as it is possible to do so (*Marleasing*)

2. **Incidental direct effect:** Directive may be given effect where national law and directive conflict and national law is disapplied, thereby giving rights, under the directive, to an individual (*CIA* and *Unilever*). Only available in exceptional circumstances

3. **State damages:** Available where an individual has suffered loss as a result of MS breach (failure to incorporate directive or other sufficiently serious breach: *Francovich*, *Pêcheur* and *Factortame*). Criteria must be satisfied

The impact of European Union law: the impact of direct effect

SOME ISSUES TO THINK ABOUT

- What impact did the Member States *originally* assume EU law would have on their national legal systems? Which important CJEU decision changed this assumption?

- What has been the impact of supremacy and direct effect on the *effectiveness* of EU law and also on the Union's success in achieving its aims and objectives?

- How has the doctrine of direct effect been developed by the CJEU? Why have these developments been considered necessary?

6 Enforcing Union law

The preceding chapters have considered why the EEC was created and how it has developed into today's EU, who 'runs' the European Union, the various sources of law that make up the Union's legal system and the relationship between national and EU law. In order to understand how the Union works in practice, we now need to consider how EU law is applied and enforced.

Because EU law forms part of each Member State's domestic legal system, rights and obligations emanating from EU law are normally enforced before **domestic (i.e. national) courts** rather than before the Court of Justice of the European Union (CJEU). This is quite logical – especially if it is remembered that EU law should be viewed as **another source of national law**. (In the UK for example, would you expect statute to be applied in a different court or in a different manner to common law?) We therefore need to consider exactly on what basis and how such enforcement takes place.

National courts have not been left totally to their own devices when applying EU law and a procedure known as 'preliminary reference' (Art 267 TFEU), which provides a valuable link between the CJEU and domestic courts, will also be considered.

While domestic courts are normally used to enforce EU law rights, there are certain actions that only the CJEU has jurisdiction to hear. These include infringement proceedings against Member States who have failed to comply with their EU obligations (Arts 258–260 TFEU) and judicial review of the acts and omissions of the Union's institutions (including Arts 263–266 TFEU). Each will be considered in turn.

I. ENFORCING EUROPEAN LAW RIGHTS BEFORE NATIONAL COURTS

As has already been considered in Chapter 5, provided certain criteria are fulfilled, Union law has direct effect, that is, it provides individuals with rights and obligations that are enforceable before national courts. We therefore need to consider which domestic courts may be employed, what procedures should be followed and what remedies should be available to individuals enforcing their EU law rights.

1. Courts

It has been left to the Member States' discretion to decide specifically which national courts will be appropriate to hear actions founded on Union law and also the procedures to be followed. (In the UK, for example, an action relating to EU employment law would be heard before an Employment Tribunal, under the usual rules and procedures of that court.)

As the CJEU stated in Case 45/76, *Comet BV v Produktschap voor Siergewassen (Comet)*:

> It is for the domestic law of each Member State to designate the courts having jurisdiction and the procedural conditions governing actions at law intended to ensure the protection of the rights which subjects derive from the direct effects of Community law.

2. Procedures

The dicta in *Comet* demonstrates that the enforcement of EU law rights in national courts has to fit in with the national systems already in place for enforcement of national law.

Harmonisation of procedures throughout the EU is not practicable due to the wide variety of approaches employed by the various Member States. Instead, in recognition of the Union's need to ensure the *effective* enforcement of EU law, while still respecting the autonomy of the Member States, the Court of Justice has laid down guidelines that the national courts are obliged to take into account. The guidelines relate to the following:

- *The principle of non-discrimination*: In the *Comet* case, the CJEU provided that its decision was contingent on 'it being understood that such conditions cannot be less favourable than those relating to similar actions of a domestic nature'. This means that although the appropriate courts and procedures are left up to the Member States, the States still have an obligation to ensure that national procedures do not discriminate against any individual wishing to enforce an EU law right, as compared to a similar national law right.

- *Availability of an action/remedy*: National procedures must not make it excessively difficult to obtain a remedy for a breach of EU law. In Case 199/82, *Amministrazione delle Finanze dello Stato v San Giorgio* (*San Giorgio Case*), the European Court explained that national rules and procedures must not make it, in practice, impossible for rights conferred by the Union to be enforced.

3. Remedies

The Court of Justice has been particularly careful to ensure that appropriate remedies are available with regard to breaches of EU law rules. In Case 33/76, *Rewe-Zentralfinanz v Landschwirtschaftskammer*, the Court explained that although it has been made possible for individuals to bring direct actions based on EU law before national courts, 'it was not intended to create new remedies in the national courts to ensure the observance of Community [now Union] law'.

Consequently, the remedies available for breaches of national law should be made available for similar breaches of EU law. However, once more, this has been qualified by guidelines laid down in decisions of the Court of Justice. Again, the provision of a remedy must not discriminate and must be made available 'on the same conditions as would apply were it a question of observing national law' (*Rewe-Zentralfinanz*). In addition, the remedy made available under national law must be an 'effective' remedy.

In Case 14/83, *Von Colson*, the Court explained that Art 10 TEC (now Art 4 TEC) provides Member States, and therefore their national courts, with the obligation of facilitating the achievement of the aims of the Union. Consequently, Member States and national courts *must* ensure that remedies available for breaches of EU law are effective, have a deterrent effect and be 'adequate in relation to the damage sustained' (in other words, be proportionate). In Case C-271/91, *Marshall (No 2)*, for example, the UK limit on the quantum of damages available rendered the remedy ineffective. As a result the UK had to amend its rules.

i. The development of a uniform Union remedy: State damages

In general, the European Union has been happy to allow national courts to protect the EU law rights of individuals by means of appropriate national procedures and remedies. There has, however, been one exception to this: the development of the Union remedy of 'State damages'.

The development of this remedy has been considered in some detail in Chapter 4. To briefly recap, in Cases C-6 and 9/90, *Francovich*, the Court of Justice provided that, where a Member State had failed to correctly implement the aims of a directive, damages were available from the State to compensate those who had suffered loss as a result of the breach. This ensures that Member States may not rely on, or benefit from, their own wrongdoings and that the remedy for doing so is uniform throughout the European Union.

The remedy is based on the obligations placed on Member States (by what was Art 10 TEC, now Art 4 TEU) and has been developed in later cases (particularly Cases C-46 and 48/93, *Brasserie du Pêcheur* and *Factortame*) to include *any* sufficiently serious breach of EU law by a State or its public

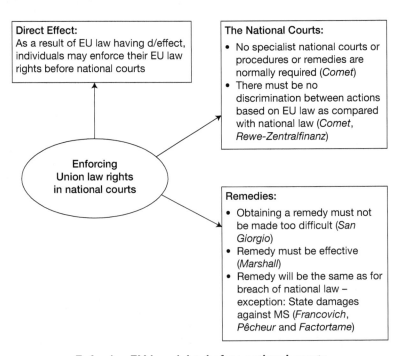

Direct Effect:
As a result of EU law having d/effect, individuals may enforce their EU law rights before national courts

The National Courts:
- No specialist national courts or procedures or remedies are normally required (*Comet*)
- There must be no discrimination between actions based on EU law as compared with national law (*Comet, Rewe-Zentralfinanz*)

Enforcing Union law rights in national courts

Remedies:
- Obtaining a remedy must not be made too difficult (*San Giorgio*)
- Remedy must be effective (*Marshall*)
- Remedy will be the same as for breach of national law – exception: State damages against MS (*Francovich, Pêcheur* and *Factortame*)

Enforcing EU law rights before national courts

bodies or, now also it would seem, private parties (*Crehan* case). A number of criteria must be fulfilled before damages can be made available and these too are considered in Chapter 4, to which you should refer.

II. PRELIMINARY REFERENCES AND RULINGS

Article 267 TFEU provides the CJEU with the jurisdiction to give preliminary rulings on the **interpretation of the Treaties** and also on the interpretation and **validity of acts of the Institutions** (in the main, secondary legislation), when requested to do so by national courts.

It should be emphasised at the outset that Art 267 does **not** give the Court authority to decide the outcome of a case but rather to interpret EU law and rule on the validity of EU legislation, other than the Treaties. This can be illustrated in *Arsenal v Reed (No 2)* [2003], where the national court refused to follow a ruling provided by the Court of Justice as they argued that the European Court had exceeded their jurisdiction by making a finding in fact.

Article 267 is often cited as evidence that EU law was always intended to have direct effect as, if national courts were not intended to enforce EU law, why would they need to make a reference to the Court of Justice.

1. The purpose of preliminary rulings

The purpose of Art 267 TFEU is to ensure the **uniform interpretation and application of Union law**. The principle of direct effect has firmly established national courts as enforcers of EU law and if interpretation were left to national courts it would not be possible to ensure uniformity, given that different legal systems employ different interpretative methods. (Consider, for example, the position in the United Kingdom, where the literal method of interpretation is favoured, as opposed to other Member States, who may employ a more purposive approach.)

2. The effects of preliminary rulings

The CJEU is not bound by precedent, which means that it does not have to follow its own previous rulings – but in reality it does so in order to ensure consistency (the Court's dicta in Cases 28–30/62, *Da Costa*, in which it repeated its *Van Gend* judgment, are a good example of this).

A referring national court will, however, be bound by the ruling of the Court of Justice and is obliged to apply the ruling obtained to the case before it. While a ruling will normally be retrospective in its effect, the

Court of Justice may limit the temporal effects of any such ruling (as it did in Case C-262/88, *Barber v Guardian Royal Exchange*, where the Court held that the ruling was effective only from the date of its judgment).

Despite national courts being bound by the rulings of the Court of Justice, the Court has, in the past, been at pains to point out that it is not 'senior' to the national courts, but merely has a different function to perform. In reality, however, the CJEU undoubtedly enjoys a superior position BUT do ensure that you always remember that it is NOT a court of appeal from the national courts.

3. Which national bodies may make a reference?

Article 267 TFEU provides that 'any court or tribunal of a Member State' may make a reference. The European Court has accepted references from a variety of national courts and tribunals, including arbitration panels, insurance officers and administrative tribunals (the reference in *Van Gend* came from a Dutch Administrative Tribunal). Consideration of case law demonstrates, however, that the Court of Justice does not have the jurisdiction to accept a reference from a body that lies outside the legal system of a Member State. In Case 102/81, *Nordsee*, for example, a request for a ruling was made by an arbitration tribunal that had been established by contract – the reference was consequently refused. Conversely, in Case 246/80, *Broekmeulen*, the Court considered that a Dutch body known as the Appeals Committee for General Medicine was an appropriate body as it operated with the consent and co-operation of the public authorities and delivered decisions which were recognised in law as final.

4. The decision to refer

A national court or tribunal will only need to make a reference where it considers that its decision in the case before it rests on a point of EU law. Article 267 TFEU makes it clear that it is for the national court to decide when a reference should be made and **not** the parties to a case or any other party or authority, *including* the Court of Justice. (National precedent should never operate to prevent a court from seeking a ruling: Cases 146 and 166/73, *Rheinmühlen-Düsseldorf*). The Treaty also distinguishes between those national courts that have the *discretion* to refer (i.e. *may* refer) and those that are *obliged* to refer (i.e. *must* make a reference).

i. The discretion to refer

Article 267(2) TFEU provides that any court 'may, if it considers that a decision on the question is necessary to enable it to give judgment, request the Court of Justice to give a ruling thereon'. The CJEU has interpreted this to mean that where an appropriate body is called upon to reach a decision which may be based on an issue of EU law, that body has the authority to make a reference to the Court of Justice (Case 92/78, *Simmenthal*) but is **not** bound to do so.

ii. The obligation to refer

Article 267(3) TFEU provides that national courts or tribunals 'against whose decisions there is no judicial remedy in national law . . . **shall** bring the matter before the Court of Justice'. Thus, any court from which there is no appeal *must* make a reference when called upon to reach a decision on a matter that relates to a point of Union law. There have been conflicting opinions, however, as to which national courts this obligation applies to.

Under what became known as the 'abstract theory', it was argued that only courts from which no appeal was available would be obliged to refer. (In the UK, for example, Lord Denning in *Bulmer v Bollinger* (1974) considered that only the House of Lords [now the Supreme Court] fell into this category.) However, under the opposing 'concrete theory' it was thought that where the parties had no automatic right of appeal, the national court was obliged to refer. This theory was considered the most persuasive, as it was supported by the CJEU in cases such as *Costa v ENEL*.

Following Case 99/00, *Lyckeskog*, the position has now been settled. In this case an appeal from a Swedish district court could only be made with the agreement of the Swedish Supreme Court. The CJEU provided that as there was a *possibility* of an appeal (even though leave to appeal could be refused) the district court was not to be considered the court of last resort. Thus it would appear that the 'abstract theory' is the approach that should be followed.

iii. Acte clair

Despite the obligation to refer provided by Art 267(3) TFEU, it should be noted that there are **three** circumstances in which the CJEU has specifically held that it may **not** be necessary for a national court to make a reference, even if circumstances suggest that the 'abstract theory' applies. This is known as *'acte clair'*. The circumstances in which *acte clair* applies were explained by the Court in Case 283/81, *CILFIT*, and are as follows:

- The question of EU law is **irrelevant** to the case being heard by the national court.
- The question of EU law has **already been interpreted by the CJEU** in a previous ruling. (This principle was first established in the *Da Costa* case. However, as the CJEU does not have to follow its own previous rulings, national courts should recognise the possibility that the Court may amend its earlier rulings and bear this in mind when taking a decision as to whether to refer or not. Two examples of the CJEU 'changing its mind' can be found in the *Lyckeskog* case set out above and in Cases C-267 and 268/91, *Keck & Mithouard*, discussed in Chapter 7.)
- The correct interpretation is so **obvious** as to leave no scope for reasonable doubt. (This rule has been criticised, as what may be 'obvious' to one national court may not be so obvious to another, possibly creating lack of uniformity.)

It should be noted that the CJEU has **not** precluded national courts from making a reference in the above circumstances; it has merely removed the obligation. In addition, the Court has explained that where a national court is under an obligation to refer (i.e. none of the above 'exceptions' apply) but does not, the State *may* be liable in damages (under the principle of *Francovich* – or State – damages, Chapter 5) for the failure of that court (Case C-224/01, *Kobler v Austria*).

5. Can the Court of Justice refuse to provide a ruling?

As already been highlighted, the decision to refer is the national courts' alone and may not be questioned by the CJEU. The Court of Justice has, however, on occasion declined to give a ruling.

We have already considered instances where the Court has refused a ruling due to the fact that the national body making the ruling lay outside the Member State's legal system. In addition, in Cases 104/79 and 244/80, *Foglia v Novello (Nos 1 and 2)*, the CJEU concluded that it had no jurisdiction to provide a ruling in a dispute which had been 'fabricated' by the parties, as their role was not to give abstract or advisory opinions. In Case C-83/91, *Meilicke*, the CJEU similarly concluded that it would exceed its jurisdiction if it answered hypothetical questions.

It has also withheld its opinion where proceedings have terminated in the national court (Case 338/85, *Pardini*) and where it has felt that it has been given insufficient information or the question was too vague (the Court has issued guidance on this matter in *'Guidance on References by National Courts for Preliminary Rulings'* [1997] 1 CMLR 78).

From examination of the above and other case law, it can be concluded that the CJEU may refuse to provide a ruling, but only in circumstances where to provide such a ruling would amount to an abuse of the preliminary reference procedure.

6. The referral procedure

Where a national court reaches the conclusion that a reference is appropriate, it must formulate a question or questions to refer to the CJEU. (Where such questions are in some way inappropriate, the Court of Justice has, in the past, shown itself willing to reformulate them in a manner that will best assist the national court, although there is growing evidence that the Court has become less willing to do this – perhaps due to pressure of work.) The national court will also need to provide issues of fact and national law relevant to the case in question. The national court must stay proceedings until the ruling of the CJEU is transmitted back to it.

Being of general interest, once the Court of Justice has received a reference, it will be translated into all official languages of the Union, notified to the Member States and EU Institutions and noted in the Official Journal. Written observations will be accepted from the parties, Member States and Institutions, and there will be a brief opportunity for oral submissions to be put before the CJEU (these will be in the official language of the national court that referred the question). The CJEU will deliberate the matter, after receiving the opinion of an Advocate General (AG), finally providing a judgment which will be reached by majority vote. This decision is then notified to the national court and also published.

It is important to remember that, while the Court of Justice has jurisdiction to pronounce on the validity of EU secondary legislation and interpret the Treaties, it is **not** the function of the Court to decide the outcome of the case before the national court. The national court must perform this function.

7. The consequences of the preliminary reference procedure

The availability of preliminary references has had a number of important consequences.

First, it has forged a link between national legal systems and the EU's legal system. Without such rulings, national courts and the CJEU would be isolated from one another. Second, the availability of a reference affords national courts (especially those of the new States) the opportunity to familiarise themselves with the EU's legal order.

Of particular importance is the manner in which the Court has used the process in order to develop the EU's legal system and constitutionalise the Treaties. The Court has clarified the extent of EU law through its development of principles such as direct effect and supremacy in seminal judgments such as *Van Gend* and *Costa* (discussed in Chapter 5). In addition, preliminary references have been the vehicle by which General Principles of EU law have been articulated (discussed in Chapter 4).

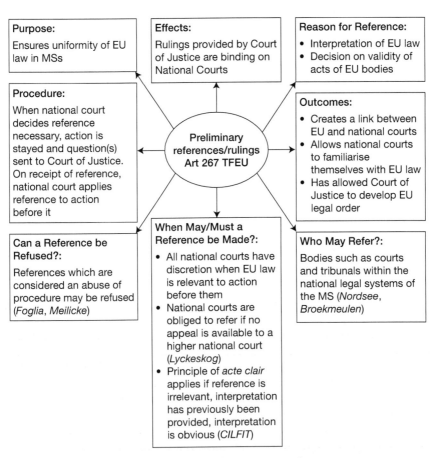

The preliminary reference procedure

In conjunction with Art 4 TEU, the Court has also been able to further extend the scope and effectiveness of the EU's legal order, developing such principles as the 'interpretative obligation' (*Von Colson*) and 'State damages' (*Francovich*) (more detail can be found in Chapter 5). Further protection has been afforded to individuals by the Court, which has ensured, for example, that the remedies available for breach of EU law rights are effective (as in *Marshall (No 2)*) and available to as many citizens as possible (such as in *Hoekstra*, discussed in Chapter 8).

Finally, it should be noted that the process can afford individuals with an alternative opportunity to challenge the validity of acts of the Institutions, an issue which is discussed further, below.

III. ENFORCEMENT ACTIONS AGAINST MEMBER STATES (ARTS 258–260 TFEU)

Member States have a duty to fulfil the obligations placed on them by EU law (for example, Art 4 TEU provides a general duty, while numerous treaty articles provide specific obligations). It is therefore necessary to consider how EU law ensures that all Member States comply with these obligations.

1. Actions brought by the Commission (Art 258 TFEU)

Should a Member State breach EU law and an individual suffer as a result, that individual may of course bring an action against the errant State (under the doctrine of direct effect etc, as discussed in Chapter 5). The TFEU, however, provides other methods of ensuring that States comply with their obligations.

Article 258 TFEU gives the Commission the authority to investigate and, if necessary bring before the CJEU, any Member State which it considers may have failed to fulfil its EU obligations. The Commission's powers are, however, discretionary and the Commission cannot be forced to act against a State (Case 48/65, *Lutticke*), although a refusal may be the subject of a complaint to the European Ombudsman (Art 228 TFEU).

It is perfectly possible for an individual to bring a direct action against a State while, at the same time, the Commission is also initiating enforcement proceedings. This can be evidenced by the *Factortame* series of cases, together with Case C-246/89R, *Commission v UK*. Both acts and omissions of the Member States are open to scrutiny (Case 167/73, *Commission v France*).

Investigation under Art 258 TFEU can be initiated by the Commission, either on its own initiative or following a complaint. (It should be noted that the complainant does not play any further role in the proceedings, as the proceedings are not intended as a means by which individuals can obtain redress.) Actions may be divided into two stages – the administrative stage and the judicial stage. The administrative stage can be further subdivided into the informal and the formal.

i. The Commission's investigative powers

Where the Commission suspects that a Member State is in breach of its EU obligations, it will enter into (informal) dialogue with the appropriate authorities within that State. This stage is very important, as the majority of alleged breaches are resolved without the need for further intervention by the Commission. (It would appear that many States fail to comply with their obligations due to ignorance or misunderstanding and, in such circumstances, they are normally quick to remedy the breach.)

If the alleged breach is not rectified at this stage, the Commission may issue a formal letter, defining the breach and requesting that the Member State submit its observations within a reasonable period of time (normally two months). If the issue remains unresolved at the end of this period, the Commission will deliver a '**reasoned opinion**', setting out how the Member State has violated its EU law obligations and allowing it a reasonable time (again usually two months, but this will depend on individual circumstances) to remedy the alleged breach. The reasoned opinion is very important in that it establishes the scope of the action and the legal arguments on which the Commission is relying.

ii. Judicial proceedings

If the breach is not remedied by the Member State within the time stated in the reasoned opinion, the Commission will proceed to the judicial stage, referring the matter to the CJEU. Even at this stage, it may be possible to settle the action before the Court gives judgment. Where judgment is given, only about one in ten decisions favour the Member State. This is not surprising, as the Commission is unlikely to proceed if its case is weak. In addition, the Court has shown itself unreceptive to the majority of defences argued by Member States.

In Case 128/78, *Commission v UK* (the *Tachograph* case), for example, the UK argued 'practical difficulties' due to trade union resistance to the introduction of tachographs in the cabs of lorries, while in Cases 227–30/85, *Commission v Belgium*, it was argued that failure of regional, rather than central, government had caused the breach. The Court accepted neither argument. In Case 101/84, *Commission v Italy*, Italy did not submit statistics required by Europe as a bomb attack on a data processing centre had destroyed relevant data. Italy argued *force majeure*, which was again not accepted by the Court.

iii. Non-compliance with the Court's judgment

If the Court of Justice finds that a Member State is in breach of its EU obligations, it will issue a declaration to that effect, requiring that the breach be remedied *immediately*. Until amendments made by the Maastricht Treaty were introduced, such judgments of the Court were of declaratory effect only, the only remedy for failure to comply being the possibility of further enforcement proceedings being initiated by the Commission, again under Art 258 TFEU.

Now however, under Art 260 TFEU, the Commission may, after giving the State an opportunity to submit its observations, once more refer the case to the Court, this time specifying an appropriate pecuniary penalty (fine) to be levied against the errant Member State. If the Court again finds against the State, it may levy a fine, not exceeding that specified by the Commission. (Since being amended by the Treaty of Lisbon, Art 260 now also includes the possibility of the Commission requesting penalties against a Member State in the *first* judgment under Article 258 TFEU but only where the case concerns the Member State's failure to adopt implementing legislation for a new directive within the deadline – so called non-communication cases.)

The ability to levy pecuniary penalties has had the effect of providing an originally rather toothless action with the necessary teeth, although it is not yet clear what the outcome would be if a Member State refused to pay any fine imposed. This question has been the topic of academic debate, with a favoured suggestion being the removal of a defaulting Member State's voting rights.

2. Actions brought by Member States

If one Member State considers that another Member State has failed to fulfil its EU obligations, then the first State may bring the matter before the CJEU under Art 259 TFEU, but the procedure first requires that the matter be brought to the attention of the Commission. Proceedings then mirror those set out under Art 258 TFEU, other than the requirement that the Commission request the observations of *both* Member States concerned.

In addition, the Commission is required to deliver a reasoned opinion within three months of the matter being brought to its attention. If the Commission fails to provide a reasoned opinion within this time, the complainant Member State may bring the matter before the Court. Should the Court find a violation, matters proceed as already set out above.

Actions brought under Art 259 TFEU are extremely rare. This is understandable, as Member States prefer to make an informal complaint to the Commission rather than choose the far more politically contentious Art 259 TFEU route.

3. The effectiveness of enforcement procedures

Although no official figures are available on the success of the informal investigative stage followed by the Commission, the administrative stage as a whole has proven itself particularly successful in resolving breaches, and the vast majority of breaches are resolved without the need to refer the matter to the Court of Justice. (Statistics can be found in the Commission's Annual Report, available on the Europa website.) This suggests that the administrative stage of enforcement procedures is particularly successful, in that it allows the Commission to 'educate' Member States and ensure that they are aware of their EU obligations.

However, also important with regard to the effectiveness of enforcement actions is the Commission's ability – or lack of it – to uncover possible breaches. The Commission has no 'police force' that it can enlist to assist in the uncovering of breaches by the Member States and it is likely that very many continue unnoticed. In recognition of this, the Commission has employed technology to encourage citizens and companies to notify them of possible breaches on their website.

The Commission has also recognised that breaches will often be the result of a Member State's failure to implement directives. The Commission has sought to remedy this by requiring that directives be published in the Official Journal and also by insisting that Member States notify them when directives are incorporated into national law.

It can be concluded that enforcement procedures, particularly the administrative stage of Art 258 TFEU, play an important role in ensuring that Union aims are achieved and Union law is upheld.

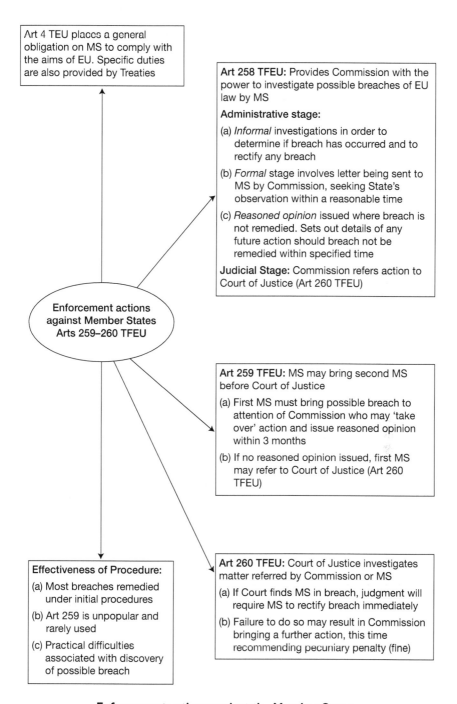

Art 4 TEU places a general obligation on MS to comply with the aims of EU. Specific duties are also provided by Treaties

Art 258 TFEU: Provides Commission with the power to investigate possible breaches of EU law by MS

Administrative stage:

(a) *Informal* investigations in order to determine if breach has occurred and to rectify any breach

(b) *Formal* stage involves letter being sent to MS by Commission, seeking State's observation within a reasonable time

(c) *Reasoned opinion* issued where breach is not remedied. Sets out details of any future action should breach not be remedied within specified time

Judicial Stage: Commission refers action to Court of Justice (Art 260 TFEU)

Enforcement actions against Member States
Arts 259–260 TFEU

Art 259 TFEU: MS may bring second MS before Court of Justice

(a) First MS must bring possible breach to attention of Commission who may 'take over' action and issue reasoned opinion within 3 months

(b) If no reasoned opinion issued, first MS may refer to Court of Justice (Art 260 TFEU)

Effectiveness of Procedure:

(a) Most breaches remedied under initial procedures

(b) Art 259 is unpopular and rarely used

(c) Practical difficulties associated with discovery of possible breach

Art 260 TFEU: Court of Justice investigates matter referred by Commission or MS

(a) If Court finds MS in breach, judgment will require MS to rectify breach immediately

(b) Failure to do so may result in Commission bringing a further action, this time recommending pecuniary penalty (fine)

Enforcement actions against the Member States

IV. ACTIONS AGAINST EU INSTITUTIONS: JUDICIAL REVIEW OF THE ACTS AND OMISSIONS OF UNION BODIES

The Treaties provide the Union's Institutions with a number of powers and obligations. As in all developed legal systems, a mechanism has been put into place through which the manner in which these obligations are discharged can be reviewed.

Judicial review is the term commonly used to describe a variety of causes of action relating to the review of acts or decisions of the Union's Institutions. It includes actions to annul (Art 263 TFEU) and actions for failure to act (Art 265 TFEU). 'Judicial review' also covers applications for interim measures relating to other judicial procedures (Art 279 TFEU). These procedures are part of the system of **'checks and balances'** which exist to ensure that the Union bodies act within the limits of the powers afforded them by the Treaties.

1. Judicial review: action to annul (Arts 263 and 264 TFEU)

Article 263 TFEU is the primary method by which the legality of the acts of the Union's Institutions may be challenged. If such a challenge is successful, the act will be declared void by the CJEU (Art 264 TFEU). Basically, this action allows the validity of rules enacted by the Institutions and other Union bodies to be challenged.

i. Whose acts may be challenged?

Article 263 TFEU provides the CJEU with the jurisdiction to review the legality of legislative acts of the Council, the Commission and the European Central Bank and of the European Parliament and European Council, where such acts are intended to produce legal effects vis à vis third parties, it shall also review the acts of bodies, offices and agencies of the Union intended to produce legal effects vis à vis third parties.

Prior to amendments introduced by the Maastricht Treaty, the TEC only referred to acts adopted by the Council and the Commission. The Court had, however, already declared the acts of the European Parliament (EP) to be reviewable prior to such amendments (Case 294/83, *Parti Ecologiste*

'*Les Verts*' *v European Parliament*, which provides a good example of EU legislation following the decisions of the CJEU).

ii. What acts may be challenged?

Consideration of the wording of Art 263 TFEU reveals that legislative acts 'other than recommendations and opinions' (neither of which have any binding force: Art 288 TFEU) may be challenged, together with acts which 'produce legal effects vis à vis third parties'. The Court has interpreted the Article broadly to include any act which is **capable of having legal effects** as challengeable (Case 22/70, *Commission v Council*, the *ERTA* case).

iii. Grounds for bringing a challenge

An action cannot be brought unless grounds for that action are specified. The Treaty lists the following grounds under which an action may be brought:

- *lack of competence* – this occurs where the Union bodies act in areas which the Treaties have not authorised them to act;
- *infringement of an essential procedural requirement* – for example, the Council failing to consult the EP (Case 138/79, *Roquette Frères v Council*);
- *infringement of the Treaties or any rule of law relating to its application* – this ground often overlaps with others. For example, it can include a breach of one of the general principles of Union law (Case 4/73, *Nold*);
- *misuse of powers* – this ground will be relevant where an EU body has used its power(s) for a purpose other than that for which they are intended.

iv. Who can bring an action?

This has proved to be a controversial area and, consequently, is often the subject of examination questions! Applicants can be divided into those with automatic *locus standi* (Glossary), that is 'privileged applicants', and those who have to prove an interest, that is 'semi-privileged' and 'non-privileged' applicants, each of which will be considered in turn:

Privileged applicants

Article 263 TFEU automatically gives *locus standi* to Member States, the European Parliament, the Council and the Commission. (The position of the EP as a litigant was again amended by the Maastricht Treaty. While the CJEU had already accepted the Parliament's right to bring an action in Case C-70/88, *European Parliament v Council* (the *Chernobyl* case), it was not until the TEU came into force that this was formalised.)

Semi-privileged applicants

In cases where their prerogatives (an exclusive right or power) are affected, Art 263 TFEU provides that the Court of Auditors, the European Central Bank and the Committee of Regions may commence an action.

Non-privileged applicants

Article 263 TFEU provides that any natural or legal person (an individual or business, for example) will have *locus standi* to bring an action in three circumstances:

(a) where the applicant is the *addressee* of an act;

(b) where an act is of 'direct and individual concern' to the applicant;

(c) where the act is a 'regulatory act', which is of direct concern to the applicant and does not entail implementing measures.

(a) Where the applicant is the addressee of an act

Where an applicant can demonstrate that s/he is the *addressee* of an act – such as a decision (read Art 288 TFEU) – they will have little problem demonstrating locus *standi*.

(b) Where an applicant has to demonstrate 'direct and individual concern'

Where an act has not been addressed to the applicant, the Article also provides *locus standi* where an act is of 'direct and individual concern' to that applicant. It therefore needs to be considered how (i) 'direct' and (ii) 'individual' concern have been interpreted by the Court.

The Court of Justice developed a 'test' to ascertain **individual concern** in Case 25/62, *Plaumann v Commission*, often referred to as the '*Plaumann Formula*'. In that case, the applicant was a clementine importer. He sought to challenge a decision addressed to the German Government, as it allowed Germany to change the duty on clementines imported from outside the EU. The CJEU prescribed that, in order to demonstrate 'individual concern', the applicant must be able to show that he was **distinguishable from other persons generally**, due to certain attributes or circumstances: in other words, he had to show he was a member of a 'closed class'. In addition, he was required to demonstrate that, by virtue of those attributes or circumstances, he should be singled out in the same way as the addressee of the Directive.

Plaumann failed in his action because, as the Court pointed out, any person could if they so chose, carry out the commercial activity in which Plaumann was involved and he was consequently not held to be part of a **'closed class'**. The test has been confirmed in a number of cases and, for example, those who have entered into a contract (Case 11/82, *Piraiki-Patraiki v Commission*) and those who have applied for a licence (Cases 106 and 107/63, *Toepfer*) have been held to come within the necessary 'closed class'. (It should be understood that an applicant does **not** have to be part of a class of *one* to be seen as in a 'closed class'.)

This test remains the seminal case in this area, despite being criticised as unduly restrictive and also despite being the subject of much judicial activity. In March 2002, AG Jacobs delivered an Opinion in Case C-50/00P, *Union de Pequeños Agricultores v Council* (the *UPA* case), in which he proposed that there be a redefinition of the test for 'individual concern'. A short time later, the Court of First Instance (CFI, now known as the General Court) appeared to support this approach in Case T-177/01, *Jégo Quéré*, also suggesting that the rather narrow definition provided in *Plaumann* be broadened and made easier to satisfy. The Court of Justice, however, rejected the positions of both the AG and the CFI, arguing that it was not for the Court to reform the conditions for *locus standi* but that it should be a matter for legislation. It was argued that this was rather a surprising stance for the CJEU to take, given its previous willingness to ensure citizens have sufficient opportunity to enforce their rights in *other* areas. It has also been pointed out that there is nothing in the wording of what was then Art 230 TEC to suggest that such a restrictive interpretation be provided.

Where the act in question is a regulation, it would appear that individual concern will not be accepted as regulations have general application (Art 288 TFEU) and cannot therefore apply to a 'closed class'. The Court has however taken a broader approach, explaining a willingness to look behind the *form* of the act to the *substance* in order to determine its true nature (e.g. Cases 41–44/70, *International Fruit Co v Commission*) thus allowing, in prescribed circumstances, that a regulation can be open to challenge.

This ensures that legislators cannot reduce the opportunity for challenge by choosing a legislative form that is not open to question by individuals. (Examples include Case C-309/89, *Cordoniu v Council*, and Cases 789 and 790/79, *Calpak*.)

Where an applicant succeeds in demonstrating 'individual concern', he must also prove that the act was of **'direct concern'** to him. According to the Court of Justice's interpretation, this requires that the applicant show that (a) the act has directly affected his legal position, and (b) a direct link exists between the act complained of and the loss/damage suffered, which can be compared to demonstrating 'causation' under Anglo-Welsh law. (An illustrative case is *International Fruit Co v Commission*.)

The CJEU has also added that a measure can only be of direct concern where no discretion is afforded to the Member State(s) with regard to its implementation (for example, Cases 10 and 18/68, *Eridania v Commission*, where a Commission Decision relating to the provision of aid was considered not to be of direct concern as authority relating to the allocation of the aid was afforded to the State).

(c) Where the act is a 'regulatory act', which is of direct concern to the applicant and does not entail implementing measures

The Treaty of Lisbon amended Art 263(4) TFEU to provide that individuals may also challenge *'regulatory acts'* but failed to provide a definition of the term. However in 2011, the CJEU delivered two separate judgments which have shed light on the matter.

In the first judgment, Case T-18/10, *Inuit*, the General Court referred to the now-defunct Constitutional Treaty, which had distinguished regulatory acts from legislative acts. Although the Court did not expressly set out which acts should be considered regulatory acts it provided that such acts include all 'acts of general application **apart from** legislative acts'. Consequently, regulatory acts can be seen as excluding acts adopted under an EU legislative procedure (such as the 'ordinary legislative procedure' set out in Art 289 TFEU).

In the second judgment, Case T-262, *Microban*, the Court confirmed its judgment in *Inuit*, adding that, in terms of 'general application' the act should produce 'legal effects with respect to categories of persons envisaged in general and in the abstract'. Consequently, acts addressed to **particular** or specific addressees would be excluded. The Court also considered the meaning of 'direct concern', clarifying that the term would continue to be interpreted in a manner consistent with pre-Lisbon Treaty case law (i.e. that relating to Art 230 TEC, as already discussed above).

Further, *Microban* can be seen as providing a helpful example of an act which 'does not entail implementing measures'. In this case the act, or measure, in question had the immediate effect of prohibiting the marketing of a substance from a prescribed date **without the need for Member State action** – in other words the act was **directly applicable**.

Consequently, the approach to differentiating between regulatory and other acts appears to be as follows:

(i) Consider the procedure under which the act, or measure, has been enacted – i.e. was it enacted under an EU legislative procedure? If it was, the act is **not** a regulatory act. *If not:*

(ii) Consider whether the act is one of general application (i.e. *not* to a particular or specific addressees). If not, the act is **not** a regulatory act. *If it* is *of general application:*

(iii) Consider whether the act is of direct concern to the applicant. If not, the act is **not** a regulatory act. *If it is:*

(iv) Consider whether the act requires implementing measures in order to gain effect. If it does, the act is **not** a regulatory act. *If not:*

(v) The act can be considered a 'regulatory act' against which a 'natural or legal person' may commence an action to annul.

v. Time limits

The Treaty imposes a time limit of two months on the bringing of an action. This time starts to run either from the publication of the measure, from its notification to the claimant, or from the day on which it came, or should have come, to the attention of the claimant.

vi. Effects of annulment

Art 264 TFEU provides that if the Court finds an application for annulment well founded, the act should be declared void. Normally, nullity will be considered to be retroactive, although the Court has shown itself willing to limit the temporal effects in appropriate circumstances, particularly where an innocent party may otherwise suffer loss (Case 81/72, *Commission v Council*).

Under Art 266 TFEU, the Institutions are obliged to comply with the judgment of the Court. The Treaty does not provide any sanction should an Institution fail to comply with a judgment (unlike the position where a Member State fails to comply), although by failing to comply, an Institution may find itself vulnerable to claims for damages under Art 340 TFEU, which is discussed below.

NOTE: Chapter 9 provides tips on how to approach problem questions relating to actions to annul, which will hopefully support your approach to answering seminar questions, coursework and examinations.

2. Judicial review: actions for failure to Act (Arts 265 and 266 TFEU)

Actions under Art 265 TFEU can be seen as the other side of the coin from actions under Art 263 TFEU. While the latter renders acts of the Institutions ineffective, the former may be used to compel an institution to fulfil its EU obligations. An action will consequently only be available where the applicant can show that such an obligation exists.

i. Whose failure to act can be challenged?

Article 265 TFEU provides that 'Should the European Parliament, the European Council, the Council, the Commission or the European Central Bank, in infringement of the Treaties, fail to act . . .' making it clear which of the Union's Institutions may be challenged. The Treaty also provides that 'This article shall apply . . . to bodies and agencies of the Union which fail to act', extending the scope of the Article.

ii. Who may make a challenge?

The Treaty provides the Member States and all Institutions with automatic *locus standi*. Natural and legal persons once more have limited *locus standi* and may only bring an action where an Institution has an obligation to address an act (other than an opinion or a recommendation) to him, her or it. The applicant must demonstrate direct and individual concern and the Court will apply the same restrictive tests as have been established for Art 263 TFEU (Case C-107/91, *ENU v Commission*).

iii. Procedure in Art 265 TFEU

Actions will only be admissible where the institution or body has first been called upon to act by the challenger, thus providing the institution concerned with the opportunity to remedy its alleged omission.

Once a request for action has been made, the institution or body must then define its position within two months of being called upon to act. Once an institution has defined its position, no further action is possible – even where the institution fails to act (Case 48/65, *Alfons Lutticke v Commission*). If the institution does *not* define its position, any action is then subject to a time limit of a further two months.

Given that an institution or body need only define its position in order to avoid an action, it is not surprising that there have not been many successful actions under Art 265!

iv. *Consequences of a successful action*

Article 266 TFEU provides that Institutions are obliged to comply with the Court's ruling under Art 265 TFEU.

3. Actions which may provide an alternative to judicial review/actions to annul

It is obvious that bringing an action under either Art 263 or 265 TFEU can present particular problems for individuals, both natural and legal, due to the difficulties associated with proving *locus standi*. In addition, neither Article provides the opportunity for claiming damages. It is therefore important to consider possible alternatives.

Such actions are considered, albeit briefly, below.

i. *Preliminary references*

As has already been considered above, the preliminary reference procedure (Art 267 TFEU) allows national courts to put questions relating to the validity of Union acts before the Court of Justice. While preliminary references do *not* provide individuals with a direct action, they may nevertheless provide a channel through which an indirect challenge may be mounted.

For example, where the time limit cannot be satisfied or where an individual has not been able to demonstrate the necessary *locus standi* to bring an action to annul (judicial review) under Art 263 TFEU, it may be possible to challenge an act through the preliminary reference procedure. This will only be possible, however, where there is a separate action before the national court – perhaps where the applicant has been brought before the court due to his/her alleged failure to comply with the act in question: it is not possible to bring such an action on the basis of a request for a preliminary reference. In addition, it should be remembered that while an applicant may ask the national court to make a reference, they cannot demand that such a reference be made.

The CJEU has, however, made it clear that the *primary* method of challenge is that under Art 263 TFEU and that a challenge brought under Art 267 (Preliminary Reference) will only be available where judicial review is *not* an option open to a claimant. This was highlighted in Case C-188/92, *Textilwerke Deggendorf (TWD)*, where the Court held that to request a ruling under Art 267 was an abuse of procedure. In this case the applicant chose not to challenge a Commission Decision under Art 230 TEC (now Art 263 TFEU) within the two-month time limit.

ii. Plea of illegality (Art 277 TFEU)

Art 227 TFEU provides a means of indirect challenge against 'an act of general application adopted by an institution, body or agency of the Union'. An example of such an act would be a regulation and, until the coming into force of the Treaty of Lisbon, the Article only referred to regulations, although the Court demonstrated flexibility by showing itself willing to look at the substance rather than just the form of an act (Case 92/78, *Simmenthal*).

A plea of illegality is not, however, an independent action (Cases 31 and 33/62, *Wohrmann and Lutticke v Commission*). It is only available as a defence, where other proceedings have been brought against the applicant, and the Court of Justice has explained that the purpose of the action is to allow individuals protection from the application of an illegal regulation. The action may be pleaded on the same grounds as those found under Art 263 TFEU.

The effect of a successful challenge is that the act will be declared inapplicable in that case, but it will not be declared void. Any measures based on the act will, however, be automatically void and subsequent measures based on the act will also be open to challenge.

4. Actions for damages (Art 340 TFEU)

i. Contractual liability

Article 340(1) TFEU provides that the 'contractual liability of the Union shall be governed by the law applicable to the contract in question'. When an individual wishes to make a claim against a Union Institution for damages in relation to a contractual matter, the action must therefore be brought in the appropriate *national* court and under the legal rules appropriate to the Member State in which the contract is enforceable.

ii. Non-contractual liability

Article 340(2) TFEU relates to the EU's non-contractual liability. Under the jurisdiction afforded to it by Art 268 TFEU, the CJEU may hear actions brought against the Union in relation to damage caused either by its:

- Institutions, including the European Central Bank (*fautes de service*), or
- Servants (staff or '*fautes personnelles*'), in the performance of their duties (the concept of vicarious liability is relevant here but has limitations, as is illustrated in Case 9/69, *Sayag v Leduc*, which is worth reading).

The liability of the Union is to be 'in accordance with the general principles common to the laws of the Member States' and consequently the Court of Justice has looked to the laws of the Member States for guidance on the application of the Article.

Locus standi and time limits

Actions brought under Art 340(2) are independent actions and as such there are no limitations on who may bring a claim: in other words, *locus standi* does not need to be demonstrated (Case 48/65, *Lutticke*). However, a time limit of five years from the time of 'injury', or from the time when the claimant should have reasonably known of it, is imposed.

Breaches may either be administrative *or* legislative in nature.

Liability for administrative acts

Where an action is brought in relation to the manner in which Union rules have been applied or the manner in which staff have carried out their duties, the EU may be liable for both wrongful acts and omissions.

Liability may, for example, involve negligence (Case 14/60, *Meroni*) or failure to consider relevant facts, to accord individuals certain procedural rights or to adequately supervise bodies to whom power has been delegated. The relative seriousness of the 'error' may also be taken into account (Case 145/83, *Adams v Commission* is a helpful case to which you may want to refer.)

Liability for legislative acts

At one time, liability in terms of legislative acts was divided into two distinct types by the Court of Justice: liability involving 'economic policy choices' and liability involving 'other' acts.

Breaches involving economic policy choices were governed by a test known as the '*Schoppenstedt* formula' following the Court's dicta in Case 5/71, *Schoppenstedt v Commission*. However, since the Court's decision in Case C-352/98P, *Bergaderm*, a single test covering both types of breach would now appear to be in favour.

The conditions for liability

In order to succeed in an action for damages, three matters must be considered:

- Was the EU rule which is alleged to have been breached **intended to confer rights on individuals**? This may include not only rights contained in legislation but also in the general principles of Union law (*Schoppenstedt*).

- Was the breach **sufficiently serious**? Issues such as the complexity of situations and difficulties in application of interpretation should be taken into account. At the heart of the modern test, however, lies the issue of discretion. Basically, where there is little or no discretion, then all that may be necessary is for the claimant to prove sufficiently serious breach on the part of the institution. However, where the institution has been provided with some degree of discretion, some degree of 'blameworthiness' must be demonstrated (Case T-351/03 *Schneider v Commission*).

- Is there a **causal link** between the breach and the damage complained of? The amount claimed must be actual, certain and concrete (Case 26/74, *Société Roquette Frères v Commission*). With regard to causation, the Court has made it clear that the applicant must demonstrate two things: the act caused the loss/damage and the chain of causation has not been broken. The chain of causation may be broken by the actions of a Member State, in which case it will be the State, as opposed to the EU, that will be liable, unless the EU has failed to adequately exercise its supervisory power over the State (*Lutticke*). If there is joint liability on the part of the Union and a Member State, the Member State will generally be considered to be primarily liable and the action should then be brought in the appropriate national court. Contributory negligence may also serve to defeat a claim or at least reduce the quantum of damages (*Adams*).

It will be evident from the above discussion that liability for damage caused to individuals by a legislative act of one or more of the Union Institutions, or their staff, bears a strong resemblance to liability under the principle of **State liability in damages** available against the Member States (discussed in Chapter 5). In Cases C 46–48/94, *Brasserie du Pêcheur*, the Court of Justice made this very clear by providing that the test for State liability and non-contractual damage should not differ.

Finally, it should be remembered that an action for damages may be brought independently *or* in addition to any claim under **Arts 263 and 265 TFEU**.

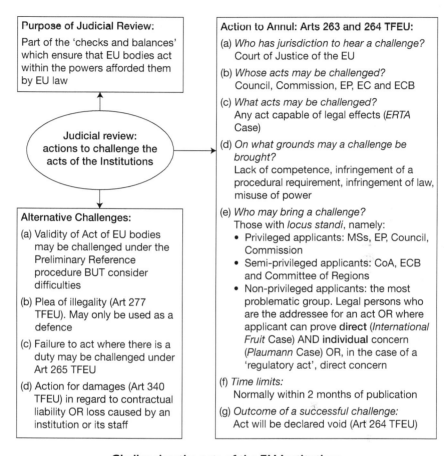

Purpose of Judicial Review:

Part of the 'checks and balances' which ensure that EU bodies act within the powers afforded them by EU law

Judicial review: actions to challenge the acts of the Institutions

Alternative Challenges:

(a) Validity of Act of EU bodies may be challenged under the Preliminary Reference procedure BUT consider difficulties

(b) Plea of illegality (Art 277 TFEU). May only be used as a defence

(c) Failure to act where there is a duty may be challenged under Art 265 TFEU

(d) Action for damages (Art 340 TFEU) in regard to contractual liability OR loss caused by an institution or its staff

Action to Annul: Arts 263 and 264 TFEU:

(a) *Who has jurisdiction to hear a challenge?*
Court of Justice of the EU

(b) *Whose acts may be challenged?*
Council, Commission, EP, EC and ECB

(c) *What acts may be challenged?*
Any act capable of legal effects (*ERTA* Case)

(d) *On what grounds may a challenge be brought?*
Lack of competence, infringement of a procedural requirement, infringement of law, misuse of power

(e) *Who may bring a challenge?*
Those with *locus standi*, namely:
• Privileged applicants: MSs, EP, Council, Commission
• Semi-privileged applicants: CoA, ECB and Committee of Regions
• Non-privileged applicants: the most problematic group. Legal persons who are the addressee for an act OR where applicant can prove **direct** (*International Fruit* Case) AND **individual** concern (*Plaumann* Case) OR, in the case of a 'regulatory act', direct concern

(f) *Time limits:*
Normally within 2 months of publication

(g) *Outcome of a successful challenge:*
Act will be declared void (Art 264 TFEU)

Challenging the acts of the EU Institutions

V. CONCLUSIONS

Union law places rights and obligations on individuals, Member States and EU Institutions alike. European Union law would, however, have little effect if such rights and obligations were unenforceable, and so the Union's legal system includes a variety of means by which it can be ensured that all comply with European law.

When an individual (natural or corporate) breaches Union law, he/she can expect to have an action brought against her/him in an appropriate national court under the doctrine of direct effect, with domestic courts being 'assisted' by the Court of Justice of the European Union under the preliminary reference procedure. (It should be remembered that the Court's role does not allow it to 'take over' the proceedings and its role is restricted to providing an interpretation of Union law and/or judgment as to the validity of legislative acts of the institutions.)

When a Member State breaches its obligations, the Treaty provides that the Commission or Member State may bring an action before the CJEU in order to ensure compliance. In addition, a Member State may find itself a

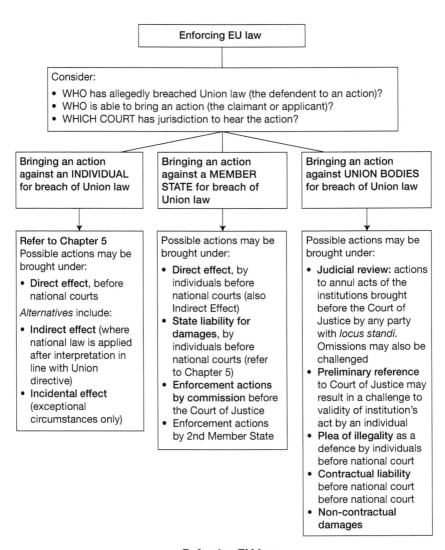

Enforcing EU law

defendant in an action before a national court under the doctrine of vertical direct effect and/or, where the claimant wishes to pursue an action for damages, under the principle of 'State damages' (*Francovich*). Often, Member States will find themselves the subject of an action brought by an individual in a national court, while at the same time being the subject of an enforcement action by the Commission.

Other than in actions relating to contractual liability, Union Institutions/ bodies will be brought before the Court of Justice if the European Union should they breach Union rules. Any challenge to the validity of legally effective acts of the institutions will normally be brought under Art 263 TFEU (action to annul), although due to the difficulties associated with proving *locus standi*, individuals should also consider the possibility of employing the preliminary reference, plea of illegality and/or 'action for damages' procedures to mount a challenge. Special notice should be taken of the differing effects of these actions, however.

SOME ISSUES TO THINK ABOUT FURTHER

- Which court(s) hear the majority of actions concerning Union law? Why is this?
- By what means can the acts of the Union's Institutions be challenged? What are the advantages and disadvantages of each? Does the TFEU encourage individuals to make such challenges?
- Through what means does the TFEU allow the Member States to be challenged for failure to comply with their EU obligations? Are there other means of challenging their compliance?

7 Free movement of goods

As previously discussed, the original European Communities were created in an attempt to ensure peace and economic stability within Europe and the Treaties set out a number of aims to be achieved through which these aspirations are to be fulfilled.

While, in the main, these aims may be categorised as economic, others have social impact, while others can be said to be political in nature. Economic integration was, however, traditionally seen as the primary area of emphasis of the EEC and the objective of creating and maintaining an internal market remains a priority for the EU. Art 26 TFEU, in particular, provides that 'the internal market shall comprise an area without internal frontiers in which the free movement of goods, persons, services and capital is ensured'. These areas of free movement have commonly become known as the 'four freedoms' and it is the first of these freedoms with which this chapter is primarily concerned.

Creating an area that has free movement of goods cannot be achieved overnight and the rules concerning its creation and maintenance are often complex. Such rules can be best understood if an incremental approach is taken, and this chapter considers some of the more important rules which apply to Member States with regard to the removal of both pecuniary (monetary/charges) and non-pecuniary (quantitative/numeric) barriers to trade.

Before moving on to consider the law relating to the internal market and the free movement of goods within it (Arts 26 to 37 TFEU) it is important to be clear about, first, who such rules are aimed at and, second, the meaning of the term 'goods'.

Reference to the relevant Treaty articles makes it clear that this area of law is directed at the Member States. It is obvious that the free movement of goods is fundamental to the achievement of the EU's aims and the Court of Justice of the EU has consequently provided a wide interpretation of the term 'State', providing that not only public bodies come within its scope but also private bodies which receive public finances and are supervised by public authorities (Case 249/81, *Commission v Ireland, 'Buy Irish' Campaign*).

The term 'goods' is not defined by the Treaty and so again it has been necessary for the Court to consider exactly what may be subject to the EU's rules. Again the Court's interpretation is broad: in Case 7/68, *Commission v Italy* (the *1st Art Treasures* case), the Court defined 'goods' as including any product which can be valued in money and which is capable of forming the subject of a commercial transaction. It is relevant to note, however, that intangible benefits have been held not to come within this definition (Case C-97/98, *Jagerskiold v Gustafsson*).

I. THE ELIMINATION OF PECUNIARY (MONETARY) BARRIERS TO TRADE

It should be remembered that prior to the EEC's inception, each State levied customs duties on goods entering and leaving its territory. In order to create an area where trade was facilitated rather than hampered, customs duties had to be removed and a new system of regulation put into place.

1. The Customs Union and Common Customs Tariff (Arts 28 to 33 TFEU)

i. What the Treaty says

Art 28 TFEU provides that the Union 'shall comprise' a Customs Union. The creation of a Customs Union involves the removal of all customs duties, together with any charge having an equivalent effect to such a duty, on goods moving between the States.

Art 28 TFEU also provides for the creation of a Common Customs Tariff (CCT). The CCT is charged on all goods imported into the Union from non-Member States. It is charged at the same rate no matter which of the Member States the goods are imported into, or where they are exported from.

Arts 28 and 29 TFEU also make it clear that once imported goods have been subject to the CCT, they are considered to be in 'free circulation' and should be treated in exactly the same manner as goods originating from within the EU. (This is the main difference between a Customs Union and a free trade area: in a free trade area goods from outside that area continue to be subject to different rules.)

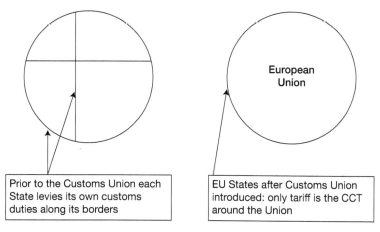

Prior to the Customs Union each State levies its own customs duties along its borders	EU States after Customs Union introduced: only tariff is the CCT around the Union

Creation of a Customs Union

It should not be confused with charges levied by the Member States as part of their own *internal* taxation systems (which are discussed in further detail below). The removal of existing customs duties was not, of course, achieved overnight and it was not until July 1968 that the final, remaining customs duties were removed and the CCT was fully introduced.

2. New customs duties and charges having equivalent effect (Art 30 TFEU)

The removal of existing customs duties has the obvious benefit of allowing trade to take place on a level playing field, allowing the consumer to be the final arbiter as to which goods will be successful and which less so. The levying of customs duties may, however, benefit Member States, allowing them an opportunity, for example, to promote domestically manufactured goods over imported goods through the imposition of high import taxes. Therefore, the possibility of a Member State imposing a *new* customs duty or similar charge cannot be ignored.

i. What the Treaty says

The removal of existing pecuniary barriers to trade would not, alone, have ensured the free movement of goods as it would not prevent Member States from re-erecting customs duties or putting into effect other charges having equivalent effect (CHEEs), in circumstances considered beneficial to that State. Art 30 TFEU consequently provides that 'Customs duties on exports or any charges having equivalent effect shall be prohibited between Member States.'

ii. The Court of Justice's interpretation and application of Art 30

Art 30 TFEU – which applies to both imports and exports alike – appears to provide reasonably clear instruction to Member States, but it has still been necessary for the CJEU to interpret its exact meaning in order to ensure uniform application of its terms throughout the Union.

The Court has also made it clear that the purpose for which the duty or charge is levied is irrelevant and that it is the effect which is significant in deciding whether or not Art 30 applies (Case 24/68, *Commission v Italy* – the *2nd Art Treasures* case).

It has also been necessary for the Court to consider which charges will come within the scope of CHEEs. In the *2nd Art Treasures* case, the Court once again provided a wide definition, holding CHEEs to include 'any pecuniary charge ... imposed ... on domestic or foreign goods by reason of the fact that they cross a frontier'.

iii. Charges which are not considered to be 'charges having equivalent effect'

Once a duty or charge has been held to come within the scope of Art 30, it is immediately deemed to be unlawful, as the Treaty provides no derogations from its prohibitions. The CJEU has, however, explained that certain charges may *not* be CHEEs. Such charges include those levied by a Member State for the provision of a service to an importer/exporter. By providing that such a charge is outside the scope of Art 30, the Court has allowed Member States to recoup costs which would otherwise have to be borne by the State – which can be considered inappropriate if that State does not benefit from the service. In addition, charges made for certain inspections *may*, similarly, not be considered a CHEE. However, before such a charge can be considered to be outside the scope of Art 30, a number of criteria must be fulfilled:

Charges levied for a service provided

Where a Member State has levied a charge for a service performed, that charge will not be considered to be a CHEE if the following criteria can be fulfilled (Case 24/68, *Commission v Italy*, the *Statistical Levy* case):

- the service rendered a specific benefit to the importer/exporter (*Statistical Levy* case);
- the charge is proportionate to quantity, not value or quality, of the goods to which the service has been rendered (Case 170/88, *Ford Espana v Spain*);
- the charge made for the service does not exceed its cost (Case 46/76, *Bauhuis*);
- no discrimination – both domestic and imported goods are treated alike (Case 87/75, *Bresciani*).

Charges levied in respect of an inspection

Where a Member State levies a charge for an inspection, it will not constitute a CHEE *provided* it can satisfy the following conditions (Case 18/87, *Commission v Germany*, the *Animal Inspection Fees* case):

- the **inspection** is mandatory under Union (or international) law (*Bauhuis*);
- the **inspection** is in the interest of the importer (*Bresciani*);
- the **inspection** is non-discriminatory (that is, both domestic and imported goods are treated alike) (Case 87/75, *Bresciani*);
- the **inspection** is in the interest of the Union and promotes the free movement of goods (*Animal Inspection Fees*) (in other words, the **inspection** is lawful – more on this later);
- the **charge** is proportionate to the quantity of the goods inspected and not their value or quality (*Bresciani*);
- the **charge** does not exceed the cost of the inspection (*Bauhuis*).

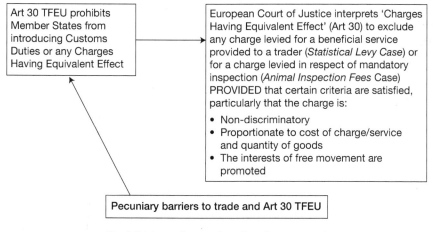

Prohibition of pecuniary barriers to trade

3. Discriminatory internal taxation (Arts 110 to 113 TFEU)

While prohibiting Member States from levying charges on goods as they move from State to State within the EU (Art 30 TFEU), the Treaty does not seek to deprive Member States of the right to levy *internal* taxes for the purpose of raising public revenue. A *genuine* internal tax can be described by reference to the well-used definition as 'a general system of internal dues applied systematically to categories of products in accordance with objective criteria irrespective of the origin of the products' (Case 90/79, *EC v France*). However, where an internal tax does not comply with this definition it will be prohibited and Art 110 can be seen as complementing the provisions contained in Art 30 TFEU.

It should be noted that the Court of Justice has made it clear that actions under Arts 30 and 110 TFEU are exclusive (that is, they are separate actions) but that it may at times be difficult to distinguish between 'charges' and unlawful internal taxation. Consequently, actions should be brought before the Court together, thereby allowing the Court the opportunity to determine which should apply in any particular circumstances (Case 77/76, *Fratelli Cucchi*).

i. What the Treaty says

Art 110 TFEU provides that: 'No Member State shall impose, directly or indirectly, on the products of other Member States any internal taxation of any kind in excess of that imposed directly or indirectly on similar domestic products.' This means that internal taxation will be unlawful if it discriminates against imported products or is protective of domestic products.

ii. The European Court's interpretation of Art 110 TFEU

Clearly, there may be an argument as to what products may be considered to be 'similar'. In Case 27/67, *Fink-Frucht*, the Court of Justice provided that goods would be regarded as similar if they came within the same tax classification, but it has also been held that products need not necessarily be the same.

For example, in Case 170/78, *Commission v UK*, it was concluded that an appropriate test may be whether a consumer might *substitute* one product for another for the purpose he has in mind, while in Case 168/78, *Commission v France* (the *French Spirits* case), France unsuccessfully attempted to distinguish alcoholic spirits made from grain and those made from fruit, characteristics such as composition, physical characteristics and consumer usage were considered.

iii. Indirectly discriminatory internal taxation

Taxation that is directly discriminatory overtly treats domestic and imported goods differently, but taxation that is indirectly discriminatory may, on the face of it, appear to comply with Union rules although, in reality, placing non-domestic goods at a disadvantage.

Case 112/84, *Humblot*, provides a helpful example of such treatment. French law decreed that the amount of car tax payable increased with the power rating of the vehicle, with cars below and above a 16CV rating being charged at different rates. No French car was rated above 16CV and therefore only imported cars fell into the higher tax rating. France's internal car taxation system was therefore considered to be covertly discriminatory and consequently unlawful under Art 110.

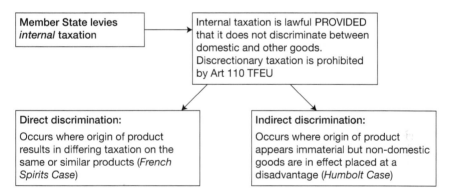

Unlawful internal taxation

4. Enforcing the rules relating to pecuniary barriers to trade

Art 30 TFEU has been held to be directly effective (*Van Gend*). Traders may therefore enforce their rights against a Member State in the appropriate national court.

Member States will normally be required to repay any charges which have been unlawfully levied (Case 199/82, *Amministrazione delle Finanze dello Stato v San Giorgio*), unless the trader has passed the costs on to his customers (Cases C-192–218/95, *Société Comateb*).

In addition, an errant State may find itself the subject of an enforcement action brought by either the Commission or another Member State, this time before the Court of Justice (Arts 258–260 TFEU, discussed in Chapter 6).

Art 110 TFEU is also directly effective (*Humblot*) and individuals may consequently enforce any rights accruing from the Article in their national courts. Once more, Member States who levy discriminatory internal taxation may also find themselves investigated by the Commission, as above.

II. THE ELIMINATION OF NON-PECUNIARY BARRIERS TO TRADE

1. The problem

The prohibition of pecuniary barriers to trade would not, alone, be sufficient to guarantee the free movement of goods within the EU. In addition to the pecuniary measures discussed above, measures of a non-pecuniary nature can also hinder free movement.

Non-pecuniary measures may include quantitative restrictions such as bans or quotas, while the imposition of compulsory inspections or trading rules relating to the composition, packaging and so on of goods are also capable of hindering trade. The Treaty consequently provides a prohibition on quantitative restrictions and measures having equivalent effect (MHEEs).

2. Quantitative restrictions and measures having equivalent effect (Arts 34–36 TFEU)

Article 34 TFEU provides that 'Quantitative restrictions on imports and all measures having equivalent effect shall be prohibited between Member States.' Art 35 TFEU provides a similar prohibition with regard to exports.

Article 36 TFEU, on the other hand, provides an opportunity for Member States to justify, or derogate from, the prohibitions in both Arts 34 and 35. The availability of such derogation – which may only be claimed in limited circumstances – is a recognition that some issues are more important than the need to ensure the creation and maintenance of the internal market, allowing State regulation and the aim of free movement of goods to be reconciled.

As one would expect, each Member State has developed its own trading rules and, while the Union has attempted to harmonise such rules, progress has been slow. In the absence of harmonising legislation (note that where there has been such legislation, Member States may **not** impose any additional requirements **unless** the harmonising legislation expressly permits it), the Court of Justice has taken the stance that national rules must not be allowed to hinder the free movement of goods, interpreting Arts 34 and 35 TFEU broadly to encompass as many restrictive measures as possible. On the other hand, Art 36 TFEU, which allows Member States to derogate, has been interpreted narrowly, ensuring that as few barriers to trade as possible exist.

i. Article 34 TFEU and imports

The extent of the legislation

As has already been touched upon above, the Court has provided a wide interpretation with regard to whose measures may be prohibited by EU rules on free movement of goods, which is primarily addressed to Member States.

In Case 249/81, *Commission v Ireland* (the *Buy Irish* case), the CJEU held that the Irish Government's support of the Irish Goods Council's campaign was sufficient to allow the body to be considered 'public' for the purposes of Art 34. It is also important to note that, in Case C-265/95, *Commission v France*, the Court declared that the actions of French farmers who had disrupted imports, came within the ambit of the French Government, as the State authorities were considered not to have taken sufficient action to ensure free movement: in other words, an *omission* to act may also be considered to be a MHEE.

Meaning of 'quantitative restrictions'

Quantitative restrictions (QRs) can be described as national measures which impose a *numerical limit* on goods of a particular type entering a domestic market. The purpose of such behaviour is often to offer protection to domestic products. The Court has provided that 'total or partial restraints' on trade fall within the scope of the term (Case 2/73, *Geddo*), thus making it clear that quotas and total bans on goods are prohibited. (It needs to be emphasised that the ban or quota must relate to goods and not to something related to the goods. If, for example, an additive is banned this is not a QR, as the goods – without the additive – would not be outlawed.)

Meaning of 'measures having equivalent effect'

As well as prohibiting quantitative restrictions, Art 34 outlaws 'measures having equivalent effect to quantitative restrictions' (MHEEs). This term has proved difficult to define and has been the subject of both secondary legislation and interpretation by the Court of Justice. In general terms, MHEEs can be seen as measures that discriminate by, for example, promoting or favouring domestic goods (consider Case 249/81, *Commission v Ireland*, the *Buy Irish* case) or which make importation of goods more difficult or costly (such as in Case 50/85, *Schloh*).

- **Commission Directive 70/50/EEC (OJ 1097 L13/29)**

Directive 70/50/EEC was adopted in an attempt to amplify the meaning of Art 34 TFEU and, although no longer in force, it is still used as a guide to the practices which are prohibited by Arts 34 and 35. The Directive makes a distinction between two types of measures:

(a) measures which apply to imports only and are therefore directly dis- criminatory: known in 'Euro-speak' as 'distinctly applicable measures' (DAMs); and

(b) measures which are applicable to both domestic and imported products alike and which therefore are not overtly discriminatory: known as 'indistinctly applicable measures' (IDAMs).

The Commission, by means of Art 2(1) of the Directive, concluded that while discriminatory measures (DAMs) would always come within the scope of Arts 34 and would consequently be prohibited (*unless* provided with a derogation under Art 36 TFEU, discussed below), IDAMs would not normally come within the scope of Art 34 *unless they place an additional burden on imports.*

- **Judicial development of the meaning of 'measures having equivalent effect'**

The Court's jurisprudence has been responsible for developing Art 34 into a formidable tool in the drive against national trading rules that restrict the free movement of goods. In an attempt to illustrate this development, the Court's decisions will be considered in chronological order.

The Dassonville 'Formula'

In Case 8/74, *Procureur du Roi v Dassonville*, the CJEU provided that:

All trading rules enacted by Member States which are capable of hindering directly or indirectly, actually or potentially, intra-Community trade are to be considered as measures having an effect equivalent to quantitative restrictions.

In what has become the **authoritative definition** of a MHEE, thc Court interpreted Art 34 extremely broadly, bringing apparently neutral measures, as well as discriminatory measures, within its scope. In *Dassonville*, the Court also provided that it is not necessary to show actual effect on trade between Member States – it is sufficient to show that the measure is *capable* of such an effect. This is a particularly all-encompassing interpretation, allowing Member States very little autonomy in regard to their trading rules.

This broad approach is hardly surprising however, given that the Court's usual approach is to ensure that any barriers to the achievement of the aims of the Union are removed.

National measures which may not be considered MHEEs:

(1) Mandatory requirements and the 'Rule of Reason': Case 120/78, *Rewe-Zentral v Bundesmonopolverwaltung fur Branntwein (Cassis)*

In the case thankfully known as '*Cassis*', the Court qualified its approach in *Dassonville* by applying a 'Rule of Reason' and providing that, **in the absence of EU harmonising legislation** a non-discriminatory national measure may be 'justifiable' and consequently not come within the scope of Art 34. However the national rule must:

(a) satisfy a **'mandatory requirement'**. (This term can perhaps be better understood when considering Case C-120/95, *Decker*, where the Court substituted 'overriding reason in the general interest' for 'mandatory', while in Case 155/80, *Obel*, the Court talked of '*legitimate interests'*.)

(b) be **'necessary'** (i.e. its aim must not be achievable through less restrictive means: also known as the general principle of *proportionality*).

The Court went on to highlight particular areas where this is likely to apply, such as:

- effectiveness of fiscal supervision;
- protection of public health;
- fairness of commercial transactions;
- consumer protection.

This list is **not** exhaustive however, and the CJEU has shown itself willing to extend this into areas such as:

- promotion of national culture (Cases 60 and 61/84, *Cinéthèque v Federation des Cinemas Francais*);

- protection of the environment (Case 302/86, *Commission v Denmark*, the *Danish Bottles* case); and
- fundamental rights (Case C-112/00, *Schmidberger v Austria*).

Prior to the introduction of the 'Rule of Reason' in *Cassis*, it was thought that *all* measures caught within the very broad *'Dassonville* Formula' would be prohibited by Art 34 *unless* they could be justified under Art 36 TFEU (discussed in detail later). Following *Cassis*, it can be concluded that *non-discriminatory* measures will not come within the scope of Art 34, if they can fulfil the criteria set out above, thus giving Member States a degree of autonomy removed by the *Dassonville* Formula.

Further, it is relevant to note that it is for the *national* court to determine whether or not the 'Rule of Reason' applies to a particular national rule (Case 145/88, *Torfaen v B&Q*).

(2) Non-discriminator 'selling arrangements': the judgment in joined Cases C-267 and 268/91, *Keck and Mithouard*

Due to confusion over the meaning of MHEEs, and the consequently high volume of cases coming before national courts and the CJEU (through the preliminary reference procedure discussed in Chapter 6), the CJEU, in *Keck*, took the opportunity to 're-examine and clarify' its case law.

While confirming *Dassonville*, the Court provided that 'contrary to what has previously been decided ... **certain** selling arrangements' are to be considered outside the scope of the *Dassonville* Formula, **providing** that they apply 'to all affected traders operating within the national territory and provided they affect in the same manner, in law and in fact, the marketing of domestic products and those from other Member States'.

Simplified, this means that:

(i) *certain* past decisions of the Court should no longer be considered 'good' law; and

(ii) 'selling arrangements' which affect all traders, in both law and fact, are outside the scope of Art 34.

While the Court's judgment was intended to clarify the law, it caused a great deal of confusion, particularly with regard to the exact meaning of 'selling arrangements' and the character of the 'effects'.

With hindsight, the Court's judgment can be recognised as distinguishing between national measures which relate to:

- the goods themselves, that is their *intrinsic* qualities, such as composition, size, labelling, packaging, weight, form and so on – known as **'product requirements'** – which continued to be prohibited, and those which relate to
- *extrinsic* matters such as advertising, who may sell goods or where or when goods may be sold – i.e. **'selling arrangements'** – which will only be prohibited if they have the propensity to have a particular effect.

The judgment in Case C-368/95, *Familiapress*, is helpful in terms of understanding how the concept of a lawful 'selling arrangement' is to be approached. In this case a German company published a magazine offering, as a marketing tool, competitions involving prizes. The publication was also distributed in Austria, which had a trading rule imposing a ban on such competitions in the press – activities which were permitted under German law. A preliminary reference was sent to the CJEU on the question of whether the Austrian rule was contrary to Art 34 TFEU requiring the Court to consider whether the national ban was a 'selling arrangement' and therefore outside the scope of Art 34. In para 11 of its judgment, the Court provided that:

> even though the relevant national legislation is directed against a method of sales promotion, in this case it bears on the actual content of the products, in so far as the competitions in question form an integral part of the magazine in which they appear. As a result, the national legislation in question as applied to the facts of the case is not concerned with a selling arrangement within the meaning of the judgment in *Keck and Mithouard*.

Consequently, even though the national ban on competitions appeared to relate to marketing, which would suggest it was a 'selling arrangement', the competitions were held to be part of the composition of the magazine, as the magazine would have had to have been altered in order to comply with Austrian law and was to be seen as a 'product requirement'. The national ban was consequently prohibited by Art 34.

While *Keck* was seen as an important case in explaining that certain national trading rules (i.e. selling arrangements) – in addition to those held to be outside the scope of Art 34 by the *Cassis* 'Rule of Reason' – will not be prohibited if non-discriminatory *in both law and fact*.

More CJEU assistance on recognising prohibited national rules and discrimination 'in law and in fact'

As has already been discussed, it is clear that national measures which directly discriminate between domestic and imported goods are prohibited by Art 34 TFEU. The Court of Justice has, however, also clearly established that measures which *appear* to apply to both domestic and imported goods in the same manner may also come within the definition of an MHEE due to their propensity to impact on the free movement of goods (under the '*Dassonville* Formula'). Such measures have been held by the CJEU to include:

(i) Measures which place a 'dual burden' on importers

Some national measures create a dual burden for importers because they place an **additional** requirement on goods. For example in *Cassis*, as explained earlier, the national rule required that all Cassis sold in Germany contain an alcohol content of 25 per cent. The national rule can be seen as placing an *additional* burden on importers of the liquor from States where no such rule applies, as the goods would have to be modified before they could be lawfully traded in the importing State.

This can be seen as having a potential impact on trade as it is likely to make importing the goods more difficult by adding to time and/or expense.

(ii) Measures which 'impede market access'

The 'dual burden' rule has been further developed by the Court in later cases and we are now aware that, where even an apparently neutral measure has the potential to impede the market access of imported goods, that measure will be prohibited.

In Cases C-34 to 36/95, *De Agostini*, for example, which related to a Swedish ban on advertising aimed at young children, the Court of Justice provided that a national rule would be prohibited by Art 34 if that rule affected domestic and imported goods in a different way. It can be argued that if goods cannot be advertised, they will have no means of becoming 'known' by consumers in the importing State, and consequently demand for them is likely to be lower – and market access will be impeded.

Similarly, in Case C-405/98, *Gourmet Foods*, Swedish law prohibited the advertising of alcoholic beverages in trade magazines. While this rule was again not directly discriminatory, being targeted at domestic and non-domestic products alike, it was argued that it was more likely to have a disadvantageous impact on (the less well-known) imported brands than on domestic brands. It was consequently determined to be a MHEE despite, at first sight, *appearing* to be a non-discriminatory 'selling arrangement', which could have removed it from the scope of Art 34 under the '*Keck* principle'.

(iii) Discrimination and 'use restrictions'

More recently the Court of Justice has considered national rules which restrict the *use* of goods: that is, while there may be no restriction on the entry of the product, there are limitations on the use to which products may be put in a State. Two cases are instructive here.

In Case C-142/05, *Mickelsson v Roos*, the Court held that a restriction on where goods (in this case jet skis) may be used was a MHEE and within the scope of Art 34, as fewer jet skis would be bought and consequently imported if they could not be used freely. (In this instance the national rule was justified under Art 36 TFEU.)

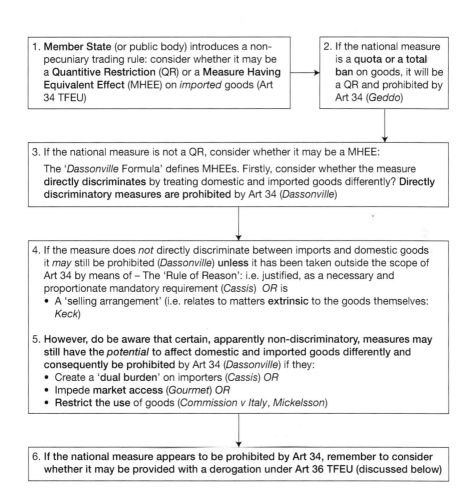

1. **Member State** (or public body) introduces a non-pecuniary trading rule: consider whether it may be a **Quantitive Restriction** (QR) or a **Measure Having Equivalent Effect** (MHEE) on *imported* goods (Art 34 TFEU)

2. If the national measure is a **quota or a total ban** on goods, it will be a QR and prohibited by Art 34 (*Geddo*)

3. If the national measure is not a QR, consider whether it may be a MHEE:

   The '*Dassonville* Formula' defines MHEEs. Firstly, consider whether the measure **directly discriminates** by treating domestic and imported goods differently? **Directly discriminatory measures are prohibited** by Art 34 (*Dassonville*)

4. If the measure does *not* directly discriminate between imports and domestic goods it *may* still be prohibited (*Dassonville*) **unless** it has been taken outside the scope of Art 34 by means of – The 'Rule of Reason': i.e. justified, as a necessary and proportionate mandatory requirement (*Cassis*) OR is
   - A 'selling arrangement' (i.e. relates to matters **extrinsic** to the goods themselves: *Keck*)

5. However, do be aware that certain, apparently non-discriminatory, measures may still have the *potential* to affect domestic and imported goods differently and consequently be prohibited by Art 34 (*Dassonville*) if they:
   - Create a '**dual burden**' on importers (*Cassis*) OR
   - Impede **market access** (*Gourmet*) OR
   - **Restrict the use** of goods (*Commission v Italy*, *Mickelsson*)

6. If the national measure appears to be prohibited by Art 34, remember to consider whether it may be provided with a derogation under Art 36 TFEU (discussed below)

Free movement of goods: applying Art 34 TFEU

Similarly, in Case C-110/05, *Commission v Italy*, following the introduction of legislation, by Italy, prohibiting motorcycles from towing trailers, the Court held that the rule hindered the market access of motorbike trailers and was in breach of Art 34 TFEU. Again, who would consider purchase if their use was limited? In this case it was held to be irrelevant that fewer domestic goods would also be sold.

It can be seen from the case law of the CJEU, the Court is keen to eliminate *any* national law that has a restrictive impact on the movement of goods within the Union.

ii. Article 35 TFEU and exports

There may be instances, although less frequent than in relation to imports, where a Member State may wish to restrict the free flow of exports and consequently the EU has responded to such a possibility.

Article 35 TFEU prohibits quantitative restrictions and all MHEEs on *exported* goods. While the prohibition contained within Art 35 *appears* to mirror that contained within Art 34, this is **not** actually the case.

This is because the case law of the Court of Justice in decisions such as *Dassonville, Cassis* and *Keck* related to the Court's interpretation of Art 34 and *not* Art 35.

While Art 34 has been held to prohibit both discriminatory measures and measures which treat domestic and other goods alike, it would appear that Art 35 only prohibits measures which discriminate (Case 15/79, *Groenveld*).

Examples of measures that have been held to be MHEEs with regard to exports include Case 237/82, *Jongeneel Kaas v Netherlands*, where inspection documents were required for exports while no such requirement was placed on goods destined for the domestic market. Also, Case C-5/94, *R v MAFF ex p Lomas*, where national authorities refused to sanction the export of live animals to Member States where slaughterhouse standards were considered to be inadequate, the Court held that such national rules were discriminatory and consequently within Art 35 TFEU.

3. Derogation from the prohibitions contained in Arts 34 and 35: Art 36 TFEU

i. What the Treaty says

The EU has recognised that certain measures put into effect by Member States, although detrimental to free movement of goods, may be necessary to fulfil important functions. In order to give effect to the recognition that the positive effects of certain measures outweigh the negative effects on trade, Art 36 TFEU provides that:

The provisions of Arts 34 and 35 shall not preclude prohibitions or restrictions on imports, exports or goods in transit justified on grounds of:

- public morality;
- public security or public policy;
- protection of the health and life of humans, animals or plants;
- protection of national treasures possessing artistic, historic or archaeological value;
- protection of industrial and commercial property.

The Article goes on to qualify this, providing that: 'Such prohibitions or restrictions shall not, however, constitute a means of arbitrary discrimination or a disguised restriction on trade between Member States.'

ii. The jurisprudence of the Court of Justice

The principle of 'mutual recognition' (the Second *Cassis* Principle)

Before considering Art 36 TFEU, it should be noted that the starting point in considering whether a national trading measure is lawful was developed in the *Cassis* case. In Case 120/78, *Rewe-Zentral v Bundesmonopolverwaltung fur Branntwein* (*Cassis*), the CJEU developed a second, important principle. The Court provided that, in the absence of harmonising legislation, there should be a *presumption* by Member States that goods which have been *lawfully* produced and marketed in one Member State will comply with the minimum requirements of the importing State, thereby limiting the need for an importing State to enact trading rules requiring certain additional standards to be met or inspections to be undertaken, for example.

The presumption can, however, be *rebutted* by evidence that further measures are necessary to ensure adequate standards are met (Case 18/84, *Commission v France*).

The principle has also been of fundamental importance to the process of harmonisation of trading rules within the EU. In order to create an integrated market, the Union recognises that trading rules within the Member States must be in harmony with one another and the Commission has since supported the principle, providing that:

Any product imported from another Member State must in principle be admitted to the territory of the importing Member State if it has been lawfully produced, that is, conforms to rules and processes of manufacture that are customarily and traditionally accepted in the exporting country, and is marketed in the territory of another.

(Commission Communication OJ 1980 256/2)

In addition, as the Member States should not automatically treat imported goods with suspicion, the need for national rules relating to the *quality* of imported goods can therefore be kept to a minimum.

The general position of the Court of Justice

As touched upon earlier, the CJEU has adopted a narrow stance with regard to its interpretation of the measures which may enjoy derogation from the prohibitions found under Arts 34 and 35 TFEU, as to do otherwise could constitute a threat to the Union's fundamental principle of free movement of goods.

It should be remembered that Art 36 TFEU cannot be used to justify a measure in areas which have been subject to harmonisation by the EU.

iii. Grounds for derogation under Art 36 TFEU

As already touched upon, the Treaty provides an exhaustive list of grounds under which a Member State may claim derogation from the prohibitions provided by Arts 34 and 35 TFEU. The Court has generally expressed unwillingness to consider any extension of these grounds, as it sees this as a matter for legislation (as evidenced by the Court's dicta in Case 113/80, *Commission v Ireland*, the *Irish Souvenirs* case). Prior to the *Cassis* judgment (the 'Rule of Reason', discussed above), Art 36 was the only means of 'saving' a prohibited measure from being outlawed under Art 34. (Art 36 TFEU is still the only means under which a measure prohibited under Art 34 TFEU may be 'saved', as the 'Rule of Reason' does not apply to Art 35.)

Public morality

Consideration of Case 34/79, *R v Henn and Darby* and Case 121/85, *Conegate Ltd v HM Customs & Excise*, provide examples of the Court's interpretation of this ground.

In *Henn and Darby*, the defendants were accused by UK authorities of illegally importing pornographic material. They argued, in their defence, that UK rules contravened Art 34. The Court of Justice found that the UK's ban on pornography was justified under Art 36, as it is for each State to determine the standards of public morality that exist within its own territory.

In *Conegate*, the defendants imported inflatable, life-size 'love dolls' into the UK. The dolls were seized and, once more, it was argued that the UK rules constituted a threat to trade. The UK rules did not contain a similar ban on the domestic manufacture of 'love dolls' and, although the Court repeated its dicta from *Henn and Darby*, it was held that a State may not rely on Art 36 'when its legislation contains no prohibition on the manufacture or marketing of the same goods in its territory'.

What can be concluded from these decisions is that, while the Member States are free to determine their own moral standards, they must not place any stricter burden on imported goods than they do on nationally produced goods.

Public policy

Case 7/78, *R v Thompson and Others* is a rare example of a successful action under this ground, involving the right to mint (and melt down) coinage.

The Court held that this ground could be successful where there is a need to protect a right that is traditionally regarded as involving a fundamental interest of the State.

Public security

This ground often goes hand in hand with a claim based on public policy. In Case 72/83, *Campus Oil Ltd v Minister for Industry and Energy*, importers of petroleum products were required to buy 35 per cent of their oil from the Irish National Petroleum Company at a fixed price. The Court of Justice accepted that this was to enable the Irish Government to maintain a viable refinery that could meet essential needs in times of crisis and that the national measure could be justified as in the interests of public security. The Court has also held that both external and internal security comes within the scope of this derogation (Case C-367/89, *Richardt*).

Protection of health and life of humans, animals or plants

This is the area most claimed by Member States in order to justify obstacles to trade. The Court of Justice has made it clear that, when considering whether or not a measure may be justified, there are a number of issues that are likely to be relevant, primarily:

- in the absence of harmonising legislation, the principle of 'mutual recognition' may be relevant. This principle is discussed in further detail above but, to briefly recap, it provides that goods lawfully produced in one Member State should be presumed to reach minimum requirement standards in all Member States (*Cassis*);

- scientific or other relevant knowledge (Case 174/82, *Officier van Justitie v Sandoz* and Case 178/84, *Commission v Germany*, the *German Beer* case, including the existence of a technical need);

- in a case involving inspections or checks in Case 4/75, *Rewe-Zentralfinanz v Landschwirtschaftskammer* (*San José Scale*), it was held that inspections will only be justified if imported products constitute a real risk not present in comparable domestic goods, while in Case 228/91, *Commission v Italy*, the Court provided that where health certificates are available, spot checks, rather than continual inspection, will be acceptable.

It should be evident that an overlap exists between measures justifiable under the 'Rule of Reason' (*Cassis*) and Art 34, particularly in the area of 'public health'. However, when Member States have previously sought to justify measures on public health grounds, the Court has chosen to consider such requests under Art 34.

Protection of national treasures

There is a paucity of definitive case law in this area and therefore little guidance as to what will be considered to be a 'national treasure' (although Directive 93/7/EEC and Regulation EEC No 3911/92 have been used to assist). Restrictions on the export of artefacts have been generally considered justifiable but in the *1st Art Treasures* case, which was brought as a result of Italy's breach of Art 30 TFEU rather than Art 34, the European Court failed to allow the Italian Government to levy an export tax on 'cultural artefacts' in an attempt to restrict their removal abroad.

Protection of industrial or commercial property

Industrial or commercial property (also known as 'intellectual property') rights may take the form of trade marks, copyright, patents and so on. Protection of such rights encourages innovation and their ownership is complemented by Art 345 TFEU, which provides that: 'The Treaty shall in no way prejudice the rules in Member States governing the system of property ownership.'

Where national rules allow such rights to be protected, an individual with an intellectual property right (IPR) can often rely on such legislation to prevent re-importation of particular goods. National legislation relating to an IPR may, however, have the result of restricting trade, which is, of course, prohibited under Union law.

The Court of Justice has struck a balance between the protection of an IPR and the principle of free movement of goods by distinguishing between the existence of an IPR and the exercise of such rights. The Court has provided that an IPR will be protected by Art 36 only when rights have not been exhausted by the subject matter of the right being put into free circulation within the EU (Case 15/74, *Centrafarm v Sterling Drug*). This is probably best understood by the provision of the following example.

An inventor (A) has patented a new invention and so an IPR exists. Should A decide to award a licence to manufacturer B, giving B the right to produce the invention, A will be said to have *exercised* his IPRs.

If the product remains within the Member State, the rights afforded by the award of a patent will be subject to the intellectual property laws of that Member State only and EU rules will be irrelevant.

If, however, the product is exported by B, A will not be able to exert any further control over the product, even if it is re-imported, as the EU provides that his rights were *exhausted* or 'used up' when he awarded B authority over the product.

The doctrine of exhaustion of rights has been held to be applicable to:

- patents – Case 15/74, *Centrafarm v Sterling Drug*;
- trade marks – Case 16/74, *Centrafarm v Winthrop*;
- copyright – Case 78/70, *Deutsche Grammophon v Metro*.

It should be noted that a certain amount of secondary legislation has been adopted by the Union with the aim of harmonising the rules in this area and such legislation, although outside the scope of this book, may need to be considered.

iv. The matter of 'arbitrary discrimination'

Article 36 specifically provides that 'prohibitions or restrictions shall not, however, constitute a means of arbitrary discrimination'. An example of such discrimination can be found in Case 152/78, *Commission v France*. In this case French advertising restrictions appeared to be biased against grain-based spirits, while favouring fruit-based spirits. The French authorities attempted to justify this on the grounds of 'public health', arguing that grain-based spirits were more likely to be injurious to health. Independent evidence, however, proved the effect on health of both spirits to be identical. (Interestingly, the French produce fruit-based spirits, while grain-based spirits are generally imported. The Court, in its judgment, considered the restriction to be capricious, constituting arbitrary discrimination.)

v. Measures which are a 'disguised restriction on trade'

In addition to 'arbitrary discrimination' being outlawed, Art 36 also provides that national measures must not constitute a 'disguised restriction on trade'. An example of such behaviour can be found in Case 40/82, *Commission v UK* (the *Newcastle Disease* case) in which the UK banned the import of poultry and poultry products from States which did not have a policy of slaughtering flocks of birds with Newcastle disease. The UK attempted to justify this on the grounds of 'health'. Evidence showed that other methods of controlling the disease were equally effective and that the ban had been imposed following pressure from UK poultry producers relating to an increase in

---

Justification under Art 36 TFEU: derogation from the prohibition contained in Arts 34 and 35

'Cassis' and Mutual Recognition:	**A national measure that appears to be prohibited by either Art 34 or 35 TFEU MAY obtain derogation (may be justified) if Art 36 applies: A derogation may be obtained on the following grounds:**
The Court of Justice has provided that goods lawfully produced in one MS should be presumed to comply with minimum requirements in all MSs.	**Grounds:** Exhaustive and interpreted narrowly by the Court of Justice, grounds are as follows:

A national measure that appears to be prohibited by either Art 34 or 35 TFEU MAY obtain derogation (may be justified) if Art 36 applies: A derogation may be obtained on the following grounds:

Grounds:

Exhaustive and interpreted narrowly by the Court of Justice, grounds are as follows:

- Public morality (*Henn & Darby* and *Conegate*)
- Public policy (*Thompson*)
- Public security (*Campus Oil*)
- Protection of health and life of humans, animals and plants: an often-claimed derogation to which 'mutual recognition' closely applies. Consider the state of scientific knowledge (*Sandoz* and the *German Beer* Case) and the need for inspections (*San Jose Scale*) and health certificates (*Commission v Italy*)
- Protection of national treasures (*Art Treasures* Case)
- Protection of industrial/commercial property. Consider the exhaustion of rights

In addition to finding the appropriate ground, the national measure must not be:

- **Arbitrary** discrimination or a **disguised restriction** on trade (consider the *Newcastle Disease Case*), and must be
- **Proportionate:** Consider whether the aim of the measure could be achieved in a less restrictive manner (*Cassis*)
- A measure will not be justified in an area which has been the subject of EU **harmonising legislation**

'Cassis' and Mutual Recognition:

The Court of Justice has provided that goods lawfully produced in one MS should be presumed to comply with minimum requirements in all MSs.

This is seen as a **starting point** in regard to the Free Movement of Goods

Justifying non-pecuniary barriers to trade

turkeys imported from France and Ireland. Furthermore, when French importers complied with UK requirements, additional restrictions were imposed. The Court of Justice concluded that the UK's restrictions therefore amounted to a disguised restriction on trade.

vi. The requirement of 'proportionality'

Although not specifically mentioned in Art 36 TFEU, it is implicit that the General Principle of proportionality will apply to any measure for which a Member State is claiming justification. The principle requires that measures be no more than strictly necessary to achieving a particular aim (Case 124/81, *Commission v UK, Re UHT Milk*). Consequently, it should always be considered whether or not the aim of a national measure can be achieved by less restrictive means.

III. CONCLUSIONS

Students who have survived this far will probably agree with a comment made at the beginning of this chapter – that is that the rules relating to the free movement of goods are complex! Remember that understanding *why* the rules have been developed in the first place and adopting a logical, incremental approach in regard to the development of the law in this area of law will allow you to master its intricacies.

SOME ISSUES TO THINK ABOUT FURTHER

- Why are rights in regard to the free movement of goods interpreted broadly, yet limitation of those rights interpreted restrictively by the Court of Justice?
- Has the CJEU changed its interpretation of 'measures having equivalent effect to quantitative restrictions on imports' since its decision in *Dassonville*?
- Why is Art 36 TFEU not applicable in areas which have been subject to harmonising measures?

8 Free movement of persons

As considered in previous chapters, economic integration between the Member States has always been a central theme of the EU. In order to ensure that this aim is achieved, the TFEU provides that all obstacles to the free movement of goods, persons, services and capital (known as the 'Four Freedoms') be abolished within the EU (Art 26 TFEU).

Although the number of languages spoken within the EU has undoubtedly had an adverse effect on cross-border mobility and, despite less than 2 per cent of EU citizens living outside their State of origin, free movement of persons is nevertheless considered fundamental to the creation of the internal market. Without a mobile workforce, workers would not, for example, be able to move around the Union to fill manpower or skills shortages. Similarly, European entrepreneurs would not be able to expand their businesses into new States, nor could service providers cross borders to provide occasional services to clients in other Member States. The consequences would be detrimental to the creation of an integrated EU and, unsurprisingly therefore, EU law gives Union citizens the right to move from their 'home' State to another Union State (the 'host' State), largely un-hampered by unnecessary restrictions.

Simple as this may initially appear, *specific* rights with regard to free movement within the EU are dependent on determining the 'status' of individuals wishing to move between States. Status largely depends on two things: **nationality** and **economic activity**. While Art 21 TFEU provides a basic right of free movement to all Union citizens, Arts 45 to 62 TFEU provide a framework of **additional rights** for those who are *also* economically active. The rights contained within the Treaty have been considerably expanded by secondary legislation and developed by the jurisprudence of the Court of Justice. European Union citizens, employees, the self-employed, family members and businesses all enjoy rights but their *exact* nature – and source – depends on the 'group' into which an individual falls. Each group is considered below, albeit comparatively briefly with regard to the self-employed, establishment and the provision of services, with the main emphasis of this chapter being placed on the rights of EU citizens and workers.

I. GAINING THE RIGHT TO 'FREE MOVEMENT'

1. EU citizenship

Rules relating to free movement of persons have changed significantly over the years. Originally, because individuals were seen as factors of production in the same way as, for example, raw materials, only those who were economically active, such as workers, the self-employed and service providers, were given rights of free movement. However, others – in their relatively new guise as European citizens – now have the right, subject to certain limitations, to move between Member States independent of their economic status and based purely on nationality.

European Union citizenship was first established by the Maastricht Treaty (TEU, 1992) when all Member State nationals became citizens of the Union. The CJEU has made it clear that EU citizenship does not replace nationality but is in addition to it: they view citizenship of the EU as the 'fundamental status of nationals of the Member States', indicating the importance placed on Union citizenship by the Court (Case C-184/99, *Grzelczyk*).

The rights of EU citizens, of which there are over 500 million, are not limited to free movement and include the right to vote and stand for election to the European Parliament (EP), the right to petition the EP and refer complaints of maladministration by EU bodies to the European Ombudsman (Art 20 TFEU). In addition, Arts 9 to 12 TEU set out rights relating to democratic participation in the governance of the Union, including the right to information, to be consulted and to invite the Commission to submit legislative proposals, should a sufficient number of citizens (at least one million) so request (known as the 'citizens' initiative': Art 24 TFEU), while the EU Charter of Fundamental Rights provides yet further rights. However, it is Union citizens' rights of free movement that are given priority in this chapter.

i. EU citizenship and free movement

It is essential to emphasise at the outset that rights relating to free movement are only provided *directly* to those who are citizens of the EU. This is evidenced by Art 21 TFEU, which provides that: 'Every **citizen** of the Union shall have the right to move and reside freely within the territory of the Member States.' It should be noted, however, that the right to move freely between Member States is not absolute and is 'subject to the limitations and conditions laid down by the Treaties and by the measures adopted to give them effect'.

As Union citizenship now provides the basic rights of free movement between Member States, these will be considered first, followed by consideration of any additional rights available to those who are economically active. The limitations on any such rights are also considered.

Before moving on, it is relevant to note that **The Schengen Agreement**, introduced with the aim of promoting integration, allows the free movement of European citizens across the majority of national borders without the need for visa or passport checks. However, given increased levels of immigration into the EU from third countries and the sensitivities of anti-immigration politics, the concept of open internal borders has become highly controversial, as it can be argued that the lack of internal borders makes it easier for migrants who have entered the EU illegally to move about undetected. As highlighted by the Commission, it is consequently essential that the European institutions maintain vigilance over the functioning of the Schengen area and are ready to respond to any challenges it faces.

ii. Who is considered a citizen of the Union?

Originally introduced by the TEU in an attempt to strengthen ties between the EU and its citizens, Art 20 TFEU (then Art 17 TEC) established the concept of Union citizenship, providing that: 'Every person holding the nationality of a Member State shall be a citizen of the Union.'

Consequently all Member State nationals are also citizens of the Union. Clearly EU citizenship is not something to be awarded or denied by the Union but is a consequence of the Member States' own, national, rules on nationality. However, a proviso appears to have been added by the CJEU in Case C-135/08, *Rottmann*, where the Court provided that while:

> the Member States have the power to lay down the conditions for the acquisition and loss of nationality, the exercise of that power, in so far as it affects the rights conferred and protected by the legal order of the Union ... is amenable to judicial review carried out in the light of European Union law

suggesting that State autonomy in this area is not totally unfettered by Union membership.

iii. Third-country nationals and free movement

While the right to move freely between the Member States is only provided *directly* to EU citizens, the EU has also moved towards developing common policies and harmonising national rules on movement in relation to third-country nationals (i.e. non-EU citizens). While Member States have formally supported this, in reality there has been reluctance by the States to relinquish too much power to the Union in what is considered to be a politically sensitive area, and any legislative initiatives in this area are subject to unanimous agreement by the States.

Title V, TFEU attempts to provide, and safeguard, the rights of third-country nationals with regard to matters such as visas, immigration and asylum and there is a developing body of harmonising legislation in this area. It would appear, however, that there is presently a question mark over the extent of any competence (Glossary) of the Union in terms of controlling movement between EU States, of third-country nationals who are legally resident in one State.

Entry into a Member State of a third-country national is still, in the main, subject to national rather than EU law, taking the matter outside the scope of this text. *However*, where third-county nationals are **family members** of a Union citizen (as defined in Arts 2 and 3 Directive 2004/38) the position is different, as such individuals may gain rights to free movement – but *indirectly*, through their relationship with the EU citizen (sometimes referred to as 'piggy-back' rights). Once family membership is established, rights, in the main, mirror those of family members who are Union citizens.

Affording **non**-EU family members rights of free movement has, however, resulted in the CJEU being presented with a number of questions as to *when* such rights can be enforced by third-country nationals. Article 3 D2004/38 appears to provide that the relevant EU citizen must have first exercised their right of free movement (i.e. by leaving their home State and entering a host State, thereby introducing an 'EU element' to the situation) *before* a third-country national family member can enjoy rights of free movement. While this was confirmed by the Court in Case C-127/08, *Metock*, in later decisions the CJEU appears to have qualified this position.

In Case C-200/02, *Chen*, for example, the EU citizen in question was the infant daughter of a third-country national. As the child had not yet exercised her right to free movement, remaining in the UK where she was born, the situation appeared to be 'wholly internal' to the UK and consequently outside the scope of EU law. The situation was further complicated by the fact that the third-country national, being an adult, was not 'dependent' on the EU citizen, who was a minor, as would appear to be a requirement under Art 2 D2004/38. The Court, however, ruled that, as an EU citizen, the minor had a right to reside anywhere in the EU and that to deny residency to her parent at a time when the child was unable to look after herself would conflict with the child's basic EU law rights – thereby making it a matter for EU law.

Later cases have further developed this theme and in Case C-34/09, *Zambrano*, the CJEU explained that consideration should be given to whether a refusal of rights to a third-country family member could deprive the EU citizen of 'genuine enjoyment of the substance of rights conferred by virtue of their status' as a Union citizen. This has become known as the '**genuine enjoyment test**' and, while the test has been reasserted in Case C-434/09, *McCarthy* and Case C-256/11, *Dereci*, the exact nature of the 'test' is still to be fully established.

Consequently, it can be concluded that free movement rights of third-county nationals are still, to a certain degree, uncertain and that this is an area in which you will need to be alert to new decisions of the Court of Justice.

iv. Rights attached to Union citizenship

Once it has been established that an individual wishing to enjoy rights of free movement between Member States is a Union citizen, it is then necessary to establish the **specific** source(s) and nature of their rights.

The original EEC Treaty was silent on the right to free movement of those who were *not* economically active, as the emphasis of the EEC and EC was economic in nature. However, in the 1990s three directives were enacted (sometimes called the '90's Directives') providing certain non-economically active European citizens i.e. students, retirees and those with sufficient resources not to be a burden on the social security system of the host State, with rights of free movement comparable with, but *not* identical to, those enjoyed by economically active Union citizens. This, together with the formal recognition of Union citizenship by the Maastricht Treaty (TEU, 1992), with its corresponding 'right to move and reside freely within the territory of the Member States' (now Art 21 TFEU), clearly signalled that rights of free movement were being extended.

In 2006 new legislation, in the form of **Directive 2004/38** (often called the 'Citizens Directive') on the rights of EU citizens and their families to move and reside freely within the EU, was introduced. It repealed the majority of earlier secondary legislation, including the '90's Directives', and **it is this Directive which now largely provides the basic rules by which Union citizens may move to, and reside in, a host State.** (It may be helpful to note that many of the rights now provided by D2004/38 were originally developed by the Court of Justice as the result of preliminary references (discussed in Chapter 6). Such case law is often very instructive and is consequently still relevant.)

In essence, **subject to limitations** which are discussed in detail later, EU citizens now have the right to:

- be **accompanied** by family members (Art 3 D2004/38);
- **exit** their home State (Art 4 D2004/38);
- **enter** a host State (Art 5, D2004/38);
- **reside temporarily** in the host State for a period of up to **three** months (Art 6 D2004/38);
- **enjoy equal treatment** with nationals of the host State during this period of temporary residence (Art 24 D2004/38).

v. Citizens' rights of exit, entry and residence

Articles 4 and 5 D2004/38 relate to rights concerned with exiting a 'home' Member State and entering a 'host' Member State. In order to ensure that a home State cannot deny exit, Art 4 states that nationals must be provided with a passport or identity card, while the Directive further holds that a host State cannot create a barrier to free movement by making it prohibitively difficult for Union citizens to enter a host State by demanding entry visas or other such documents (Art 5 D2004/38).

As already touched upon, once in a host State, all Union citizens have the right to reside temporarily in the host State for a period of up to **three months** (Art 6 D2004/38). This right is extended (by Art 7 D2004/38) where the citizen is:

- a worker; or
- self-employed; or
- has sufficient means not to be a financial burden on the state

Once an EU citizen has been legally resident in a host State for a continuous period of **five years**, Art 16 D2004/38 provides that they gain the right of **permanent** residence.

Continuity of residence is not affected by temporary absences from the host State of up to six months in any twelve-month period or absences due to 'important reasons' such as pregnancy or illness. The right of permanent residency can, however, be lost by an absence exceeding two consecutive years (Art 16 D2004/38).

vi. EU citizens and the extent of their right to equal treatment with host-State nationals

It is unlikely that nationals of one Member State would want to move to another State if the host State were permitted to treat them differently to their own nationals. Consequently, the EU has recognised the importance of prohibiting discrimination and requires equality of treatment between Union citizens, irrespective of their nationality.

While Art 18 TFEU provides a general prohibition on discrimination based on nationality, Art 24 D2004/38 is more specific, making it clear that Union citizens, and their families, 'shall enjoy equal treatment with nationals' of the host State in which they are residing.

Equality may, however, be **limited** in regard to '**social assistance**' (welfare benefits) available to migrants during the first three months of residence *unless* the individual is a worker or self-employed (Art 24(2) D2004/38). The Court has made it clear that Art 24(2) of the Directive and Art 18 TFEU should be read in conjunction with one another and has cautioned Member States against the application of conditions which are liable to deter citizens from making use of their right to free movement, explaining that such restrictions can only be justified if 'based on objective considerations of public interest independent of the nationality of the persons concerned and if it is proportionate to the legitimate objective pursued by the provisions of national law' (Joined Cases C-11/06, *Morgan* and C-12/06, *Iris Butcher*).

In regard to migrant students and the availability of grants and similar benefits, the Court has stated that, while they may rely on Art 18 TFEU, it is not unreasonable for the host State to require a certain level of integration to be demonstrated (such as residence in the host State for a certain period of time) before such support is made available (Case C-209/03, *Bidar* and Case C-158/07, *Forster*).

From these cases it is possible to see that the Court, in an attempt to encourage movement between Member States, places strong emphasis on equality and that Member States are increasingly being required to justify any discriminatory rules likely to discourage free movement. However, in the more recent judgment of C-333/13, *Dano*, which related to Germany's refusal of a claim for social assistance, the Court of Justice re-emphasised the exception to equal treatment set out in Art 24(2) D2004/38, providing that:

A Member State must therefore have the possibility of refusing to grant social benefits to economically inactive Union citizens who exercise their right to freedom of movement solely in order to obtain another Member

147

State's social assistance although they do not have sufficient resources to claim a right of residence

prompting argument that this may be the Court's response to concerns about 'benefit tourism'.

vii. Citizens' rights and family members

It is self-evident that those with rights of free movement would be less likely to make use of those rights if they were unable to take family members with them when they took up residence in a host State. As has been touched on previously, Art 3 D2004/38 consequently provides EU citizens with the right to be accompanied by family members when they move from one Member State to another. This right exists irrespective of the nationality of the family member, as we have seen when considering the rights of third-country nationals, above.

Arts 2 and 3 D2004/38 provide that 'family member' includes:

- a **spouse**: the approach of the CJEU has been to interpret the term restrictively to include **legally married persons** only (Case 59/85, *Reed*);
- an individual with whom the Union citizen has a **registered partnership**, *provided* that the host State recognises such partnerships as equivalent to marriage;
- direct **descendants** under 21, *or* dependants of the citizen or his/her spouse or partner;
- direct **ascendants** dependent on the citizen, spouse or partner;
- other **dependent** family members who, in the country from where the citizen has migrated, were **resident in the household** *or* who have serious **health problems** requiring personal care; and
- a partner with whom the citizen has a **durable relationship**: it is for the host State to investigate this and to justify any denial of entry or residence. (In *Reed* the Court explained that, in a host State where a stable relationship enjoyed by an unmarried couple was accorded similar status to marriage, to treat such couples differently would amount to discrimination. This is now formally recognised by Art 3 D2004/38.)

viii. 'Piggy-back' rights enjoyed by family members

Where a family member is an EU citizen, the Treaty (Art 20 TFEU) and secondary legislation (Art 6 D2004/38) provide them with the right of free movement for a minimum period of up to three months, independent of their family relationships. However, where the family member is either a third-country national *or* wishes to reside *beyond* the three-month period without themselves being able to satisfy the requirement either of 'sufficient means' or of 'economic activity', the family member will need to rely on the rights afforded them indirectly as a result of their relationship with the EU citizen.

II. LIMITATIONS ON CITIZENS' RIGHTS TO FREE MOVEMENT

1. Restrictions on exit, entry and residence on grounds of public policy, public security and public health

The EU recognises that there are certain circumstances under which it is neither reasonable nor desirable to allow EU citizens, or their family members, the right to move freely within the EU. Union law therefore provides that Member States may restrict rights in certain circumstances and on specific grounds – and some limitations have already been touched upon, such as the three-month limit on residency for those who are likely to be, or become, an economic burden on the host State.

While Art 21 TFEU makes it clear that rights to free movement are 'subject to the limitations and conditions laid down by the Treaties and by the measures adopted to give them effect', Art 27 D2004/38 is more specific, stating that:

> Member States may restrict the freedom of movement and residence of Union citizens and their family members, irrespective of nationality, on grounds of public policy, public security and public health.

i. Public policy and public security

It is made clear, by D2004/38, that EU law does not give Member States *carte blanche* to deny individuals their rights, on the grounds listed. For example, in regard to public policy and public security, national measures:

- must 'not be invoked to serve **economic** ends': e.g. a State should not refuse entry or expel an individual due to the cost to the State should they remain;

149

- must 'also comply with the principle of **proportionality**': e.g. a State should not expel for a minor reason or where no equivalent sanction would be placed on a national. In Cases 115 & 116/81, *Adoui* (the *French Prostitutes* case), the CJEU held that expulsion of a migrant where similar conduct by a national would not incur a similarly restrictive sanction conflicted with the principle of proportionality. In this case French nationals were denied entry to Belgium due to their 'moral standards', despite the fact that prostitution was not illegal in Belgium (this measure also breached the principle of equality);

- must be 'based exclusively on the **personal conduct** of the individual': in Case 41/74, *Van Duyn*, the CJEU held that participation in activities and/or identification with the aims of a group *could* constitute 'personal conduct' and that the conduct need not be criminal;

- must 'represent a **genuine, present and sufficiently serious threat**, affecting one of the **fundamental interests** of society': in Case 36/75, *Rutili*, a trade unionist was restricted to living in a particular area of France, despite not being shown to be a genuine or sufficiently serious threat. In Case 30/77, *Bouchereau*, a migrant convicted of drug offences was threatened with deportation. The CJEU provided that, in order to be deported, an individual must show a propensity to act in the same way in the future;

- 'previous **criminal convictions** shall not in themselves constitute grounds.' In addition 'considerations of a general nature shall not be accepted', e.g. Case 67/74, *Bonsignore*, in which B, an Italian working in Germany, accidentally shot his brother. He was convicted of unlawful possession of a firearm and was ordered to be deported. On reference to the CJEU, the Court held that deportation could not be ordered as a general preventative measure.

ii. Public health

Article 29 D2004/38 provides that States may refuse entry or expel individuals on health grounds. The Directive also outlines the diseases for which entry and expulsion is allowed as being:

> diseases with epidemic potential as defined by the World Health Organization and other infectious or contagious parasitic diseases if they are the subject of protective provisions applying to nationals.

Where it is considered necessary, a host State may (within three months of arrival) require individuals to undergo a health check. The host State must not charge for these checks and must not conduct the checks as a matter of routine. Where a decision to expel is considered on health grounds, diseases which occur after three months of entry into a host State will *not* constitute grounds for expulsion.

iii. *Protection against expulsion and procedural safeguards*

In order to ascertain whether an individual presents a threat, certain procedures apply. For example, when issuing a registration certificate or residence card or, in the absence of a registration system, no later than three months after the entry of the individual into a host State, Art 27 D2004/38 provides that a host State may investigate a migrant's background by requesting the home State to provide information relating to the previous police record of the individual. A home State is required to provide an answer within two months.

Article 28 D2004/38 also provides the matters that a host State should take into consideration before taking the decision to expel on **public policy and/or security grounds**. These include:

- length of residence in the host State;
- age;
- health;
- family;
- economic situation;
- social and cultural integration into the host State; and
- links with country of origin.

Where the individual has the right of *permanent* residence, a decision to expel can only be taken where the grounds are *serious*. Additionally, where the individual has resided in the host State for **10 years** or is a **minor** (unless in the best interests of the child, as provided by the UN Convention on the Rights of the Child) no expulsion may take place **except** on 'imperative grounds of public security'.

The Directive also provides that any decision to expel must normally be provided in full and **in writing** (Art 30) and that there must be an **appeal** process available (Art 31). In addition, those who are excluded may submit an application to have the expulsion order lifted, after a reasonable period, which should be no longer than five years (Art 32).

2. Free movement of those with 'sufficient resources', job seekers and 'economically active' persons

i. Those with 'sufficient resources'

As already mentioned, where an EU citizen can demonstrate that they:

> have **sufficient resources** for themselves and their family members not to become a burden on the social assistance system of the host Member State during their period of residence in the host Member State and have comprehensive **sickness insurance** cover in the host Member State

their right of residence is **extended *beyond* three months** (Art 7 D2004/38) – unless the subject of limitations set out under Art 27 D2004/38 as discussed above.

ii. Job seekers

In Case C-292/89, *Antonissen*, the CJEU considered the status of individuals who wish to move to a host State in order to seek work. In reply to this question, which came before the Court of Justice before the enactment of D2004/38, the Court still provided that, although not considered a 'worker' within the full definition of the term (set out below), a job seeker should be allowed to enter and remain in a host State for a 'reasonable' amount of time provided they had a genuine chance of finding work.

This situation is now covered by Arts 6 and 14, D2004/38, which provide that Union citizens may reside in a host State for up to three months without the usual formalities, providing they have a passport or a valid identity card, which obviously includes job seekers.

Due to the wording of Art 14(1) D2004/38, it was originally thought that the rights of those *searching* for work were not as extensive as those of a worker and that host States were not bound to provide social assistance during this three-month period. However, the Court of Justice has since made it clear that it is no longer possible for a host State to routinely deny citizens benefits of a financial nature which are intended to facilitate access to employment, such as Job Seekers' Allowance, **unless** objectively justifiable for reasons unrelated to nationality (Case C-138/02, *Collins*, and Case C258/04, *Ioannidis*), as this would discourage integration.

iii. Those who are 'economically active'

In addition to those who have 'sufficient resources', those who are 'economically active' are also able to enjoy extended rights of residence, together with a number of additional rights. Consequently, the issue of 'economic activity' needs to be considered in further detail.

While secondary legislation, in the form of D2004/38, now provides the majority of rights to free movement enjoyed by Union citizens, originally primary legislation was the main source of rights and it is primary legislation (now the TFEU) that provides *additional* rights to those who are economically active.

The TFEU differentiates between categories of economic activity, namely:

- *workers* – Arts 45 to 48 TFEU relate to the rights of wage and salary earners;

- *self-employment/establishment* – Arts 49 to 55 TFEU relate to the rights of the self-employed and businesses to establish a permanent base in a host State; and

- *service providers* – Arts 56 to 62 TFEU provide the right to enter a host State in order to provide services, normally on a **temporary** basis.

These rights are, of course, in addition to other provisions which underpin the free movement of *all* EU citizens, such as Art 18 TFEU, which provides a general prohibition on discrimination on the grounds of nationality, which should always be read in conjunction with free movement rights.

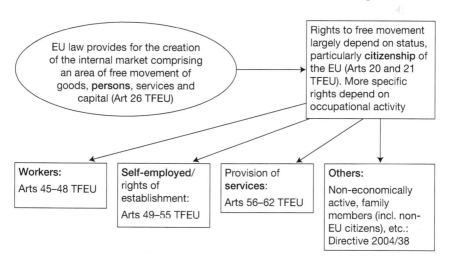

Overview of free movement of persons

III. FREE MOVEMENT: WORKERS' RIGHTS (ARTS 45–48 TFEU)

1. Definition of the term 'worker'

Neither the Treaty nor secondary legislation provide a definition of the term 'worker', but the CJEU has made it clear that 'worker' is a Union concept that the Court alone has jurisdiction to define (Case 75/63, *Hoekstra*). This ensures that the Member States cannot restrict rights by developing a narrow definition. While case law makes it clear that 'worker' refers to an employed person, the term has been **interpreted very widely**, allowing as many citizens as possible to enjoy the rights provided and thus promoting free movement.

The following decisions provide a flavour of the Court's broad and inclusive interpretation of 'worker':

- Case 75/63, *Hoekstra* – a worker who had lost his job but was capable of finding another should be considered a worker;
- Case 53/81, *Levin* – a part-time employee is to be considered a worker, provided the work is 'real' or genuine work of an economic nature and not nominal or minimal;
- Case 139/85, *Kempf* – a part-time music teacher (from Germany), even though in receipt of supplementary benefit (in the Netherlands) to bring his wage up to minimum levels, came within the term;
- Case 196/87, *Steymann* – a member of a religious community provided with board and lodge and pocket money, but not formal wages, was held to be a worker;
- Case C-413/01, *Ninni-Orasche* – it is the nature, rather than the extent, of the work which determines status and being employed on a fixed-term contract will still amount to 'work'; and
- Case 344/87, *Bettray* – an important case demonstrating the *limits* of the term 'worker'. It was held that, as the position was artificially created by the government as part of a drug rehabilitation programme, he could not be considered to be engaged in economic activity of a genuine nature.

2. Additional rights afforded to workers by EU law

Article 45 TFEU contains the principal provisions relating to migrant workers. These include:

- the right to accept offers of employment actually made and to move freely within the host State for this purpose;
- the right to reside in the host State, for the purpose of employment, under the same rules as enjoyed by nationals; and
- the right to remain in the host State after having been employed in that State (following retirement or incapacity).

i. Extension of rights relating to residence

While all EU citizens have the right to reside in a host State for up to three months, subject to the limitations already considered, a worker will also have an *immediate* right to reside beyond this period (Art 7 D2004/38), subject to any necessary administrative formalities (Art 8 D2004/38).

ii. Additional rights relating to equality with nationals

While Art 18 TFEU and Art 24 D2004/38 provide rights relating to non-discrimination and equality, as means of encouraging free movement, Art 45(3)(c) TFEU provides that migrant workers must not be discriminated against on the basis of their nationality, *in terms of their employment, remuneration and other conditions of work and employment*. Regulation 492/11 (which replaced Regulation 1612/68) expands upon equality in employment, specifically providing that migrant workers should also be treated equally with nationals in areas outside employment, such as the provision of social advantages, access to vocational training and housing *immediately* when they enter the host State.

While discrimination on the basis of nationality is clearly outlawed, EU law also recognises that apparently discriminatory conditions sometimes need to be applied by reason of the nature of the post to be filled, for example the need to ensure **linguistic proficiency**. In Case 379/87, *Groener v Minister of Education*, the CJEU provided some assistance in understanding how such conditions should be applied. Groener, a Dutch national, was not appointed to a teaching post at an Irish college when she failed an oral test. The test, which related to her competency in Gaelic, applied to both nationals and migrant workers alike (i.e. it was not *directly* discriminatory) and had been introduced as part of a policy to encourage the use of the language. The Court explained that such policies must not be disproportionate to the aim to be achieved by that policy, nor should the manner in which they are applied discriminate against migrant workers. The Irish rule satisfied these criteria and was therefore held to be lawful.

iii. Further development of the rules on discrimination

While EU rules unquestionably prohibit direct discrimination on grounds of nationality, the CJEU also outlawed **indirect discrimination**, for example the imposition of national rules that are *more easily satisfied* by nationals than by migrants. This can be evidenced by Case C-237/94, *O'Flynn* where the Court was prepared to recognise that an apparently neutral UK rule which allowed workers to claim burial grants – but only when the burial was held in the UK – was indirectly discriminatory and consequently contrary to Union law. (This can be compared to the manner in which both distinctly and indistinctly applicable measures may be prohibited under rules relating to the free movement of goods, discussed in Chapter 7.)

The Court has been prepared to go even further by providing that any measure that *discourages* free movement may also be prohibited. In Case C-415/93, *Bosman*, for example, the transnational transfer system relating to footballers, although not discriminating on the basis of nationality, was held to be an excessive obstacle to free movement, as it was *capable* of preventing players from obtaining employment in other Member States.

It should be noted, however, that **indirect discrimination** may be subject to **objective justification** by a host State. In Case C-55/94, *Gebhard*, the CJEU provided that 'national measures liable to hinder or make less attractive the exercise of fundamental freedoms guaranteed by the Treaty must fulfil four conditions', if they are not to fall foul of Union law. The Court went on to list the following conditions that must be satisfied if the national rule is to be justified, namely:

- they must be **applied** in a non-discriminatory manner;
- they must be **justified** by imperative requirements in the general interest;
- they must be **suitable** for securing the attainment of the objective which they pursue; and
- they must **not go beyond what is necessary** to attain it (proportionality).

(This approach can again be compared to the Court's approach in relation to free movement of goods (Chapter 7). In *Cassis*, the CJEU developed the 'Rule of Reason' which provides circumstances in which a restrictive measure can be justified. It can be argued that the Court's jurisprudence in both areas has developed on the basis of similar reasoning.)

iv. Additional rights of workers to remain after employment has ceased

Article 45(d) TFEU provides workers with the right to remain in a host State after being employed in that State.

The right of a worker to remain in a host State on retirement or where she/he ceases to be employed as a result of permanent incapacity is now expanded upon by Art 17 D2004/38 and, while the right of permanent residence is provided to all EU citizens who have been lawfully resident for a continuous **five**-year period (Art 16 D2004/38), workers (and the self-employed) who reach the retirement age of the host State will enjoy the right to remain earlier, in particular after:

- working in that State for at least the **12 months** preceeding retirement; and

- having resided there continuously for **three** years.

Similarly, those who are permanently incapacitated as a result of an industrial accident or occupational disease will enjoy permanent rights of residence **irrespective of how long they have resided** in that State. Those who are incapacitated by other illnesses will, however, be required to have completed **two years'** continuous residence in order to be entitled to reside permanently.

v. Rights of workers who live in one State but work in another

Certain workers may find themselves working in one host State while residing in another. Providing such workers can demonstrate:

- three years' continuous residence and employment in the territory of a host State where they wish to remain; and

- that they return at least once a week to that State they will have the right of permanent residency in the State in which they are domiciled, after ceasing work in the second host State (Art 17, D2004/38).

vi. Rights and workers' families

Primary legislation does not refer to a migrant worker's right to be joined by his/her family in a host State. This has been left to secondary legislation and D2004/38 now provides rights in relation to workers' families. Such 'family rights' can be summarised as follows.

Family rights of exit, entry and residence

Articles 4 to 7 and 16 D2004/38, provide the rights of exit, entry and residence to all EU citizens, as already explained above. However, where a family member is a third-country national, they will also gain, under Arts 6, 7 and 10 D2004/38, a right of entry as a result of their familial relationship with the EU citizen, subject to satisfying formalities as set out under Art 5 D2004/38.

Once family members, who are EU citizens, have been legally resident in the host State for a continuous period of five years, they will have the right of permanent residency in the host State (Arts 16 and 17 D2004/38). Those who are non-EU citizens also enjoy a similar right, provided by Art 18 D2004/38.

Should the EU citizen who is the source of the 'family rights' leave the host State or die, the rights of family members who are EU citizens will remain unchanged. This is also the position of third-country nationals, *providing* that they have resided in the host State as a family member for at least 12 months, although they will *not* gain rights of permanent residency unless they have 'sufficient means' or are 'economically active'. Children of the relevant EU citizen, and their parent/guardian, may stay in the host State in order to complete their studies (Art 12 D2004/38).

Families' right to take up employment

If the family member is an EU citizen, the right to take up employment (or become self-employed) is provided by Art 45 TFEU. Taking up employment in a host State will, of course, give the family member *independent* rights and, consequently, they will no longer need to depend on rights provided by their family relationship. Article 23 D2004/38 also extends the right to take up employment to non-EU family members who have the right of residence.

Families and the right to education

Under Reg 492/2011, children of a worker residing in a host State enjoy access to general educational, apprenticeship and vocational training schemes. This has been broadly interpreted by the CJEU, which has held that the children of migrant workers are entitled to *exactly the same benefits as children of domestic workers*, including educational grants (Case 76/72,

Michel S), and it would appear that the *exception* to this – contained in Art 24 D2004/38 – has been interpreted by the CJEU in a particularly restrictive manner. (Case C-209/03, *Bidar*, where, Bidar, a French national resident with his grandmother in the UK, failed to meet the residence requirement of three years in order to obtain a grant. It was argued that, as an EU citizen, he should be entitled to a grant on the same terms as UK citizens, a proposition with which the Court agreed.)

The broad interpretative approach of the Court can also be evidenced by decisions such as Cases 389 and 390/87, *Echternach* and *Moritz*, where the Court held that children of migrant workers may remain in the host State to finish their education, even if their parents had returned home. Similarly, in Case C-7/94, *Gaal*, the Court provided that educational rights include the right to complete a course, even after a once dependent child reaches the age of 21, as to act otherwise would discourage integration.

It is not as clear whether workers' spouses/partners enjoy such wide rights in relation to education, but they have been held to be entitled to equal access to educational, apprenticeship or vocational training schemes by reason of non-discrimination provisions enshrined in Art 18 TFEU (for example, Case 152/82, *Forcheri*). Such rights are further strengthened by the requirement in Art 24 D2004/38 that workers and their family members, whether EU nationals or not, should be treated equally with nationals.

Families and the right to remain: death or divorce

D2004/38 not only details the rights of workers to remain in a host State, but also provides that the residence rights of a worker's family will normally remain unchanged should the worker die or leave the host State, although the right to remain of family members who are non-EU citizens will be reliant on their having resided with the worker, in the host State, for at least 12 months prior to the worker's death (Art 12). The CJEU has also confirmed that the surviving family of a deceased worker will enjoy equality of treatment with nationals of that State (Case 32/75, *Cristini*).

Divorce, annulment or termination of a registered partnership should also not affect the right of family members to reside (Art 13 D2004/38), although conditions relating to the length of the relationship, custody of children and so on, may apply where the spouse/partner is a third-country national.

Other rights relating to family members

As has already been established, the rights afforded to workers' families often flow from their relationship with the worker. It should also be remembered that Art 18 TFEU provides *all* EU citizens with a general right

159

not to be discriminated against on grounds of their nationality, while Art 24 D2004/38 extends this right to family members who are non-EU citizens.

More specifically, the CJEU has elaborated on the extent of dependants' rights in a number of cases, particularly with regard to 'social advantages'. In Case 32/75, *Cristini v SNCF*, the Court held that the right 'cannot be interpreted restrictively', as to do so would hamper integration, and case law such as this can be used to support arguments for extension of rights.

3. Limitations placed on workers' rights: work in the public sector

While workers' rights to move freely within the EU can be limited in the same way as citizens' rights, that is on grounds of public policy, public security or public health (Art 27 D2004/38 and Art 45(3) TFEU), which have been considered above, Art 45(4) TFEU also provides that the provisions of Art 45 'shall not apply to employment in the public service'.

While Art 45(4) TFEU **does not allow a host State to refuse entry or expel a worker**, it can prevent a worker from taking up a job in the 'public sector' of the host State.

The exact scope of 'public service' is not defined by legislation but, unsurprisingly, as it provides an exception to the fundamental EU principle of equality, the concept has been narrowly interpreted by the CJEU. The Court has shed light on the extent and application of the rule and a number of cases are particularly enlightening.

The Court has held that Art 45(4) TFEU cannot be invoked by Member States in relation to the terms and conditions of employment, as it applies only to *access* to employment (Case 152/73, *Sotguit*), while in Case 149/79, *Commission v Belgium (Re Public Employees)*, Belgian law reserving **all** posts in the public service for Belgian nationals, irrespective of the duties performed, was held to be unlawful under Art 45(4) TFEU. To come within Art 45(4), the Court has held that employment must involve 'direct or indirect participation in the exercise of powers conferred by public law and duties designed to safeguard the general interests of the State or other public authorities'. While it is evident that high-level posts are the most likely to come within the scope of Art 45(4), lower-level posts – with, for example, access to 'sensitive' information, such as cleaners and night-watchmen – *may* also be included in appropriate circumstances.

The implication of this is that posts in which the worker owes a particular allegiance to the State may be included (e.g. the armed forces, police,

Workers' rights:

- **Art 45 TFEU** provides the right to take up employment on the same basis as nationals of the host State. Workers also given the right to remain when employment ceases
- **Reg 1612/68** sets out further rules on eligibility for employment, equality and family rights
- **Dir 2004/38** expands rights, including equal treatment outside employment (social advantages), the right to be accompanied by family members
- **Dir 2004/38** also provides administrative detail in regard to entry, exit and residence

Limiting workers' rights:

- **Art 45** provides that MSs may deny workers rights of free movement on grounds of public policy, security and health
- **Art 45** also provides that workers' right to take up public-sector employment may be limited by State
- **Dir 2004/38** provides additional detail in regard to limitation of workers' rights and expulsion, including procedural safeguards

The status of 'worker':
Term is defined by the Court of Justice. Workers must demonstrate that they undertake genuine work of an economic nature (*Levin*)

Citizens' and workers' rights to free movement within the EU

Job seekers and students:
Citizenship of EU provides non-economically active citizens with limited rights to free movement to seek employment and study, provided they do not place a burden on the State (**Art 20 TFEU** and **Dir 2004/38**)

Non-economically active EU citizens:

- All EU citizens have the right to free movement for up to 3 months (**Dir 2004/38**)
- Further right to reside dependent on not being a financial burden on the host State
- Citizens' right to equality increasingly developed by Court of Justice

Workers' families:

- Family members (as set out in **Dir 2004/38** given right to accompany worker (includes non-EU citizens) and reside
- Family members enjoy equal rights with nationals, including social advantages, right to remain, etc.

Rights of free movement: citizens and workers

judiciary, tax authorities and high-ranking civil servants, etc.). This view was reinforced by a Notice in 1988 (OJ No 72/2), in which the Commission provided guidance as to which jobs would be included, concluding that the following would be *unlikely* to be covered:

- public health services;
- teaching in State educational establishments;
- Research for non-military purposes in public establishments; and
- public bodies responsible for administering commercial services.

While the EU recognises a need for Member States to preserve their own national identity, the Union is clearly not prepared to allow them to do this to the detriment of free movement.

IV. FREEDOM OF ESTABLISHMENT AND THE PROVISION OF SERVICES

In addition to promoting the free movement between Member States of EU citizens in general, and also of workers and their families within the EU, EU law also provides rights to the self-employed, businesses wishing to establish themselves in a host Member State and also those wishing to provide or receive a service in a host State.

Articles 49 to 55 TFEU prohibit discriminatory restrictions from being placed on those who wish to establish themselves (self-employed and businesses) in a host State, while Arts 56 to 62 TFEU afford the right of free movement to those who wish to provide a service in a host State, normally *without* having a base there.

In addition to the 'Citizens Directive' (Directive 2004/38), which provides rights to EU citizens and their family members, as explained earlier, the TFEU provides three sets of provisions covering the free movement of the three different 'groups' and the Court has emphasised that much common ground exists between these 'groups'. In Case 48/75, *Royer*, for example, the CJEU observed that the free movement of workers, freedom of establishment and freedom to provide services are all:

> based on the same principles in so far as they concern the entry into and the residence in the territory of Member States of persons covered by Community [now Union] law and the prohibition of all discrimination between them on grounds of nationality.

It should be borne in mind, however, that while the *principles* behind the various provisions have much in common, the *rules* applying to businesses can be quite different. In view of the constraints of this text, both right of establishment and provision of services are provided in outline only.

1. Right of establishment (Arts 49 to 55 TFEU)

The CJEU has defined establishment as the 'pursuit of an economic activity through a fixed establishment in another Member State for an indefinite period' (Case C-221/89, *Factortame*).

i. What amounts to 'establishment'?

Articles 49 and 54 TFEU can be read as providing the right of any business, already having a base in one Member State, to establish a further permanent base in a host State, under the same conditions as those enjoyed by nationals. This right includes the setting up of permanent agencies, branches or subsidiaries of companies or firms that have already been established in another State. In addition, EU citizens wishing to work on a self-employed basis in a host State are also provided with the right to move to do so.

Such businesses and individuals are required to comply with national laws applicable in the host State *unless* those laws can be shown to discriminate on the basis of nationality. Such discrimination is prohibited both by Art 49 and, in a more general manner, by Art 18 TFEU. Discriminatory rules will be seen as conflicting with Union law and must be set aside by the host State.

Once more, the relevant primary legislation is supported and expanded upon by secondary legislation and decisions of the Court of Justice.

ii. Natural legal persons

In some situations there may be initial confusion over whether someone is employed or self-employed. The Court has, however, made it clear that anyone who is working under the control of another and is receiving a wage or salary will be considered a worker, while those involved in the setting up and running of a business for themselves, rather than on behalf of another, will be considered to be self-employed (Case C-456/02, *Trojani*).

iii. Artificial legal persons

As has already been touched on, in addition to natural legal persons who wish to establish themselves as self-employed in a host State, artificial legal persons are also afforded rights of establishment. (Art 54 TFEU should be read here, as it provides a list of 'artificial persons' who may benefit from rules on establishment.)

To enjoy such rights, companies must demonstrate that they are legally established in one Member State, known as the 'primary State', and wish to conduct business in a second Member, or 'secondary', State (Art 54 TFEU).

This has, on occasion, been problematic, as companies registered in one State and established in a second State have then moved their main place of business to the second State in order to benefit, for example, from a more lax regulatory regime (as in Case 81/87, *Daily Mail*, or where the business was able to avoid onerous taxation rules in its 'home' State). The Court of Justice has provided that only the *primary* State can raise objections to such behaviour (Case C-212/97, *Centros*).

iv. Rights of the self-employed and their families: exit, entry and residence

Article 7 D2004/38 is quite specific in that it provides rights *not only* for workers and their families but *also* self-employed persons and their families. Consequently, the rights outlined above will apply in the same manner to the self-employed and their families as they do to citizens, workers and their families and so do not need be reiterated here.

As the CJEU has also provided that the rules relating to workers and the self-employed are **based on the same principles** (*Royer*), it can safely be assumed that an analogous approach can be taken in regard to their interpretation and application.

v. Equality and establishment: what amounts to 'discrimination'?

In line with its case law in other areas of free movement, the CJEU has provided that both directly and indirectly discriminatory rules may breach Art 49 TFEU.

While national rules which apply to non-nationals *only* will be *prima facie* discriminatory, domestic laws which appear to apply equally to non-nationals and nationals alike may also breach Art 49 TFEU (Case 71/76, *Thieffry*). In Case 143/87, *Stanton*, the Court explained that any national rules, whether discriminatory or not, which may 'place Community [now EU] citizens at a disadvantage' will be prohibited *unless* it can be objectively justifiable by the State wishing to rely on them.

'Reverse discrimination' (which occurs when the discrimination complained of takes place within the national's *home* State) has also been held to be prohibited by Art 49 TFEU. An illustration of this can be found in Case 115/78, *Knoors*, where qualifications obtained by Mr Knoors, a Dutch national, while resident in Belgium were not recognised by the Dutch State when he returned home to the Netherlands.

It is clear that any rule which discourages free movement is likely to be prohibited by Union law – unless it is indirectly discriminatory, in which case it may be objectively justified. (The issue of 'justification' of indirectly discriminatory measures has already been discussed above, together with a list of the conditions that must be fulfilled if a rule is not to fall foul of Union law, as provided by the Court in the case of *Gebhard*.)

vi. Recognition of qualifications

National rules relating to qualifications can result in a significant barrier to the free movement of persons. An example of this can be found with regard to solicitors in England and Wales, whose qualifications must comply with rules set out by the Solicitors Regulation Authority. Failure to comply with such rules will result in an individual being prohibited from carrying out his/her profession, thus creating a barrier to lawyers from other States practising their profession in the United Kingdom.

Article 53 TFEU provides the Council with the authority to issue directives relating to recognition of training and qualifications obtained within the Union and, as a result, harmonising legislation has been enacted. (You may want to visit the Europa website to research this in more detail in regard to specific professions and also in regard to D2005/36, which applies to regulated professions wishing to practise in a Member State other than the State in which their qualifications were obtained, particularly as the Directive is presently under review and likely to be amended in 2014.)

The CJEU approach provides insight as it has held that national authorities have an obligation to consider the training and/or qualifications held by a migrant and compare it to domestic provisions. Where they are found to be equivalent, the host State is required to recognise them as such (Case 340/89, *Vlassopoulou*). Where they are found not to be equivalent, the host State is placed under an obligation to provide reasons for its decision, which must be open to judicial review (Case 222/86, *Heylens*). Where qualifications are found to be 'part equivalent', a host State may require further training to be undertaken in order to 'make up the difference'.

vii. Limitations on freedom of establishment

As we have already seen in relation to EU citizens in general, restrictive measures put in place by Member States may be justified on grounds of public policy, security and health, and also with regard to employment of workers in the public sector. Similar grounds may also be argued in relation to establishment (and the provision of services).

Limitation on grounds of 'public policy, public service and public health'

Article 53 TFEU provides for limitation of rights 'on grounds of public policy, public security or public health' and the CJEU has held that these grounds should be applied in a similar manner to those found under Art 45(3) TFEU (Case 36/74, *Walrave and Koch*), while secondary legislation (D2004/38) specifically refers to workers *and* establishment).

The exercise of 'official authority' limitation

Article 51 TFEU provides that rights relating to establishment may not be available in regard to the 'exercise of official authority'.

This exception will be relevant in relation to the exercise of an official (State) power. The Court has confirmed that it is to be applied in a similar manner to the exception found under Art 45(4) TFEU, that is, the 'employment in the public service' exception to free movement of workers (Case 2/74, *Rayners*). As the CJEU has interpreted the 'public service' exception narrowly with regard to Art 45(4), a similar approach can be assumed in regard to establishment.

2. Free movement and the provision of services (Arts 56 to 62 TFEU)

While rights of establishment are rights enjoyed by EU citizens (and businesses) who wish to establish a permanent base in a host State (that is, for an unspecified period), rights of free movement to provide services normally relate to the carrying out of an economic activity for a *temporary* period and where the provider has no permanent base in that State.

The distinction can be difficult to draw, however: for example, in *Gebhard* it was ruled that a service provider may have an office or other base in the host State from which he provides his (temporary) service(s). The CJEU also provided that 'the temporary nature of the activities in question has to be determined in the light not only of the duration of the provision of the service, but also of its regularity, periodicity or continuity'.

Article 56 TFEU has also been held to prohibit measures that restrict the provision of services, where the *recipient* **moves** to a host State to obtain a service (Joined Cases 286/82 and 26/83, *Luisi* and *Carbone*, and Case 186/87, *Cowan*). It also appears to cover situations where the service moves but neither provider nor recipient move (e.g. internet-provided services), *or* where both parties move to a third Member State – **what is important is that there is an inter-State element to the transaction**. Directive 2006/123, on services in the internal market, is residual, in that it only applies where no other EU legislative act applies, and its provisions cover both services and establishment. The text incorporates principles first developed by the case law of the CJEU and one of its main innovations is that it attempts to simplify procedures found in different Member States.

i. What amounts to a 'service'?

Article 57 TFEU provides that to be considered a 'service', the service must be 'provided for remuneration' (which has been supported by the CJEU in Case 52/79, *Debauve*, where the Court made it clear that services provided gratuitously are not included). The Treaty Article also provides examples, such as activities of an industrial or commercial nature, of craftsmen and of the professions.

The Court has interpreted 'services' widely to include medical services, vocational training and tourism, and is likely to include any (lawful) temporary presence in a host State, *unless* specifically covered by another area of the Treaty.

ii. Rights of service providers

Rights of service providers (and recipients) include the following:

Rights of exit and entry

Rights include the right to exit a home State and enter a host State, as provided to all EU citizens by D2004/38. However, as those wishing to provide – or receive – a service do not wish to establish a permanent base in a host State, **rights do not include residence rights** for either the provider, receiver or family members.

Protection from discrimination

Article 56 TFEU requires the elimination of all discrimination based on nationality, against non-national providers (or receivers) of services. This Article is supported by the more general Art 18 TFEU, as well as Art 24

TFEU, which requires the elimination of all discrimination based on nationality.

As for other groups, the elimination of discrimination has been extended to national measures which impede free movement, without necessarily *directly* discriminating (Case C-384/93, *Alpine Investments*). Again, where the national rule is not directly discriminatory, it may be objectively justified (in Cases C-369 and C-376/96, *Arblade*, the principles developed in *Gebhard* – already discussed above – were more applied).

iii. *Exceptions to the right of free movement to provide services*

Member States may derogate from their obligations to provide rights of free movement of services on similar grounds to those already considered in regard to citizens, workers and 'establishment'. As has already been discussed, exceptions to the right of free movement have been interpreted restrictively by the Court, thus ensuring that restrictions on free movement are kept to a minimum. Unsurprisingly, as all 'four freedoms' are intended to support the creation of a single market, the Court's approach here mirrors its approach in relation to free movement of other groups.

Public policy, public security and public health limitations

Article 62 TFEU specifically provides that the derogations, relating to establishment, found in Arts 51 to 54 TFEU will also apply to the right to move freely to provide a service. Consequently, the discussion provided above in relation to such derogations will be relevant to consider in relation to services.

'Exercise of official authority' limitation

Article 62 TFEU also provides that the derogation relating to the exercise of official authority found in Art 51 TFEU will apply in the same manner to services.

V. ENFORCING RIGHTS TO FREE MOVEMENT

In addition to understanding that EU law *provides* EU citizens, workers, the self-employed, businesses and service providers and receivers with rights to free movement throughout the European Union, it is also necessary to consider how these rights may be enforced and against whom.

Under the doctrine of direct effect, individuals may normally enforce their EU law rights before national courts, under the doctrine of direct effect (Chapter 5). The CJEU has been concerned to emphasise that Art 45 TFEU, which provides rights to workers, is both vertically and horizontally directly effective. In *Bosman*, for example, the defendants in the action were, among others, the Belgium Football Association, while in Case C-282/98, *Roman Angonese v Cassa di Risparmio di Bolzana Spa*, the Court of Justice specifically explained that the Union principle of free movement of workers places obligations not only on public bodies but also on *private* persons (in this case a bank). In Case 167/73, *Commission v France* (the *French Seamen* case), the Court also held that as Art 45 is 'directly applicable in the legal system

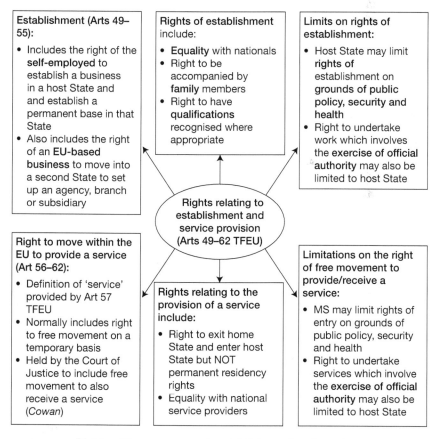

Rights of free movement: establishment and services

169

of every Member State', all conflicting national law should be rendered inapplicable.

Similarly, the CJEU has provided that Art 49 TFEU, relating to the rights of the self-employed and businesses, is directly effective (Case 2/74, *Reyners*), while in Case 36/74, *Walrave and Koch*, the Court again appeared to extend the scope of the legislation beyond the actions of public authorities. Meanwhile Case 33/74, *Van Binsbergen*, provides authority that Art 56 TFEU, which relates to services, also has direct effect.

Enforcing rights emanating from a directive is, of course, a different matter, and rights contained in D2004/38 should take effect by means of national implementing legislation (Art 288 TFEU). However, research into the extent to which Member States have implemented the Directive has not been particularly positive in the case of a number of Member States, which can make enforcement of rights far more difficult for recipients. (This was considered in Chapter 5.)

Of course, should a Member State fail to comply with its obligations in relation to free movement, the Commission (or second State) may initiate enforcement proceedings against that State (Arts 258 to 260 TFEU, discussed in Chapter 6), while a sufficiently serious breach by a Member State failure could result in an action for damages against the State (Chapter 5).

NOTE: Chapter 9 provides tips on how to approach problem questions relating to free movement of persons, which will hopefully support your approach to answering seminar questions, coursework and examinations.

SOME ISSUES TO THINK ABOUT FURTHER

- Why does EU law see it as so important to ensure free movement between Member States?
- Can you distinguish between the various groups who enjoy rights of free movement between Member States?
- In outline, consider what rights are enjoyed by such groups? What are the main differences between the rights of the various groups?
- What limitations have been placed on rights of free movement?

9 Assessment

This book is not intended to be a revision workbook or a guide on how to pass assessments but some hopefully helpful tips are provided below.

I. SUGGESTED APPROACHES TO COURSEWORK

It would be wrong to suggest that there is only one way to approach coursework. Sometimes a student will take a novel approach that is highly successful. However, students often complain that they don't know where to start; hopefully this chapter will give them some ideas which they can successfully utilise and develop.

First things first: when you are given a coursework question, set aside sufficient time to analyse (breakdown) the specific requirements of that question. As experienced examiners will confirm, too many answers take a 'tell all you know on the topic' approach rather than targeting the *specific* question set. For example, a question on Action to Annul (Art 263 TFEU, discussed in Chapter 6) could take the form of a problem in which an individual must be advised on the application of the law to a given scenario OR an essay on the availability of such actions to individuals. In such circumstances, the advice given in relation to the problem question is likely to require consideration - and application to the facts – of matters such as what, and whose, acts may be challenged, by whom and on on what grounds. The 'essay' question, on the other hand, will probably need to focus on the controversial matter of what a 'natural or legal person' needs to demonstrate in order to prove sufficient standing, and demand a far more evaluative approach.

Before you begin to write, think carefully about the resources you will need to access. Some students believe that utilising their lecture notes, together with a number of textbooks is sufficient but, while textbooks certainly have their place in developing an overall view of the law, reading more than one text is rarely a good use of time (cases and materials excepted) as the same law will normally be set out in each. Better to 'bite the bullet' and access primary sources (treaties, secondary legislation, case law and so on) and articles in appropriate journals, which should certainly deepen both knowledge and understanding.

Once *sufficient* research has been carried out, it is time to plan the structure of your answer. What should be set out in your introduction? (Be aware that an introduction is normally an essential element of an answer to an 'essay' question but not of an answer to a 'problem' question.) A brief – *never* ramble – introduction can be seen as an opportunity to 'set the scene', provide relevant background information and/or demonstrate an understanding of how the subject matter of your answer relates to the wider EU context. Alternatively, if you find this problematic, an introduction can be used to **briefly** explain to the reader what needs to be discussed – and *why* – in order to answer the question but be aware that this is unlikely to provide any extra marks.

The 'main' part of your answer should contain the 'meat': i.e. the law and its application (problem) or evaluation (essay). When planning your answer, you should not only decide what you need to write, but also the **order** in which it is most effectively set out. This will ensure that your answer flows logically and that arguments can be clearly developed.

If you have been asked to 'advise', this will normally require you to *first* set out the relevant law and *then* consider how a court is likely to apply that law to the facts of the scenario which you have been given. How will you know how a court is likely to do this? – By looking at how they have applied the law in the *past* (i.e. by referring to case law). Where the material facts of a scenario are sufficiently similar to those of a decided case, this should guide your argument and provide supporting authority for it. What you are doing in essence is 'second guessing' how a court is likely to decide a case based on what has been decided in the past.

Accept that there may be no right or wrong answer. If you have been provided with insufficient facts, for example, or where there are conflicting precedents, discuss all possible outcomes and recognise that you may not be able to provide a definite answer – although if one argument is stronger than another, be prepared to say so. In an essay-type question, it is usually relevant to consider – and weigh-up – the opinions of noteworthy academics but remember that these are only opinions, albeit important ones, and again they do not necessarily provide a definitive answer.

Questions (both coursework and examination) require you to reach a conclusion that answers the specific question set. *Never* forget to do this. You may have been asked to advise someone, consider a proposition or comment on the development of law, for example and to ensure that you have answered the question asked, *and not the one you would like to have been asked*, **re-read the question** before embarking on your conclusion. If you discover that you have wandered from the point or missed an important point, you will then still have the opportunity to rein yourself in! Be wary of making any new points in your conclusion and do not be tempted to repeat arguments, although emphasising key issues is normally appropriate. It is often sufficient to say: 'In conclusion, based on the arguments (or discussion or facts) provided above, I would advise Joe that . . .'

YOU WILL NEED PRACTICE TO PERFECT YOUR TECHNIQUE, SO ENSURE THAT YOU USE YOUR SEMINAR PREPARATION TIME WISELY.

An example of what you may wish to consider when answering a problem question on direct effect and/or supremacy:

---

1. Is there more than one possible **source of law which may give rights**? I.e. (i) EU law and (ii) national law? If so, it's appropriate to explain the principle of **supremacy** (*Costa*) and apply to the scenario.

2. If the likely source of rights is EU law, explain the (two-pronged) principle of **direct effect** (*Van Gend*).

3. Do all sources of EU law have direct effect? Explain the (3) **criteria** which must first be satisfied (*Van Gend/Reyners* criteria).

4. Consider who EU rights may be enforced against. **Is the defendant a private or public body**? If public, rights may be enforceable through vertical direct effect, if private party, through horizontal direct effect (*Defrenne v Sabena*).

5. What is the specific EU legal source?
   - **Treaty article**: *Van Gend* criteria must be satisfied, capable of horizontal and vertical direct effect (*Defrenne*)
   - **Regulation**: as for Treaty article
   - **Directive**: more problematic (particularly in the light of *Art 288 TFEU*). Directives must satisfy the *Van Gend* criteria but will not be able to satisfy the 3rd until the date given for implementation has past (*Ratti*). Also, directives may only be enforced vertically (*Marshall*). [Consider the broad definition given to '**emanation of the state**' by the Court of Justice and the guidance provided in *Foster v British Gas*.]

6. Apply to the scenario/facts provided. If it appears unlikely that a directive will be directly effective, consider possible alternatives, particularly:
   - **Indirect Effect/Interpretive Obligation** (*Von Colson*)
   - **State Liability in damages** (*Francovich* and also *Brasserie and Factortame* case)

7. Consider: how would you sum up your arguments in a **conclusion**?

An example of what you may wish to consider when answering a problem question on free movement of citizens and/or workers:

---

1. **Question analysis**: does it appear that a Member State has placed an obstacle to free movement into effect? If yes, *consider*:

2. Why is it necessary to ascertain the status of the individual concerned?

3. What is the status of the individual concerned? What are the possibilities?

4. Why is nationality relevant?

5. What are the legislative SOURCES of the rights to free movement of the various types of status?

6. What are the outline rights of the individual concerned (relevant to his/her status)?

7. How do these rights apply to the scenario provided? (Case law of the Court of Justice interprets the legislation and indicates the likely approach of the courts to the situation outlined in the scenario and is consequently relevant.)

8. Are there any limitations on these rights? How are they likely to be applied to the scenario?

9. Conclusion

II. SUGGESTED APPROACHES TO REVISION

Obvious though it may seem, ensure that you are familiar with the syllabus of your course and the format of your assessment. It is very unlikely that you will be expected to know everything that you have studied in order to succeed in an unseen assessment, as undergraduate examinations tend to require you to answer three questions from a choice of six, or four from a choice of eight. (But don't make the mistake of only learning three topics if you only, for example, have to answer three questions: what if you don't understand a question? Always ensure you have 'back-up' by revising one or two additional areas of the syllabus.)

Plan your revision in advance, ensuring that you start early enough to complete it *and* have some time for relaxation! Drawing up a revision timetable which clearly demonstrates that you have enough time to complete your revision can be invaluable in calming pre- assessment nerves.

Trying to 'learn' EU law by rote is boring, hard work and unlikely to produce particularly good results. Although some rote learning is inevitable (legal authorities are an example), what you should endeavour to do is try to ensure that you *understand* the law, particularly *why* it has developed as it has. This is because success at this level is rarely based on knowledge alone and assessment will require you to also demonstrate an ability to analyse, evaluate and apply the law in order to achieve the best marks.

If you have worked consistently throughout your course, **particularly if you have prepared adequately for seminars**, you should have few problems, as all you need to do is ensure that what you have learned throughout the academic year is brought back to the forefront of your memory. One of the most important things to do is to discover what you know and what areas need a little more work – there is little point in spending excessive time on areas that you have sufficient knowledge and understanding of! One of the best ways of testing your knowledge is to obtain **past examination papers**, old seminar questions or even pick out appropriate questions from a revision workbook. Sit down and attempt to answer the questions – preferably in full and under similar constraints as will be imposed in the examination room. Check your answers against your notes or textbook which should highlight which are your weak areas, allowing you the opportunity to concentrate the majority of your revision time on these. Remember that revision is a skill: it needs thought and practice if it is to develop fully, just like all other skills.

As touched on above, sitting down with your notes or textbook and trying to learn by rote is unlikely to be particularly effective. It is far more productive to read around the areas that you are finding difficult as widely as time allows, perhaps making your own notes, and then attempt to answer further questions, again under examination conditions.

If you make your own notes, which is always a good idea as it aids memory, make sure that they are not too detailed. If they are, it probably indicates a lack of understanding and you may also find that there is little advantage in consulting them over a textbook. Briefer notes also tend to be the most helpful for last minute revision. You may find it helpful to develop 'spider diagrams' or flowcharts, which can also be very useful when constructing answer plans. (There are plenty of examples of this in this textbook.) Brainstorming is another useful way to 'encourage' your memory – don't discount it without giving it a try!

III. EXAMINATION TECHNIQUE

Success in examinations cannot be entirely put down to good (or bad) exam technique, as without an appropriate level of knowledge and understanding it is unlikely that exam success will be enjoyed. *But* good exam technique can make the difference between achieving, or just missing, a grade.

As already emphasised above, first, **always** ensure that you spend an adequate amount of time carefully **analysing** the requirements of the question and then prepare your answer **plan**. You may feel that there is little time for such luxuries in a time-constrained assessment but, in reality, you will save time, as unplanned answers often ramble and points may be repeated or irrelevant issues discussed. Your plan need not be long or complex; often a few key words, placed in an appropriate order, will be sufficient. I can't emphasise enough that no tutor will ask you to 'tell all you know' on a particular topic, so don't think that this approach will *ever* impress.

As for coursework, exam answers should normally have an introduction, a 'main' part or parts, and a conclusion. The introduction is something that you can think about at the revision stage but remember that, if you are short of time, an introduction, *particularly* in answer to a problem-type question, can be seen as an unnecessary luxury.

As well as planning your answers, do not forget to plan your time. Many undergraduate examinations are three hours in length; some have additional 'reading time'. Divide this time carefully between the number of questions that have to be answered and ensure that you do not spend too long on one answer to the detriment of the others. It is **very important** to ensure that you answer the requisite number of questions. If you are required, for example, to answer four questions, you are unlikely to obtain as many marks by answering three questions particularly well as you would by answering four reasonably well.

I hope that it is unnecessary to remind you to check the date, time and place of the examination! Do, however, ensure that you are aware of what you may take into the examination room with you. For example, it is often possible to take in an unannotated copy of EU legislation – which you should find invaluable *if* you have referred to it diligently throughout your course.

All that remains now is for me to wish you every success! (Yes, your tutors *do* want you to do well!!)

Index

absolute majority 62

acte clair 93–4

action to annul 33, 37, 47, 102

    acts to be challenged 103

    applicants 103–7

    effects of annulment 105

    grounds 103

    relevant bodies 102–3

    time limits 105

Assembly *see* European Parliament

'assent' procedure *see* consent
    procedure

barriers to trade *see* free movement of
    goods

'benefit tourism' 147–8

budgetary role of European
    Parliament 32

case law 64

case names 5, 6

citizens *see* EU citizenship

CJEU *see* Court of Justice of the
    European Union

co-decision procedure 14, 16, 17,
                              31, 32

    see also 'ordinary' legislative
      procedure

codes of conduct 58

Commission 46

    administrative and executive
      role 40

    Commission President 49

    composition of 38, 39

    enforcement actions against
      member states 97–9

    functions of 39

    legislative role 39

    powers of 38, 41

    representing the interests of
      the EU as a whole 38, 39

    supervisory functions 40

Committee of Permanent
    Representatives (COREPER) 35

Committee of the Regions (CoR) 45

Committees of Inquiry 33

Common Customs Tariff
    (CCT) 118, 119

common market 4, 10

competence: allocation of 27

    application of 27–8

    types of 27

competition rules 40

conciliation committee 32

conferral principle 25, 26, 27

consent procedure 32, 61

constitution for Europe 18

consultation procedure 31, 32, 61

co-operation procedure ... 12, 14, 31, 32
Copenhagen criteria 21
COREPER 35
Council 46
    composition of 35
    decision making 36–7
    functions 35–6, 37
    legislative role 36
    representing the interests of
        the governments of the
        Member States 36, 37
Council of Europe 7–8, 66, 67
Council of Ministers 11
    see also Council
coursework, approach to 171–4
Court of Auditors (CoA) ... 14, 44–5, 46
Court of First Instance (CFI) 12, 41
    see also General Court
Court of Justice of the European
    Union (CJEU) 41, 44, 46
    composition of 41–2
    functions of 42
    General Court 43
    judicial activism and interpretive
        methods 42–3
    jurisdiction 42
    procedure before the Court 43
criteria for membership 21
customs union 118, 119

damages: actions against
    Institutions 110–13
    see also State liability for
        damages
Dassonville 'Formula' 126–7, 131
decisions 57, 58
    direct effect 77
declarations 55

delegated acts 62–3
'democratic deficit' 48
direct effect: conditions for 76
    creation of doctrine 74–5
    decisions 77
    Directives 77–9
    international agreements 77
    Regulations 77
    source of EU right 85
    Treaty articles 76–7
Directives 57, 58
    direct effect, and 77–9
    'incidental effect' 81, 85
    'indirect effect' 79–81, 85
directorates-general (DGs) 39
discrimination: discriminatory
    internal taxation 122, 123
    establishment 164–5
    service providers, against 167–8
    see also equality principle
dualist States 71–3

ECB 14, 44, 46
'economically active' persons:
    free movement 153
Economic and Social Committee
    (ESC) 45
ECSC 8, 9
education: rights of workers'
    families 158–9
employment: rights of workers'
    families 158
    see also job seekers
    workers' rights
'empty chair' policy 37
EMU 14
enforcement 87, 113, 114, 115
    see also preliminary rulings;
        references to European Court

enforcement action against EU
  institutions 102, 112
  actions for damages 110–13
  judicial review 102–9
  plea of illegality 110
  preliminary references 109
enforcement actions against
  Member States 97, 101
  brought by Commission 97–9
  brought by Member States .. 99–100
  effectiveness of enforcement
    procedures 100
  see also State liability for
    damages
enforcement of individuals'
  EU rights before national
  courts 88, 90
  appropriate courts 88
  procedures 88–9
  remedies 89–91
enlargement 17, 21
entry rights see free movement
  of persons
equality principle 65–6
  EU citizens 147–8
  workers' families 159–60
  workers' rights 155–7
  see also discrimination
EU citizenship 14, 142, 143
  equal treatment, right to 147–8
  family members, right to
    be accompanied by 148
  family members,
    rights of 148–9
  free movement,
    right to 142–3, 145–6, 161
  limitations on citizens' rights
    to free movement 149–51
  rights 142

EU law: importance of 1
European Atomic Energy
  Community (EURATOM) 9
European Central Bank (ECB) 14, 44, 46
European Coal and Steel
  Community (ECSC): aims of 9
  creation of 8
European Communities 7–10
  development of 10–22
European Community (EC) 4
European Convention on
  Human Rights 7–8, 15–16, 66, 67
European Council 12, 34, 35, 46
  composition of 34
  role of 34
European Court of Human
  Rights (ECtHR) 8
European Court of Justice see
  Court of Justice of the European
  Union
European Defence Community 9
European Economic Community
  (EEC) 4
  aims of 10
  creation of 10
European Investment Bank
  (EIB) 45
European Monetary Union
  (EMU) 14
European Ombudsman 14, 33, 97
European Parliament (EP) 46
  budgetary role 32
  composition of 30
  functions 30
  interests of EU citizens 30
  legislative role 31–2
  powers 33–4
  supervisory role 32–3

European Political Community 9

European Union (EU): complexity
  of 22

  creation of 4, 7, 14, 15, 22–3

Eurozone 44

  debt crisis 20

examination technique 175–6

exclusive competence 27

exit rights *see* free movement of
  persons

exports: quantitative restrictions
  and measures having equivalent
  effect 132

  see also free movement of goods

failure to act: judicial review 108–9

family members: EU
  citizens 148, 149

  self-employed, of the 164

  third country nationals,
    and 144–5

  see also workers' families,
    rights of

federalism 25–6

fiscal compact 20

Francovich principle *see* State
  liability for damages

freedom of establishment 162, 169

  artificial legal persons 163–5

  discrimination 164–5

  'establishment', definition of 163

  limitations 166

  natural legal persons 163

  recognition of qualifications 165

  self-employed and their
    families, rights of 164

freedom to provide
  services 162, 166, 167, 169

  limitations 168

  rights of service providers 167–8

  'service', definition of 167

free movement of goods 117–18

  non-pecuniary barriers
    to trade 124–39

  pecuniary barriers to
    trade 118–24

free movement of
  persons 141–2, 153, 161

  'economically active'
    persons 153

  enforcement of
    rights 168, 169, 170

  EU citizenship 142–3, 145–9

  job seekers 152

  limitations on citizens'
    rights 149–51

  'sufficient resources' 152

  third-country nationals 144–5

  see also freedom of establishment;
    freedom to provide services;
    workers' rights

fundamental rights 18, 66–9

General Court (GC) 43

  see also Court of Justice of the
    European Union

general principles of EU law 64

  equality principle 65–6

  function and status of 65

  fundamental rights 66–9

  proportionality principle 28, 50,
    64, 127, 139, 150

  subsidiarity principle 27, 28,
    49, 50, 59, 64, 67

glossary 4

government, functions of 30

guidelines 58

harmonisation 57, 133, 134

High Authority 11
  see also Commission

human rights 66–9
  European Convention on
    Human Rights 7–8, 15–16,
                               66, 67
  European Court of Human
    Rights (ECtHR) 8

imports: quantitative restrictions
  and measures having
  equivalent effect 125–32
  see also free movement of
    goods

information sources 3

Institutions 29–30, 50
  functions of government 30
  institutional structure 46
  legitimacy, accountability
    and democracy 48–50
  and Member States, power
    sharing 25–9, 47, 49, 50
  power balance/sharing
    between institutions 47–8, 49
  see also enforcement action
    against EU institutions

intellectual property rights
  (IPRs) 136–7

intergovernmental
  conferences 34, 55

intergovernmentalism 26

internal market 11, 12, 168

international agreements 69
  direct effect 77

jargon 3–4

job seekers: free movement 152

judicial review: action for
  failure to act 108–9
  action to annul 33, 37, 47, 102–7

Laeken Declaration 18

lectures: attending 2

legal base of secondary
  legislation 59

legal personality, EU 19, 69

legitimacy, accountability and
  democracy: Institutions 48–50

locus standi 33, 103, 104, 105,
                          108, 109, 111, 115

Luxembourg Accords 11, 22, 37

maladministration, allegations
  of 33

Marshall Plan 7

Member States (MS): and Institutions,
  power sharing 25–9, 47, 49, 50
  see also enforcement actions
    against Member States;
    national legal systems and
    EU law; State liability for
    damages

migrant workers *see* workers' rights

monetary barriers to trade *see*
  pecuniary barriers to trade

monist States 72

'mutual recognition'
  principle 133–4, 135–6, 138

national legal systems and EU law
  71–4, 81, 84
  see also direct effect; State liability
    for damages; supremacy
    of EU law

national treasures, protection of 136

non-pecuniary barriers to trade 124

   derogation from
      prohibitions 132–9

   quantitative restrictions
      and measures having
      equivalent effect 124–32

non-privileged applicants 104–7

'official authority': limitation
   on establishment right 166

   limitation on provision of
      services 168

Official Journal 43, 56, 57, 95, 100

opinions 57, 58

'ordinary' legislative
   procedure 32, 36, 49, 58, 63

Ordinary Revision Procedure 55, 56

participative democracy 49

pecuniary barriers to trade:

   charges having equivalent
      effect 119–20

   charges levied for a service
      provided 120–1

   charges levied in respect of
      an inspection 121

   Common Customs Tariff ... 118, 119

   discriminatory internal
      taxation 122, 123

   enforcing rules 123–4

   prohibition of 118–23

plea of illegality 110

power sharing: between
   Institutions 47–8, 49

   Institutions and Member
      States 25–9, 47, 49, 50

preliminary rulings 89

   effects of 89–94

purpose of 89

   refusal to provide a ruling 94–5

primary sources of EU law 54–5

   revising primary legislation 55–6

privileged applicants 103–4

proportionality principle 28, 50,
                64, 127, 139, 150

protocols 55

public health 135–6, 150–1, 166, 168

public morality 134–5

public policy 135, 149, 150,
                 151, 166, 168

public security 135, 149, 150,
                 151, 166, 168

public service 160, 166

qualifications, recognition of 165

qualified majority voting
   (QMV) 12, 13, 17, 19, 36,
                      37, 62

quantitative restrictions and
   measures having equivalent
   effect 124–32

recommendations 57, 58

references to European
   Court 109

   acte clair 93–4

   appropriate bodies 92

   consequences of preliminary
      reference procedure 95, 96, 97

   decision to refer 92–3

   discretion to refer 93

   obligation to refer 93

   referral procedure 95, 96

Regulations 56–7, 58

   direct effect 77

'representative democracy' 48

residence rights *see* free movement
of persons

revision 174–5

'Rule of Reason' principle 127, 128,
129, 131, 136,
156–7

Schengen Agreement 143

secondary legislation 16, 56–8

enacting 58–60, 63

implementing law 63

secondary sources of EU law:

case law 64

general principles of
EU law 64–9

international agreements 69

secondary legislation 56–63

self-employed and their families:

rights of 153, 164, 170

seminars: attending 2

semi-privileged applicants 104

shared competence 27

simple majority 36, 62

Simplified Revision
Procedure 55, 56

single market 11, 12, 168

'soft law' 57, 58

sources of EU law 53, 69

primary sources 54–6

secondary sources 56–69

Spaak Report 9, 10

'special' legislative
procedures 32, 36, 61, 63

'State', definition of 79

State liability for damages
(*Francovich* principle) 85, 90, 89

development of the
principle 82–3

extension of principle to actions
against private parties 84

failure to fulfil obligations
of EU law 82

'sufficiently serious' breach 83

study approach 2, 4, 6

case names 5, 6

coursework 171–4

examinations 175–6

information sources 3

jargon 3–4

lectures 2

revision 174–5

seminars 2

typical syllabus 5

subsidiarity principle 27, 28, 49,
50, 59, 64, 67

supporting, co-ordinating
or supplementing acts of
Member States 27

supranationalism 26

supremacy of EU law 72–4

taxation: discriminatory
internal taxation 122, 123

terminology 3–4

third-country nationals:

free movement 144–5

'three pillared'
structure 14, 15, 16, 20

trade barriers *see* free movement
of goods

transparency 15, 18, 37, 48, 49

Treaties 54–5

declarations 55

direct effect 76–7

protocols 55

revising treaties 55–6

tutorials: attending 2

'Twin Pillars' 72

   see also direct effect

   supremacy of EU law

unanimity 36, 62

uniform interpretation and
   application of EU law 89

United Kingdom (UK):

   application for membership 21

veto power 11, 12, 14, 31, 36, 37, 62

voting procedures 62

   absolute majority 62

   qualified majority voting 12, 13, 17,
                  19, 36, 37, 62

   simple majority 36, 62

   unanimity 36, 62

workers' families,

   rights of 157–8, 159–60, 161

   education 158–9

   exit, entry and residence 158

   right to remain after death
      or divorce 159

   taking up employment 158

workers' rights: definition
   of 'worker' 154

   equality 155–7

   extended residence 155

   family members 157–60

   free movement 155, 161

   limitations 160, 162

   living in one State but
      working in another 157

   remaining after employment
      has ceased 157